ZERO TO ZERO: THE MYSTIC CIRCLE

THE JOURNEY FROM EMPTINESS TO ENLIGHTENMENT

The Life, Teachings, and Divine Messages of His Holiness
Sri Sri Sri Vidya Narayana Theertha Swaminaha
Sri Jagadguru Shankaracharya Samsthanam,
Dwaraka Badarikashram, and Sri Vidya Narayana Foundation,
Bengaluru

Compiled, Crafted, and Curated by

DR. HARI CHINTHAKUNTA

With Divine Grace and Blessings from His Holiness
Sri Sri Vidya Narayana Theertha

INDIA • SINGAPORE • MALAYSIA

A Reverent Offering

At the Sacred Lotus Feet of Sri Sri Sri Vidyanarayana Theertha,
the Eternal Light of Wisdom: A Heartfelt Tribute to
the Divine Mystic Circle.

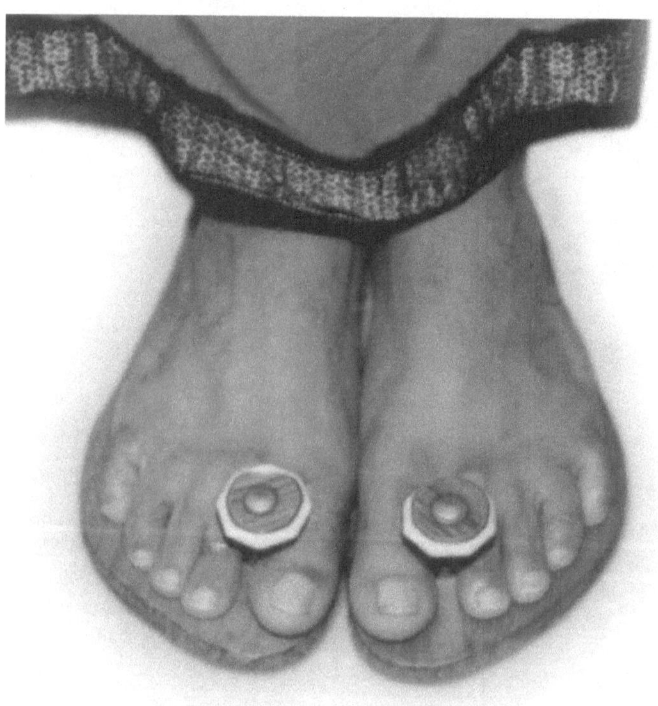

Contents

"Biographical Overview of His Holiness Sri Vidyanarayana Theertha"

His Holiness Sri Vidyanarayana Theertha, a revered spiritual leader and Peetadhipathi of the Sri Jagadguru Shankaracharya Samsthanam, Dwaraka, Badarikashram, has dedicated over 50 years of his life to monkhood, serving humanity with unparalleled wisdom, compassion, and guidance. A doctor by profession, he seamlessly integrates his medical expertise with spiritual guidance, focusing on the holistic well-being of humanity. His compassionate approach and deep understanding have earned him immense respect across various communities. Sri Vidyanarayana Theertha's ability to bridge modern science and ancient spiritual wisdom has inspired countless individuals to seek a deeper understanding of life and health. His journey from a doctor to a highly respected ascetic embodies the essence of spiritual transformation.

As the Peetadhipathi of the prestigious Dwaraka Badarikashram, His Holiness has played an instrumental role in guiding and inspiring spiritual seekers from all walks of life. His teachings emphasize the importance of transcending material pursuits and focusing on higher truths, encouraging individuals to embark on a path of self-realization, humility, and compassion. His Holiness' insights on health, both physical and spiritual, have helped countless individuals understand the holistic nature of well-being.

In addition to his spiritual work, His Holiness is the founder of the Sri Vidyanarayana Foundation in Bengaluru, a charitable organization that focuses on improving the lives of underprivileged children and communities. The foundation provides vital healthcare services and educational opportunities to those in need, ensuring that future generations have the tools and resources to thrive. Through his vision and leadership, Sri Vidyanarayana Theertha has made a significant impact on society, offering hope and support to those who need it the most.

For over five decades, Sri Vidyanarayana Theertha has selflessly dedicated his life to the service of humanity, blending medical knowledge with spiritual wisdom. His life serves as an inspiring example of the power of inner transformation, and his teachings continue to guide individuals toward achieving spiritual enlightenment, self-realization, and a life of service. His Holiness' unwavering commitment to the welfare of others and his deep spiritual insights have left a lasting legacy, shaping countless lives and inspiring future generations.

Soulful Surrender

A Sacred Offering to His Holiness Sri Sri Sri Vidyanarayana Theertha Swamy

"ZERO to ZERO: The Mystic Circle" transcends the concept of a book; it is a spiritual offering laid at the lotus feet of His Holiness Sri Sri Sri Vidyanarayana Theertha Swamy—a living embodiment of divine wisdom and infinite compassion. This magnum opus rises above the mundane realm of literature, standing as an odyssey into eternal truth and the transformative power of surrender.

Through its sacred pages, the Guru's grace illuminates the path for seekers, guiding them to self-realization by unraveling the veils of ignorance. The work reflects the timeless wisdom of Swamiji's life and philosophy, resonating with those who yearn for peace, wisdom, and spiritual awakening.

The Spiritual Essence

At its core, *"ZERO to ZERO: The Mystic Circle"* serves as a bridge across the profound philosophies of Vedanta—Advaita, Dvaita, and Vishishtadvaita. It brings these streams into a harmonious confluence, revealing the singular truth beyond dualities. Each concept finds its resonance in ancient scriptures like the Ramayana, Mahabharata, and the Bhagavad Gita, which are not merely cited but reimagined in the light of contemporary spiritual challenges.

This spiritual masterpiece serves as an experiential guide to Vedantic truths, inspiring seekers to rediscover the eternal relevance of these sacred texts in an age where technology and materialism often obscure human connection. The book weaves Swamiji's teachings into every chapter, transforming abstract philosophy into practical wisdom for modern living.

Research as a Path to Spiritual Insight

The journey of this book is as much about rigorous inquiry as it is about divine inspiration. Grounded in the intersection of spirituality and psychology, it offers a comprehensive exploration of the human mind, body, and spirit. By combining Vedantic insights with modern research on consciousness, it demonstrates how ancient truths can align with cutting-edge scientific discoveries, bridging faith and reason.

This approach not only affirms the timelessness of spiritual teachings but also emphasizes their relevance to seekers in today's world. The work is enriched by references to historical sages, empirical studies on mindfulness, and modern applications of meditative practices, making it a beacon for those navigating the complexities of contemporary life.

The Guru's Divine Mission

Sri Vidyanarayana Theertha Swamy's life is a testament to his divine purpose as the choicest son of the Cosmic Mother. His teachings transcend individual enlightenment, calling for universal harmony and the realization of oneness. By dissolving illusions of separateness, Swamiji guides humanity to embrace its divine essence.

This sacred work encapsulates his mission, awakening readers to their inner divinity and inspiring them to lead lives of love, compassion, and truth. It reminds us that the journey from ZERO to ZERO is a return to the eternal source—a journey not of endings, but of infinite beginnings.

An Invitation to Transformation

"ZERO to ZERO: The Mystic Circle" calls all seekers to embark on an inward journey of profound transformation. It dismantles the illusions of ego, inviting the reader to embrace a reality where the finite dissolves into the infinite. The mystic circle reflects the cyclical nature of existence, where the journey of the self culminates in the realization of the divine.

This sacred text challenges us to see beyond dualities, offering a path of surrender that leads to divine grace. Through Swamiji's teachings, it reminds us that the greatest transformation begins within and that the ultimate destination is unity with the Divine.

A Beacon of Light for Seekers

In a world marked by uncertainty, *"ZERO to ZERO: The Mystic Circle"* stands as a lighthouse, guiding seekers toward clarity, peace, and ultimate realization. It offers practical teachings interwoven with the Guru's grace, reminding us that divinity is present in every moment and every interaction.

This sacred offering not only inspires the heart but also empowers the intellect, encouraging seekers to explore their spiritual potential while grounding them in timeless truths.

A Spiritual Testament

"ZERO to ZERO: The Mystic Circle" is more than a book—it is a spiritual testament, a call to awaken to the highest truths, and a guide for those seeking the light of divine realization. It encapsulates the teachings of His Holiness Sri Vidyanarayana Theertha Swamy, inviting seekers to journey from ignorance to enlightenment and from duality to unity.

This work is a sacred guide for modern seekers, offering timeless wisdom while addressing contemporary challenges. It inspires the reader to surrender with faith, embrace the journey from ZERO to ZERO, and realize their oneness with the Divine.

A Prayer for Divine Grace

O Cosmic Mother, Source of Light,
Guide our hearts to infinite height.
Cleanse our souls, dissolve our strife,
Lead us to the path of eternal life.

With every breath, may wisdom flow,
Reveal the truth all seekers must know.
Grant us peace, pure and bright,
Unite us in Your boundless light.

Om Shanti Shanti Shanti.

With humility and boundless devotion,

— **Dr. Hari Chinthakunta**

Tributes of Gratitude

With profound humility and unwavering gratitude, I bow down in reverence to Lord Vinayaka, the remover of obstacles. I seek His divine blessings to remove all hindrances from my spiritual path and grant me the wisdom and clarity to overcome every challenge. To Lord Subramanyeswara, I offer my heartfelt prayers for strength, courage, and discernment to pursue the truth, along with His divine protection from all negative influences that may impede my progress.

To Goddess Bala Tripura Sundari, I humbly seek Her sacred grace to purify my heart and mind, guide my thoughts with wisdom, and lead me toward the highest spiritual fulfilment. I offer my gratitude for Her eternal love, which bathes the soul in divine light.

I also bow before Lord Venkateshwara, the Lord of Seven Hills, Kaliyuga Daivam. I seek His divine blessings, praying that His graceful hands always rest upon my head, guiding and protecting me on my spiritual journey. May His staunch Bhakti fill my heart with unwavering devotion, and may His eternal protection lead me to wisdom and peace.

My heartfelt thanks are due to the Saints, Sages, and Seers of the traditional spiritual lineage, whose illuminating wisdom has been the guiding light for countless spiritual seekers throughout the ages.

I extend my deepest gratitude to my divine parents, Avadootha Nanna and Karunamayi Amma, whose unconditional love and nurturing have shaped my soul's journey. I also express my deep gratitude to my divine sister, Sai Niveditha, and my brothers, Naga Yogiraj and Balayogi Ganesh, for their unwavering support, love, and strength, which have sustained me through every challenge.

Above all, I offer my eternal and boundless gratitude to my revered Gurudev, His Holiness Sri Vidyanarayana Theertha Swamy. It is through His divine grace that I have been chosen as His humble instrument, His pen, to bring this work into the world.

It is He who guides my every step, and it is through His divine energy that this book has come to life. Through His grace, I have come to understand that it is not the individual ego, but the Cosmic Mother—the ultimate force that governs and directs the universe— that shapes and guides our lives. In truth, His soul, acting through me, created this offering, and He is the true author of this work, the architect of my soul. I am but a vessel, guided by the divine forces of the universe, to express the sacred teachings He has shared with me.

Swamy has graciously offered ZERO to ZERO: The Mystic Circle as a spiritual journey, reflecting the cyclical nature of existence—from ignorance (*ZERO*) to the realization of truth (*ZERO*). This journey is not about the individual self, but about surrendering to the divine will, recognizing that we are mere instruments in the hands of the

Cosmic Mother. As we traverse the *"Mystic Circle,"* it is She who leads, purifies, and guides us toward self-realization. She holds the hand that guides the soul, and the same divine hand creates the stars.

It is with the deepest reverence that I offer this book as a tool for spiritual awakening, hoping it will serve as a reminder to each reader that they are not separate from the Divine, but one with it.

As we move from the first *"ZERO"* of ignorance to the second *"ZERO"* of enlightenment, we come to realize that we are all instruments in the divine play, dancing to the rhythm of the Universe, each step an expression of the eternal truth.

"May the wisdom imparted within these pages serve as a radiant beacon, inspiring and uplifting all who read, guiding them toward deeper understanding and spiritual fulfilment. As the Cosmic Mother tenderly leads each soul toward self-realization, may they be enveloped in her grace. I offer my heartfelt gratitude to Sree Lekha, Sai Leela, Mounamuni and Savithri for their unwavering moral support and to Mrs. Konanki Lakshmi Kala, K.Madhava and Vinod Kumar for their meticulous proofreading.

Bhagwan Sri Ram SIR is a master trainer and a guiding light, whose presence has profoundly shaped my life. His name embodies divine wisdom and grace—"Bhagwan" reflecting his sacred nature, "Sri" signifying respect, and "Ram" evoking qualities of righteousness, compassion, and love. The title "SIR" speaks to his role as a teacher and mentor, inspiring others to reach their highest potential.

His wisdom has been a constant source of inspiration, motivating me to compile two books—Whispers of Divine Light and Hidden Radiance—each a reflection of the light he has sparked within me.

In deepest reverence, I bow to Bhagwan Sri Ram SIR, whose guidance, though invisible, is ever-present and deeply cherished. His unconditional love strengthens me, providing the inspiration and enlightenment needed to walk the path he has illuminated.

Such rare individuals serve as mirrors to our potential, catalysts for growth, and sources of creativity. In Bhagwan Sri Ram SIR, I have found not just a mentor, but a transformative guide whose presence empowers me to fulfill my purpose and uncover my hidden strengths.

With boundless love and reverence,

— **Dr. Hari Chinthakunta**

Prologue

From His Holiness Sri Vidyanarayana Theertha

In the modern, fast-paced world, where life revolves around material pursuits, we often overlook the profound significance of the concept of *"Zero."* Zero is not just a number; it symbolizes potential, the essence of existence, and the infinite power within. Unfortunately, most people only realize its importance when faced with setbacks—when it is often too late to act.

Throughout my journey as a seeker and a sanyasi, I have encountered many enlightened souls. Two saints stand out as extraordinary influences in my life.

The first is Sri Sivananda Swamy of the Divine Life Society in Rishikesh, whom I met in the 1960s. He foresaw my future even when I was still contemplating my path. At that time, I told him of my ambition to serve as a doctor in the Royal Medical College. He smiled knowingly and predicted that I would eventually embrace the path of renunciation, becoming a sanyasi—a spiritual doctor serving humanity. His words proved prophetic.

The second saint is Dr. C. Nagaraj (Naga Yogi Raj), a fellow physician and a divinely inspired soul whom I encountered in the late 1990s. At that time, he was pursuing an MD degree, and I remarked, *"Why strive for an MD in medicine when you are already advancing towards the Master of Divinity (MD)?"* His spiritual journey was a profound reminder of the transformative power of inner realization.

Dr. Nagaraj comes from a family steeped in divinity, with his parents embodying extraordinary spiritual grace. Each member of his family is known for their divine inclinations, and they have always held a special place in my heart. Our connection transcends this lifetime, as our souls have shared journeys together in previous lives, bound by a deep spiritual affinity.

This book, *Zero to Zero: The Mystic Circle*, is the result of my *Sankalpa* (*divine resolve*) to document my life, teachings, and spiritual messages. I entrusted Dr. Hari Chinthakunta, a devoted disciple and an eloquent writer, to compile and develop this work with clarity and purpose.

ZERO to ZERO: The Mystic Circle

In this book, *Zero to Zero: The Mystic Circle,* I have endeavoured to present a spiritual journey that begins and ends with the same concept of "ZERO." The first, "ZERO", represents our state of ignorance and unawareness of our divine nature. This is where most of us begin—caught in the illusions of the material world, unaware of our true essence. The second "ZERO" symbolizes the realization of truth—the awakening to our divine self, which transcends the limitations of the physical world and connects us with the eternal.

The "*Mystic Circle*" reflects the cyclic nature of life and spiritual growth. It is a journey that moves inwards, where the outer distractions are left behind, and the seeker turns to their inner divinity. As we navigate this circle, we encounter various experiences that shape us, purify us, and ultimately bring us to a point of self-realization. We come to understand that the beginning and the end are not separate; they are part of the same infinite whole. This realization allows us to experience the oneness with all creation.

Through this book, I seek to help you understand that life is not just about external achievements but about discovering your own divine essence. True peace, true joy, and true fulfilment are found not in the external world but within. The essence of this teaching is to move from a state of ignorance (*ZERO*) to a state of enlightenment (*ZERO*), where the self merges with the divine.

I humbly offer this work to you as a tool for spiritual awakening, a guide to deepen your understanding of your divine nature and a reminder that all journeys, no matter how varied they may seem, ultimately lead to the same truth. I pray that you find strength, inspiration, and guidance through these words and that they help you move closer to your own self-realization. May you experience the bliss of being one with the divine, and may your path be illuminated with wisdom and love.

I bless Dr. Hari, who, by my divine will, carried out this sacred task with humility and excellence. His dedication and insight have been instrumental in bringing this work to fruition.

Dr Hari has previously authored two enlightening books—*The Hidden Radiance: Unveiling the Untold Story of a Quiet Yogi* and *Whispers of Divine Light: Unlocking the Secrets of Faith and Joy.* Both are profound works that inspire and guide spiritual seekers on their path. I wholeheartedly commend them to all who wish to deepen their understanding of faith and spirituality.

The proceeds from the sale of this book will support the education and healthcare of underprivileged and deserving children. Empowering young minds through education and providing health support to those in need is a vital aspect of our collective spiritual responsibility. By contributing to this cause, you are not only engaging in a noble act of service but also becoming a part of the greater circle of compassion and humanity.

"I hope this work, *ZERO TO ZERO: THE MYSTIC CIRCLE*, beckons all seekers to embark on a transformative journey—one that leads from zero, the illusion of separateness, to zero, the realization of divine oneness. Just as Hanuma's unwavering reverence for Lord Rama, his immense power, and his disciplined devotion enabled him to transcend every obstacle, may this journey inspire you to break through the barriers of your own limitations.

Within these pages lie timeless truths, profound insights, and mystical wisdom that invite you to explore the deepest recesses of your being. As you read, may you unlock the infinite potential that resides within your soul and awaken to the transformative power that not only guides you toward your highest self but also empowers society to rise in unity and harmony.

With divine blessings,

— His Holiness Sri Vidyanarayana Theertha

Sri Jagadguru Shankaracharya Samsthanam

Dwaraka Badarikashram, Bangalore

The Master's Touch: A Journey of Inspiration

My obeisance to our most beloved Guru,
H.H. Sri Sri Vidyanarayana Thirtha Maha Swamiji.

Self-realization is the ultimate goal of human life. As the great sage Patanjali once said, *"Yoga is the cessation of the fluctuations of the mind"* (Yogashchitta Vritti Nirodhah). It is through the dissolution of the ego and the surrender of the mind that one can attain true self-awareness. This state is achieved through the succession of Chaturvidha Purushartha—Dharma, Artha, Kaama, and Moksha. The first, Dharma, is of two types—Samanya Dharma and Vishesha Dharma.

Samanya Dharma outlines the principles of living a righteous life—practicing truth, helping the needy, eliminating the ego, cultivating contentment, maintaining purity in thoughts and actions, and offering work as service to God. As the Bhagavad Gita emphasizes, *"Perform your duty, but do not become attached to the results"* (Gita 2.47). Yet, many struggle to practice Samanya Dharma, let alone attempt or even speak of Vishesha Dharma, the path of extraordinary virtue.

But when the Guru bestows grace upon the fortunate, the path to perfection becomes much easier. Confusions are cleared, and direction is provided by the realized Master, the Guru. As Sri Krishna tells Arjuna, *"When you are endowed with a divine nature, you will be able to see the truth clearly and will not be swayed by worldly attachments"* (Gita 15.19). A true Guru guides us to transcend our limitations and awaken the divine within.

In these modern times, it is difficult to recognize a true Guru, as the title is often misused. The true Guru is described in the ancient shloka from Sri Sringeri Sannidhanam:

Matrutaha Pitrutaha Shudhaha, Shudha bhaavo jitendriyaha,
Sarvagamana Saragaha, Sarva Shaastraartha Tatvavitu,
Paropakaara nirataha, Japa poojaadi Tatparaha,
Amoghavachanaha shantaha, Veda Vedaanga paaragaha,
Yoga Maargaanu Sandhaayi, Devata Hrudayangamaha
Ityadi Guna Sampannaha, Gururaagama Sammataha.

This means that a true Guru is one whose lineage is noble, who has mastered control over senses, and is a master of the Shastras. A Guru is selfless, dedicated to the well-being of others, engaged in worship and meditation, and ever peaceful. *"The true Guru resides in the heart of the disciple, guiding them toward the path of liberation"* (Brahma Sutra 1.1.4). Such a person keeps God in their heart and teaches with love and wisdom.

It is rare to find a Guru who embodies all these virtues, and even rarer to find one who is easily accessible and humble despite their immense powers. H.H. Sri Sri Vidyanarayana Thirtha Maha Swamiji, an Avadhoota, walks with the common people, leading a simple and humble life. In over 30 years of association with him, I have learned that he never claimed to be the great master nor sought special treatment. Yet, he is quick to correct those who admit their mistakes and strive for self-improvement. Always alert, intelligent, and sensitive to the feelings of his devotees, Sri Swamiji serves as a beacon of guidance. *"A true master is not one who demands respect but one who earns it through actions of compassion and wisdom."*

The Significance of ZERO TO ZERO: THE MYSTIC CIRCLE

ZERO TO ZERO: THE MYSTIC CIRCLE is more than just a book; it is a journey into the heart of spirituality, offering profound insights into the teachings of Sri Swamiji. It captures the essence of his wisdom, showing how his guidance transforms lives and elevates the soul. As the Upanishads state, *"Tat Tvam Asi"* (That Thou Art), the divine presence is within all of us, and through this work, we are reminded of our inherent connection to the universe.

The book is not about the mastery of language or philosophical intricacies but about the simplicity and profundity of spiritual truth. Dr. Hari has done a commendable job of compiling and presenting these teachings with clarity, making them accessible to all seekers. As the Bhagavad Gita beautifully declares, *"The highest knowledge is that which leads to liberation, transcending all worldly desires"* (Gita 9.22).

Sri Swamiji's teachings are not confined to lofty ideals but are deeply practical, urging each reader to reflect upon their life and take actionable steps toward spiritual growth. Through Dr. Hari's earnest efforts, these teachings are made available to anyone willing to listen, ponder, and apply them in their lives. The book provides clarity and direction, helping the reader understand the essence of dharma, the nature of self-realization, and the path to liberation.

Through this work, Dr. Hari has not merely compiled teachings; he has prayed for Sri Swamiji's wisdom to flow into every heart and home. Much like the purity of the ghee, which represents the Divine Mother's love, this book flows with love, compassion, and wisdom, guiding readers with each page.

"Love is the divine essence that connects us all; it is through love that the soul awakens to its true nature"
— (Srimad Bhagavatam 10.10.34).

In the spirit of Sri Swamiji's teaching, *"I am Pure... I will make you Pure!"*, this book becomes a guide for anyone looking to find purity of thought, action, and heart. It is a source of light for those walking the path of self-realization. As Lord Rama's devotion to Lord Krishna is exemplified in the Ramayana, we see how the highest form of discipline is achieved through love and devotion.

The book encourages readers to embark on a transformative journey where the mundane meets the divine and the ordinary becomes extraordinary. It provides clarity and direction in the pursuit of peace, balance, contentment, and spiritual growth. As Hanuman's devotion to Lord Rama teaches us, "In service to the Lord, one can achieve the highest power and wisdom" (Ramayana, Sundara Kanda).

Through this book, Dr. Hari has faithfully shared the life-changing wisdom of Sri Swamiji, inviting each reader to experience the transformative power of divine grace. May this humble submission at the lotus feet of Sri Swamiji continue to bring comfort, light, and peace to all who are fortunate enough to engage with it.

At the Lotus feet of H.H. Sri Sri Swamiji,

A Fortunate Servant,

— Kiran M Nadigar

The Light That Transforms

I offer my deepest salutations and humble prostrations to His Holiness, Sri Sri Vidyanarayana Thirtha Maha Swamiji, whose divine grace has illuminated my path.

My chance to be associated with a born Master, ordained by divine will to become a saint, has become an immeasurable blessing in my life. A true Guru transforms the ignorant, guiding them to realize the true nature of the Self. The Master, the realized one, sees the Self as The Absolute Zero. For an ordinary soul like mine, the journey is from point A to point B, from ignorance to knowledge, from confusion to clarity.

The wisdom encapsulated in Zero to Zero: The Mystic Circle by Swamiji succinctly presents the ultimate truth — all is one, and one is all. Zero, in this context, is the unmanifest, the beginning and the end. Life, on the other hand, is the manifest, the play of the unmanifest in time and space. We come from Zero and must return to Zero.

For the Master, there is no change; in the deepest reality, nothing changes. Zero represents absolute stillness, the state of pure bliss, in which the Master constantly dwells. This is Swamiji's eternal, all-encompassing nature. To Him, the nature of existence is one of profound peace, untouched by the fluctuations of the material world.

For someone like me, life is an endless journey of happiness and sorrow, joy and pain, light and darkness. But in the presence of Swamiji, these dualities dissolve. He transcends the limitations of the material world and guides us to experience the unchanging, ever-present reality within. In His presence, we witness the supreme truth that all is one — that we are one with the universe, and the universe is one with us.

Swamiji's wisdom extends far beyond mere words. He embodies humility, egolessness, and a deep love for all beings. There is a special resonance between a true Saint and a true Soldier, both of whom live selflessly in service and sacrifice. Swamiji holds a natural affinity for those in uniform, recognizing the path of selfless service as a reflection of the true spiritual journey.

Dr. Hari, known to Swamiji for over three decades, has made this sacred work possible due to the soul of Swamiji acting through him, guiding his hand and heart to compile these teachings for all seekers. The wisdom contained within Zero to Zero is not merely the work of a devoted disciple, but the manifestation of Swamiji's presence in the world, blessing every reader who comes across it.

The teachings of Zero to Zero encapsulate the profound simplicity of Swamiji's spiritual wisdom. This book is a sacred offering that brings the reader closer to understanding their own divine nature. It speaks to the seeker within us all, guiding us back to the source, to the Zero from which we came. I humbly seek the blessings of the revered Master at His holy feet, and I pray that His teachings continue to illuminate the lives of all who read these words and lead them to the truth of their own existence.

At the Lotus feet of H.H. Sri Sri Swamiji,

A Fortunate Servant

With Pranams.

— Lt Gen (Retd.) BNBM Prasad, SM, VSM, PHS

Former DGHS (AF)

Reflections of a True Guide

A Tribute to His Holiness Sri Vidya Narayana Thirtha: A Beacon of Wisdom and Devotion

It is both an honor and a privilege to pen these words for the spiritual biography of His Holiness Sri Vidya Narayana Thirtha, *"The Connection to ZERO to ZERO: The Mystic Circle."* His life stands as a beacon of wisdom, spirituality, and unwavering devotion. This monumental work marks the golden milestone of fifty years of Sanyasa and Chaturmasya Deeksha, a testament to His Holiness's unparalleled dedication to the dharmic path.

In an era often marked by distractions and turbulence, Sri Vidya Narayana Thirtha is a lighthouse of inner peace and resilience. His life, grounded in Vedantic principles, serves as a living scripture, inspiring countless seekers to pursue righteousness, service, and self-realization.

As a soldier, I am profoundly moved by His Holiness's disciplined approach to spiritual life. Just as the Army upholds its duty to protect the nation's sovereignty, Sri Vidya Narayana Thirtha has devoted himself to safeguarding and promoting our spiritual heritage. The discipline of Sanyasa and the rigor of Chaturmasya Deeksha reflect the commitment required of a soldier, but on the battlefield of the inner self.

This biography is not just a chronicle of His Holiness's journey, but a guide for all those seeking purpose and spiritual growth. It encapsulates his teachings, his unwavering faith, and the transformative impact he has had on the lives of countless devotees.

I would also like to extend my heartfelt congratulations to Dr. Hari, whose dedication and insightful curation of this work have been shaped by the extreme blessings and grace of Pujya Gurudev. Dr.

Hari's efforts to craft, compile, and preserve this profound work stand as a tribute to the wisdom he has received and continues to pass on.

May this work inspire future generations to follow the path of Dharma and find light in the teachings of His Holiness Sri Vidya Narayana Thirtha.

Jai Hind!

— Major General Nandiraju Srinivas Rao (Retd)

Hyderabad

The Divine Voice Speaks

"In the stillness of life, the Divine Voice calls us back to our true self. *Zero to Zero: The Mystic Circle* is a journey that begins and ends in the realization of the infinite within us all."

In the silence of existence, a voice rises—a voice that transcends time, space, and individual identities. It is the **Divine Voice**, calling us back to our true nature, urging us to embark on a journey of self-discovery and enlightenment. **"Zero to Zero: The Mystic Circle"** is a profound exploration of this journey, a spiritual path that begins and ends in the same place: the realization of the infinite within the finite, the eternal within the transient. The voice that speaks in this book is not of one individual, but of the **Divine Presence** that resides in all of us.

The Concept of "Zero"

The term **"zero"** holds deep significance in many spiritual traditions. It symbolizes the void—the place before creation, before thoughts, before distinctions. It is the pure, unmanifested state, the infinite potential that lies at the heart of all existence. When we begin our spiritual journey, we start in this state of **zero**—lost in the distractions of life, unaware of our true nature. Yet, the journey is about returning to this very **zero**, not in ignorance, but in enlightened awareness.

In **"Zero to Zero: The Mystic Circle,"** the concept of zero is explored not as a negative space, but as the origin of all that is. It is the beginning of consciousness, the undivided unity that transcends dualities. This journey from **zero** to **zero** represents a profound transformation—a return to our essential being, where we shed the layers of ego, illusion, and separation, and merge with the Divine essence.

The Cycle of Existence

The journey described in this book is cyclical. We begin at zero and move through life's experiences—learning, growing, and evolving—until we return to **zero** in the form of spiritual realization. This **mystic circle** is the endless cycle of life, death, and rebirth, where the seeker constantly transforms, shedding the old and embracing the new.

This cycle is not linear but a continuous spiral, where each turn brings deeper understanding, greater wisdom, and a closer connection to the Divine. In the **mystic circle**, the seeker moves inward, into the heart of their being, to uncover the ultimate truth that transcends time and space. This circle is not just a symbol, but a living process that each individual undergoes as they seek to know themselves and the Divine.

The Mystical Journey Within

The **mystic circle** invites us to embark on a journey of inward exploration. It is a journey that requires patience, introspection, and the willingness to face the deepest parts of ourselves. The **Divine Voice** speaks not through words, but through silence, through moments of stillness, through the whispers of our own soul.

In this book, the reader is not simply learning abstract concepts; they are being guided through their own spiritual path. This journey is deeply personal, but it is also universal. The experiences of awakening, realization, and transformation that are explored in these pages are available to all who are willing to listen—to listen to the **Divine Voice** that resides within.

Practical Insights for the Seeker

While **"Zero to Zero"** is filled with profound spiritual wisdom, it also offers practical insights for the modern seeker. How can we listen to the **Divine Voice** in our everyday lives? How can we begin to hear the whispers of the Divine in the midst of our busy, chaotic world?

1. **Embrace Silence**: To hear the Divine Voice, we must first cultivate silence within. This does not necessarily mean physical silence but mental and emotional quietude. Set aside time each day for meditation or reflection, allowing your mind to rest and your heart to open.

2. **Practice Presence**: The Divine Voice speaks in the present moment. Be fully present in everything you do—whether it's a simple task or a profound experience. In presence, we become attuned to the deeper truths of life.

3. **Self-Inquiry**: Ask yourself the question: "Who am I?" This is the key to discovering your true nature. Self-inquiry is a powerful tool for understanding the ego, transcending its limitations, and realizing the deeper, unchanging essence of the self.

4. **Trust the Process**: Spiritual transformation is a gradual process. Trust in the journey, knowing that every step brings you closer to the truth of who you are.

The Call to Action

As you journey through these pages, take a moment to reflect on your own path. Where are you on your journey from **zero to zero**?

Have you encountered moments of awakening or deep realization? How can you embrace the concept of **zero** in your life?

This book is not just for intellectual understanding; it is a call to action. It invites you to embark on your own mystical journey, to listen for the **Divine Voice** within, and to return to your true self. The journey from **zero to zero** is the most profound one you will ever take. Embrace it with an open heart, and let the Divine Voice guide you every step of the way.

Conclusion

In the end, **"Zero to Zero: The Mystic Circle"** is about returning to the source—the place of pure consciousness and infinite potential. It reminds us that we are all part of a vast, interconnected universe, and through the mystical circle, we find our way back to the Divine. This book is not just a spiritual discourse but a transformative guide for anyone seeking to awaken to the truth of their being.

The **Divine Voice** speaks to all who are willing to listen. It speaks through the silence, through the heart, and through the whispers of the soul. It is a call to return to **zero**, to the pure state of being where all is possible, and all is one.

Chapter-1

A Journey of Divine Wisdom and Liberation

The Transformation of Dr. Chandrasekhar to His Holiness Sri Vidya Narayana Tirtha

Great saints, though born in the human realm, often carry within them a divine mission that transcends ordinary existence. Their births and lives are marked by a profound purpose—to guide humanity toward spiritual awakening, to alleviate suffering, and to show the path to liberation. These saints, though divine in essence, experience human suffering, pain, and joy, just like everyone else. Their lives reflect the unique balance between their spiritual greatness and human vulnerability.

Take the example of Ramakrishna Paramahamsa. Born into a humble family, he was gripped by an intense yearning for divine realization. His experiences of intense spiritual practices, visions, and deep communion with the Divine show that even saints endure the struggles of the human condition. Yet, their suffering is transformative, as it leads them to the highest realms of consciousness, where they become a beacon for others. Ramakrishna's life exemplified how saints transcend worldly suffering by embracing it and transforming it into divine wisdom and compassion.

Similarly, Ramana Maharshi was a young boy who experienced a sudden spiritual awakening. Although he appeared to be a normal child in the early years of his life, a profound spiritual event catapulted him into self-inquiry, and he realized his true nature. Despite facing personal losses and the hardships of isolation, Ramana Maharshi's life serves as a testament to how saints embrace their challenges and then serve humanity through their boundless compassion and wisdom.

Shirdi Sai Baba, another beloved saint, was born under mysterious circumstances, with no clear knowledge of his origins. He lived a life of simplicity, serving both Hindu and Muslim communities. His life was full of suffering, yet he endured pain for the sake of others, guiding them toward peace, healing, and spiritual awakening. Sai Baba's presence in Shirdi was a manifestation of how a saint becomes a vessel of compassion, taking on the suffering of others and alleviating it with divine love.

The Kanchi Paramacharya, Sri Chandrasekharendra Saraswati Swamigal, is another shining example of how a saint's life is filled with divine grace and struggle. Born with a great spiritual legacy, he faced many challenges, yet he guided people with his wisdom and unwavering devotion to dharma. His life showed how a saint, while living in the world, remains detached from worldly desires and yet offers immense service to humanity through his selfless love and teachings.

These saints were not immune to suffering or pain. In fact, they embraced it, as it became a part of their divine mission. Their incarnations were not only to demonstrate spiritual truth but also to bear the weight of human suffering and transform it into divine compassion. Their lives reflect the true essence of selflessness—suffering for the benefit of others, guiding them toward spiritual fulfilment.

In the same vein, the journey of Sri Sri Sri Sadguru Swamy Srividya Narayana Tirtha reflects this deep connection between divine wisdom, human suffering, and the path to liberation. Just as the great saints have lived to uplift humanity, His Holiness Sri Srividya Narayana Tirtha's life is a living example of how a saint's struggles and compassion are interwoven with their divine purpose. His teachings continue to guide us, urging us to embrace the divine wisdom that transcends the material world and leads us to the eternal truth.

The Life Story of the Sadguru

Sadguru Sri Vidyanarayana Theertha, born as Dr. Chandrashekhar Kaipa, was a person of great honour and reverence, widely recognized as the Sadguru, Sri Vidyanarayana Theertha. India has been the home to many yogis and spiritual guides, and Southern India, particularly Andhra Pradesh, has been blessed with the birth of many eminent saints. Andhra Pradesh, with its sacred land and the blessed town of Nellore on the eastern coast, witnessed the birth of Sadguru Sri Vidyanarayana Theertha on the auspicious day of Kartika Pournami, February 23, 1950, to Sri Lakshmi Parimala and Sri Ranganatha, a holy couple.

The Blessing of Avadhuta Venkayya

Upon receiving this joyous news, a visit was made to the sacred Guru Avadhuta Sri Venkayya Ashram in Nellore, where the news was shared with them. The revered Guru, with divine grace and a gentle smile, responded with words of blessing, "Oh...oh...oh...A beautiful pearl has emerged from a shell with universal power. Good...good...go...go...attend to the work," and named the child Chandrashekhar. Though the words of Avadhuta Venkayya were not aimed at attracting the external world with spiritual meanings and terms, they resonated deeply within the soul, bringing love and compassion.

A Royal Childhood

The young boy Chandrashekhar Kaipa, who grew up like a prince, was free from any pain, discomfort, or financial struggles. His parents were prominent political leaders, lawyers, and tea estate owners, who were busy managing their business and political lives during the period of 1950-1970.

Guided by a Grandfather's Wisdom

The first 20 years of Chandrashekhar Kaipa's life were spent in the presence of his paternal grandfather, the late Justice K. S. (father's father), a man who had retired as a judge and held great respect for nature and spiritual culture. Under the guidance of his grandfather, the seeds of spiritual wisdom were sown in him.

A Compassionate Spirit

Despite his royal upbringing, Chandrashekhar Kaipa remained deeply compassionate toward the poor and suffering, believing his life's purpose was to uplift and serve the downtrodden. He expressed this sentiment to his grandfather in a heartfelt manner, and the great souls around him shared their wisdom, predicting his future role in society.

Academic Excellence

In 1954, Chandrashekhar Kaipa was enrolled in the famous Bishop Cotton School in Bangalore, which was affiliated with the prestigious Eaton Bishop School in the UK. Always striving to the best of his ability, he stood first in every class. From 5th to 7th grade, he received double promotions. He completed his Senior Cambridge between 1964 and 1965.

Spiritual Foundations

While his parents were deeply involved in politics and the legal profession, young Chandrashekhar Kaipa grew up under his grandfather's care and spiritual influence, developing a deep interest in spiritual matters. Through his grandfather's guidance, he began to understand the teachings of the Bhagavad Gita and spiritual texts, attaining spiritual maturity.

Guided by Enlightened Sages

From 1963 to 1973, Chandrashekhar Kaipa came into contact with a 75-year-old spiritually enlightened sage from the Reddy community. Under his mentorship, Chandrashekhar Kaipa furthered his spiritual progress. He also received blessings from the famous sage Shankar Madhava, who visited Chandrashekhar's home.

Inspired by Great Spiritual Leaders

Chandrashekhar Kaipa was greatly influenced by the teachings of renowned spiritual leaders like the late Swami Sivananda, Swami Chinmayananda, and the founder of ISKCON, Srila Prabhupada. He also learned the significance of the *Rama Nama Mahatmyam* and *Vishnu Sahasranama Mahatmyam* from the great scholar and sage, Veda Brahma Anantarama Dikshitar. This is a brief overview of the life and spiritual journey of Sadguru Sri Vidyanarayana Theertha, the incarnation of divine grace and wisdom.

The Harmony of Music and Spirituality

Young Chandrashekhar Kaipa was a music enthusiast. He learned music as an expression of divine sound (*Nādabrahma*) under the guidance of Sri Sammengudi Srinivasa Iyer. Recognizing his interest, his teacher imparted spiritual songs that resonated with his background and devotion.

Excellence in Education and Service

During his higher education, Chandrashekhar Kaipa maintained a sense of equality between the rich and poor, earning recognition as an exemplary student. He completed his medical education at the highest level and became known as Dr. Chandrashekhar Kaipa. Alongside his studies, he pursued hobbies like flying planes, horse riding, playing tennis, and teaching subjects such as chemistry to his friends. His enthusiasm for teaching and his dedication to education stood out among his peers.

A Flourishing Medical Career

After completing his MBBS, Dr. Chandrashekhar Kaipa pursued a postgraduate degree in General Medicine while teaching undergraduate students. He enjoyed a joyful life and was well-loved by his friends. He continued his medical career at Manipal Medical College. From 1950 to 1974, he balanced a royal lifestyle with a deeply spiritual life, embodying harmony between material and spiritual pursuits.

The Maternal Role of Mrs. Sarojamma

Another important figure in his life was Mrs. Sarojamma. With his parents deeply involved in politics and law, they appointed Mrs. Sarojamma as his guardian. Though she had three sons of her own, she treated Chandrashekhar Kaipa as her child. A spiritually accomplished woman, Mrs. Sarojamma played a pivotal role in shaping him into a well-educated, cultured, and spiritually inclined individual. From 1958 to 2000, she fulfilled her role as a maternal figure with immense dedication, ensuring his upbringing was filled with joy and guidance.

A Tragic Turn and Transcendence

During this time, a tragic incident deeply impacted Dr. Chandrashekhar Kaipa's life. While working as a tutor in General Medicine in 1973, he received news from his grandfather's household manager, Sri Ramachandra Rao, that his parents had been politically murdered in Switzerland, and their bodies had been found. The news brought immense grief to Dr. Kaipa. However, drawing upon the spiritual teachings he had received from his grandfather and Mrs. Sarojamma, he found the courage to confront this devastating loss. Through their guidance, he grasped the transcendental truth beyond life and death, finding strength in the profound spiritual wisdom he had cultivated.

A Sole Heir in the Midst of Grief

Chandrashekhar Kaipa, the only son and sole heir to his parents' fortune, found himself surrounded by a heavy, grief-stricken atmosphere following their untimely passing. Dignitaries, including the Chief Justice of the High Court, IAS and ICS officers, prominent farmers, family Vedantic scholars, and notable personalities like Shivaji Ganeshan, M.S. Subbulakshmi, and Semmengudi Srinivasa Iyer, gathered to pay their respects. Chandrashekhar, amidst this immense gathering, was deeply consoled by those mourning his parents' untimely passing.

A Tribute to a Devoted Mother

Chandrashekhar's mother, Lakshmi Parimala, was not only a prominent lawyer at the Bengaluru High Court but also a devoted follower of Lord Krishna of Udupi. Her unwavering devotion left a lasting impression on her son. In his grief, Chandrashekhar penned heartfelt verses in her honor, reflecting her steadfast faith and enduring legacy. The family's devotion to Shirdi Sai Baba spanned three generations, enriching their spiritual heritage.

Family Discord and Loss

Amidst the mourning, familial discord emerged. Chandrashekhar's father, Sri Ranganatha K. Rao, had married his mother's sister, who chose to remain in London, prioritizing financial interests over familial bonds. This created a stark contrast to the atmosphere of grief, as many relatives focused on the family's inheritance rather than the spiritual and emotional significance of the moment.

A House of Sorrow and Devotion

The family home became a place of profound mourning, where Chandrashekhar sought solace with his grandmother, embracing her as he shared his sorrow. His grandfather, Justice K.S., offered comfort and wisdom during this challenging time. The family's Alsatian dog, too, stayed by Chandrashekhar's side, offering silent consolation in a time of despair.

A Double Tragedy

In the midst of mourning his parents, Chandrashekhar received the devastating news of his grandparents' passing. His grandmother, overwhelmed with grief, prepared herself spiritually for her final moments. Draped in a Kanchi silk saree and adorned with flowers, she chanted the name of Sai Ram with devotion before peacefully merging with the eternal. Her passing deepened Chandrashekhar's sorrow, leaving him in search of answers amidst the series of tragic events.

Grandfather's Wisdom: Transcending Illusion

Turning to his grandfather, Justice K.S., for solace, Chandrashekhar expressed his anguish over the inexplicable losses. Justice K.S., a spiritually enlightened soul, offered profound wisdom: "The world is full of illusion. Only the spiritual path can guide us beyond this illusion. Patience and wisdom are essential to transcend life's trials.

God's plans are beyond human comprehension, and you must strive to fulfil His divine purpose with courage and faith."

A Call to Spiritual Purpose

Justice K.S. encouraged Chandrashekhar to reflect on his life's divine purpose, urging him to rise above worldly pleasures and illusions. With spiritual strength and patience, Chandrashekhar was reminded of his higher calling—to lead a life that fulfils God's will and contributes meaningfully to the world. This conversation marked a pivotal moment, infusing Chandrashekhar with the strength to pursue a life of spiritual and purposeful living.

The Final Words of Justice K.S. Kaipa

In his last moments, Justice K.S. Kaipa imparted a profound message to his grandson, Chandrashekhar Kaipa: "Well, my boy, I'm about to leave you now. The drama is over. The next act in the journey of your meaningful life begins now. Invite all the great Gurus to witness your play on the stage of the future." With these words, Justice K.S. Kaipa peacefully passed away, leaving Chandrashekhar to grapple with the weight of his loss.

A House Deep in Mourning

Chandrashekhar, having already suffered the loss of his parents, was struck with even greater sorrow as the death of his beloved grandmother followed. The atmosphere in their residence grew darker as the preparations for the funerary rites of the four deceased unfolded. Malicious Brahmin priests sought to exploit the situation for money, further intensifying the emotional turmoil. Despite the anger of his friends, Chandrashekhar took charge of the funeral ceremonies, reflecting his strength and resilience amidst the turmoil.

Grief Amidst Greed and Family Discord

The passing of his parents and grandmother was compounded by the selfish actions of Chandrashekhar's stepmother, who, along with her sisters in London, focused on securing her share of the family's wealth. Despite the worldly flaws surrounding him, Chandrashekhar remained grounded in his spiritual foundation, striving to overcome these challenges with patience and wisdom.

Guided by Divine Wisdom

Chandrashekhar, drawing strength from his grandfather's final teachings, recognized that the time had come to transcend worldly attachments and pursue spiritual awakening. Inspired by Advaita philosophy, the teachings of Sri Adi Shankaracharya, and the wisdom of Lord Krishna's Bhagavad Gita, he resolved to seek the truth and fulfil his divine purpose.

A Spiritual Awakening

With the divine blessings of Lord Dattatreya, Avadhuta Venkatayya, and Shirdi Sai Baba, Chandrashekhar Kaipa felt the call to embark on a spiritual journey. He saw the challenges in his life as a means to break free from worldly illusions and move toward spiritual enlightenment. Despite the adversity, he remained focused on his higher calling, guided by the divine wisdom passed down through generations.

The Path to Spiritual Leadership

Chandrashekhar Kaipa's journey took him to sacred places like Kashi, in search of a Guru. After meeting several saints and ascetics, he became a disciple of Karapathra Swami and, later, Sri Vidya Abhinava Sachidananda Theertha, who imparted divine blessings upon him. Embracing the teachings of Lord Krishna and Advaita philosophy, Chandrashekhar Kaipa deepened his spiritual practice and embraced the vows of a renunciant.

A Life Dedicated to Spiritual Service

For over 50 years, Chandrashekhar Kaipa has led a life of spiritual dedication. As the leader of the Dwarka-Badrinath Peetam, he has contributed to the welfare of humanity, establishing temples, performing consecrations, and ensuring the preservation of sacred traditions. His spiritual leadership has touched many lives, guiding others toward spiritual awakening.

The Divine Mission of Sri Vidyanarayana Theertha

Sri Vidyanarayana Theertha, a revered spiritual guide, has also devoted his life to the welfare of all beings. Through his consecrations of temples, unearthing sacred sites, and performing grand ceremonies, he has fulfilled his divine mission of spreading spiritual knowledge and practices.

Fulfilling the Divine Will

The essence of this story is the recognition that divine will prevails in all circumstances. Through the guidance of saints and the practice of righteous duties, we fulfil our ultimate purpose in life. The true offering to our Guru is to live by their teachings, lead a righteous life, and contribute to the welfare of all beings, ensuring the well-being of all through our actions, thoughts, and words.

The Essence of His Teachings:

Sadguru Srividyanarayana Tirtha's teachings centre around the Guru as the divine guide to liberation. He often teaches:

- **Guru as the Embodiment of the Trinity:** The Guru is not just a teacher but is the physical manifestation of Brahma, Vishnu, and Shiva.

- **The Illusion of the Material World:** Life is transient, and worldly suffering is an illusion. Realizing the impermanence of life is key to spiritual awakening.

- **Service and Devotion:** Service to the Guru is the path to spiritual progress. By dedicating oneself to the Guru, one overcomes the ego and reaches enlightenment.

- **Path to Liberation:** Liberation (moksha) can only be achieved through devotion, knowledge, and detachment from worldly desires.

His words echo the wisdom of the divine:

"In this world of illusion (Maya), where every joy and sorrow is fleeting, your soul is the eternal truth. Only through devotion to the Guru can one realize this truth and be freed from the chains of material attachment."

The Divine Journey: Becoming Sadguru Srividya Narayana Tirtha

Chandrasekhar Kaipaa underwent a profound inner transformation as he continued on his spiritual path. His search for truth led him to the realization that only through devotion to the Guru could one truly experience liberation. He recognized the Guru as the embodiment of divine wisdom, the guide who could lead him to the ultimate realization of his true nature.

Through years of self-discipline, meditation, and devotion, Chandrasekhar Kaipaa became Sadguru Srividya Narayana Tirtha, a spiritual leader of unparalleled wisdom and compassion. His teachings emphasized the importance of surrendering the ego and transcending the illusions of the world. He became a guiding light for those seeking to overcome the distractions of life and find their true purpose.

Insights and Inferences:

- **The Illusion of Materialism:** Dr. Chandrasekhar's transformation emphasizes the fleeting nature of worldly attachments and the transient nature of suffering. The material world, with all its distractions, is an illusion—ultimately leading nowhere. His story urges us to question our attachments and desires, prompting us to seek deeper, spiritual truths.

- **The Role of Grief in Awakening:** His journey shows that grief and loss, while painful, can be the catalyst for spiritual growth. Rather than a barrier, sorrow becomes a path to awakening, pushing us to go beyond surface-level existence and search for meaning that transcends material life.

- **Spiritual Legacy and Lineage:** The wisdom passed down through generations, especially from his maternal grandfather and other key figures in his life, highlights the importance of spiritual lineage. The teachings of great masters form the foundation upon which seekers build their spiritual practices, and this transmission of knowledge is a sacred duty.

- **The Role of the Guru:** Sadguru Srividya Narayana Tirtha's emphasis on the Guru as a divine guide underscores the essential role that a spiritual mentor plays in leading a disciple to liberation. The Guru is not just a teacher but the embodiment of divine wisdom, guiding the soul toward self-realization.

- **Detachment and Self-Realization:** His renunciation of the material world demonstrates the power of detachment—not as a rejection of life, but as a way to focus the mind on higher truths. True freedom lies in overcoming ego and desire, allowing the soul to unite with the divine.

- **Service and Compassion:** Despite his personal tragedies and the challenges of the material world, Sadguru Srividya

Narayana Tirtha's life reflects the power of selfless service. The idea that serving the Guru and others leads to spiritual growth is central to his teachings. Through service, one purifies the mind and heart, cultivating humility and compassion.

- **Awakening to Divine Truth:** The ultimate insight is the realization that liberation, or moksha, is not an external goal but an internal awakening. True wisdom lies in recognizing one's divine nature and understanding the impermanence of the material world.

The life of Sadguru Srividya Narayana Tirtha teaches us that spiritual growth is not a linear path, but a profound process of inner transformation. From his early struggles with loss and grief to his eventual realization of divine truth, His Holiness exemplifies the journey of self-realization through unwavering devotion, wisdom, and detachment. His teachings serve as a guiding light for those seeking to rise above the distractions of the material world and discover the eternal truth within.

Sadguru Srividya Narayana Tirtha's wisdom continues to resonate deeply with all who seek to understand their spiritual essence. His life and message remind us that the true purpose of existence is not the accumulation of material wealth or the pursuit of external success but the awakening to the divine presence that resides within us all. Through devotion, service, and detachment, we can attain the peace and liberation that reflect our true nature.

Conclusion: The Eternal Truth

The life and teachings of Sadguru Srividya Narayana Tirtha stand as a living testament to the transformative power of devotion, wisdom, and detachment. His journey—from personal suffering to divine realization—reveals that spiritual growth is not an escape from life's challenges, but a process of embracing them to uncover deeper truths. Through his guidance, we learn that the path to self-realization lies not in the pursuit of material wealth, but in awakening to the divine presence that resides within.

His wisdom continues to inspire spiritual seekers, urging us to transcend the distractions of the material world. By surrendering the ego, practicing devotion, and serving the Guru, we can experience liberation from the illusion of worldly suffering. The true purpose of life, as taught by Sadguru Tirtha, is to find inner peace, align with the divine, and live a life of purpose and spiritual fulfilment.

In a world increasingly focused on external achievements and material success, Sadguru Srividya Narayana Tirtha's teachings offer a timeless reminder: the most profound treasures are those found within. His life and wisdom serve as a beacon, reminding us that spiritual awakening is within reach for all who seek the truth with sincerity and devotion.

A Prayer

O Divine Guru,
You are the beacon of light in the darkness,
The eternal truth that transcends all illusions.
Guide us on the path of wisdom,
Teach us to see beyond the material world,
To embrace the impermanence of life with grace.

Grant us the strength to renounce our desires,
To serve with compassion, and
To live in constant remembrance of your divine presence.

May we awaken to the truth that lies within,
May we transcend the suffering of the material world,
And may we find eternal peace in your divine light.

Om Shanti, Shanti, Shanti.

Chapter-2

The Spiritual Path: Wisdom from the Vedas

Swami Vidyanarayana's commitment to self-realization was deeply rooted in the timeless wisdom of the Vedas and Upanishads, the sacred scriptures that illuminate the path to divine truth. The Vedas proclaim, *"True knowledge is that which leads to Self-realization."* Inspired by this profound insight, Swami Vidyanarayana adopted the name *Vidyanarayana*, meaning *the source of knowledge*, symbolizing his unwavering pursuit of spiritual enlightenment. Through his diligent study and interpretation of these ancient texts, he emphasized that true spirituality arises from awakening the inner self, cultivating mindfulness, and practising compassionate action as fundamental elements of a fulfilled life.

At the core of his teachings lay the wisdom from the *Upanishads*, such as the famous phrase from the *Chandogya Upanishad*: *"Tat Tvam Asi"* (Thou Art That). This assertion embodies the realization that the individual soul (*Atman*) is one with the ultimate reality (*Brahman*). Swami Vidyanarayana guided his followers to seek this oneness through introspection and spiritual practice, explaining that self-realization is the key to understanding the essence of life itself.

One guiding principle of his teachings was: *"He who knows the Self knows the essence of life."* Swami Vidyanarayana often compared the external world to a mirror, reflecting the state of the inner self. He encouraged seekers to first find peace within, for only then could they hope to transform the world around them. For him, spirituality was not a distant ideal but a living, breathing practice—woven into every thought, word, and deed. Quoting the Bhagavad Gita, he reminded his followers: *"Act without attachment to outcomes,"* urging them to engage in selfless action, detached from the results.

The Power of Service: Compassion in Action

Central to Swami Vidyanarayana's teachings was his firm belief that *"Service to humanity is the highest form of devotion."* He demonstrated this through his tireless efforts to uplift the underprivileged, establishing schools, orphanages, and healthcare centres. His actions were not only aimed at addressing physical needs but also at nurturing the spiritual growth of individuals and communities. Through his example, he embodied the ideal of merging social service with spiritual practice, showing that true devotion is expressed in acts of compassion and kindness.

Swami Vidyanarayana taught that in serving others, we serve the divine. *"In serving others, we serve the divine,"* he would say, emphasizing that the act of giving not only transforms the lives of those helped but also brings the giver closer to the divine. His work in uplifting humanity served as a living testament to the power of love in action—showing that true spirituality manifests in making a tangible difference in others' lives.

Bridging Ancient Wisdom with Modern Life

Though deeply grounded in the ancient wisdom of the Vedas, Swami Vidyanarayana's teachings were profoundly relevant to the complexities of modern life. He rejected the notion that spirituality required retreat from the world, instead advocating for a balance between material pursuits and spiritual growth. His message was clear: spiritual practice should elevate both the individual and society.

He often defined success not in terms of wealth or fame, but as the realization of one's divine nature. Swami Vidyanarayana encouraged individuals to live lives of integrity, purpose, and selflessness, guided by love, truth, and spiritual values. In a world dominated by materialism, his words served as a beacon, urging seekers to find their true purpose and align their lives with divine principles.

Swami Vidyanarayana's teachings also shed light on how ancient wisdom could be applied to address contemporary challenges. He believed that spiritual principles should guide practical action in areas such as environmental sustainability, mental well-being, and community building, demonstrating the timeless relevance of the Vedas in today's world.

Legacy of Wisdom: A Lifelong Commitment to Service

Swami Vidyanarayana's influence extended far beyond his immediate community, inspiring countless individuals to pursue lives of greater meaning and purpose. His teachings endure, not only through the institutions he established but also through the countless lives he touched. His core message—aligning with the divine, living harmoniously with others, and dedicating oneself to service—continues to resonate.

His legacy stands as a reminder that spirituality is not an escape from life's challenges but a deepening of one's ability to engage with the world in a meaningful way. By embodying these principles, individuals discover the true essence of a life well-lived—a life of peace, purpose, and spiritual fulfilment.

Reflections of Swami Vidyanarayana: Thoughts from the Soul

Swami Vidyanarayana's teachings continue to inspire introspection and action. His reflections provide wisdom for those on the path of self-realization, inviting seekers to look inward for guidance:

- *"In the silence of your mind, you will hear the divine calling."* True peace is found in stillness, where one becomes attuned to the infinite.

- *"True strength is not the power to control the world, but the power to surrender to the divine will."* Strength lies not in resistance, but in trust and surrender.

- *"Service to others is the highest form of devotion, for in serving others, we serve the divine."* Compassionate acts are the most sacred expressions of spirituality.

- *"To know the Self is to know the universe, for the Self is the universe in its most sacred form."* The journey inward reveals the mysteries of existence.

Life's Palette: Lessons in Embracing Its Full Spectrum

Swami Vidyanarayana often compared life to a vibrant canvas, painted with all hues of joy, sorrow, triumph, and struggle. *"Life's richness lies in its contrasts, for even bitterness has its role in revealing the sweetness of grace."* He believed that the interplay of light and shadow in life was not a contradiction but an opportunity for spiritual growth.

For Swami Vidyanarayana, spirituality was not about escaping life's challenges but embracing them with trust and devotion. Through his heartfelt mantra—*"I love you, Krishna. I care for you, Krishna. I trust you, Krishna. I surrender to your holy feet"*—he exemplified a relationship with the divine rooted in love, faith, and complete surrender.

He encouraged his followers to welcome life's complexities, not as burdens, but as teachers guiding the soul closer to its ultimate purpose. Spirituality, to him, was woven into the fabric of everyday life—manifest in acts of kindness, resilience in hardships, and the courage to rejoice in fleeting moments of beauty.

Transforming Challenges into Divine Opportunities

Swami Vidyanarayana viewed life's challenges as divine opportunities. *"In every experience, God is speaking to us; listen closely, and you will hear His voice,"* he often said. Every obstacle, to him, was an invitation to deepen one's faith and spiritual connection. He encouraged his followers: *"Surrender to the divine, and even the darkest times will shine with the light of grace."*

His teachings illuminated a path to inner peace that transcended external circumstances. It was not the challenges themselves that defined the spiritual journey, but how one responded to them.

Brief Insights for Reflection

Before concluding, it is essential to pause and reflect on the teachings of Swami Vidyanarayana, which are both profound and practical in their application to our everyday lives:

- **Self-Knowledge and Inner Peace:** Recognizing the interconnectedness of all beings begins with understanding the Self. When we seek inner peace, we align with the divine order, allowing us to act harmoniously in the world.

- **True Service is Divine:** Compassionate action is the highest form of spiritual expression. When we serve others selflessly, we transcend ego and directly connect with the divine, making service not a duty, but a privilege.

- **Embrace Life's Contrasts:** Life's complexities are not obstacles but opportunities for growth. Embracing both joy and sorrow allows us to cultivate wisdom and resilience.

- **Divine Guidance in Every Moment:** The challenges we face are divine messages guiding us on our spiritual journey. Each moment of adversity is an invitation to deepen our faith and expand our understanding of divine grace.

The Eternal Truth

Swami Vidyanarayana's life and teachings are a beacon of divine wisdom that transcends time and place. His journey from personal challenges to spiritual enlightenment is a testament to the transformative power of devotion, wisdom, and selfless service. His message urges us to look inward, find peace within, and dedicate ourselves to serving others, for in serving others, we serve the divine.

In a world filled with distractions, his message is timeless: true success lies in realizing one's divine nature, not in the accumulation of material wealth. By embracing the divine within, we awaken to our highest purpose and find fulfilment that transcends the fleeting nature of worldly achievements.

Swami Vidyanarayana reminds us that spirituality is not about withdrawing from the world but living fully within it, with love, humility, and devotion to the divine. His legacy continues to inspire us to live with purpose, compassion, and spiritual integrity.

Prayer

O Divine Lord,
Grant us the strength to face life's trials with courage and grace,
The wisdom to see Your divine presence in all experiences,
And the compassion to serve others selflessly, as shown through the life of
Swami Vidyanarayana.
May our actions be guided by love, humility, and dedication,
And may we always strive to serve the divine in every moment.
Lead us on the path of self-realization,
And let our lives reflect Your infinite grace.
Om Shanti, Shanti, Shanti.

Chapter-3

Embracing Divine Wisdom: A Journey of Truth, Compassion, and Spiritual Awakening

The Chosen Child of the Cosmic Mother

In the vast, boundless ocean of existence, amidst the ceaseless waves of time and space, there emerges a soul destined to carry the light of divine wisdom to all corners of creation. This soul is none other than His Holiness Sri Sri Sri Vidyanarayana Thirtha Swamiji, the choicest child of the Cosmic Mother. Born of pure love and divine grace, Swamiji is a beacon of compassion and spiritual enlightenment, leading us through the darkest shadows of ignorance toward the radiant light of self-realization.

Like a tender child embraced by the Cosmic Mother, Swamiji embodies humility, love, and boundless wisdom. His heart, compassionate and kind, resonates with the essence of divinity. He moves with the people, understanding their struggles, wiping their tears, and lifting them up to a higher consciousness. His words are laced with love, offering solace and guidance to all who seek truth. In every gesture, in every glance, Swamiji reflects the boundless love of the Mother, showing us how to live with purity, devotion, and grace.

Swamiji's presence is not confined to a temple or a distant realm but is found in the hearts of every soul he touches. He is a living embodiment of the eternal truth that God resides within all beings, and it is through devotion, compassion, and surrender that we can awaken to this divine presence.

In the divine tapestry of creation, where cosmic forces converge, the sacred forms and names carry profound significance. As elucidated by Lakshmi Seetharamanjaneyua Sharma Srishti, the incarnations of divine beings like Dakshinamurthy, Dattatreya, and Jaganmata are deeply interwoven with the principles of Srividya and spiritual awakening.

Interpretation:

1. **Divine Incarnations as Gurumurthy:**

   - **Parameshwara as Dakshinamurthy:** The form of Shiva as Dakshinamurthy represents divine wisdom, the supreme teacher.

   - **Lord Vishnu as Dattatreya:** When Vishnu incarnates as Gurumurthy, it is understood as Dattatreya, the embodiment of unity and divine knowledge.

   - **Jaganmata as Srirajashyamala:** The universal mother, Jaganmata, manifests as Srirajashyamala, embodying nurturing and protective aspects of divinity.

2. **Essence of Srividya:**

   - Srividya encapsulates the balance between Shiva (*as Dakshinamurthy*) and Shakti (*as Srirajashyamala*), revealing the cosmic energies of creation and destruction.

   - The sound of Narayana resonates with Dattatreya, completing the divine symphony that forms the essence of this sacred knowledge.

3. **Sri Vidyanarayana Tirtha Sabda:**

    o   Sri Vidyanarayana Tirtha represents the unity of Dakshinamurthy, Srirajashyamala (*Jaganmata*), and Dattatreya, symbolizing Amma, Ayya, and Guru.

    o   The teachings of Sri Vidyanarayana Tirtha guide followers of the Avadhuta tradition, leading them toward higher spiritual understanding.

The term **Gurumurthy** refers to the divine form of a teacher, an embodiment of wisdom who imparts spiritual guidance. Swamiji's teachings bridge the divine manifestations and cosmic energies, guiding us to realize the unity of all divine forces.

Swamiji's Message: Divine Presence Within

Swamiji's profound message is simple yet all-encompassing:

"Do not search for me in temples, mosques, or churches, for I am closer to you than your breath. I am the silent witness of your thoughts and the eternal presence within you. I see through your eyes, hear through your ears, speak through your voice, and walk through your feet. I guide your heart and mind, silently dwelling in every beat and thought."

Swamiji reminds us that the Divine is not far away but resides within us, in every moment and action. By turning inward and cultivating sincerity, truth, and compassion, we can awaken to the divine presence that has always been within us.

"Be kind and compassionate to all beings, as you would to your own self. Let sincerity, truth, and love light your path. Release the burdens of selfishness and ego, for they hide your true divine nature. Turn your body into a sacred temple and prepare your heart as a pure altar where I can dwell. Invite me into your soul with devotion, and I will fill it with the light of divine truth."

Through complete surrender, we begin to realize the infinite nature of the Divine. When we open our hearts to this truth, we recognize the Divine not only within ourselves but in all things: in the light of the sun, the whisper of the wind, the stillness of the night, and the love that unites all beings.

"Know that I am with you at all times and in all places. In this realization, you will find peace that cannot be shaken, love that is eternal, and the light of enlightenment that removes all darkness. Walk with faith, live with purity, and let my presence inspire you to be a vessel of truth, love, and divinity in this world."

Inferences for Reflection: Thoughts to Ponder

- **Divine Wisdom is Innate:** Swamiji's teachings remind us that divine wisdom resides within us. Our search for the Divine should not be in distant temples but in the stillness of our hearts, where we find peace and connection with the Infinite.

- **The Path of Self-Realization:** True spirituality is a journey of self-discovery. By surrendering our ego and embracing humility, we open ourselves to the divine light that guides our every step. This path is not one of outward rituals but inward transformation.

- **Compassion as the Key to Liberation:** Compassion is at the core of Swamiji's teachings. By cultivating kindness toward all beings, we align ourselves with divine truth. In every act of love and kindness, we experience the Divine in its purest form.

- **Unity of the Divine Forces:** The unity of divine manifestations, as shown in the interpretations of Dakshinamurthy, Dattatreya, and Jaganmata, teaches us that all aspects of the Divine work together in harmony. This unity is the foundation of all spiritual paths.

- **Living with Purity and Devotion:** Swamiji emphasizes the importance of living with purity and devotion. When we purify our hearts and surrender fully to the Divine, we can witness miracles of transformation, both within and around us.

- **Divinity in Everyday Life:** Swamiji's message encourages us to see the Divine not only in sacred spaces but also in the mundane moments of life. The divine is present in every breath, thought, and action. By cultivating awareness, we can experience the sacred in all things.

- **Embrace of Love and Faith:** Through love and faith, we are guided to higher planes of spiritual understanding. Trusting the Divine and surrendering to its guidance allows us to live a life filled with peace, joy, and eternal truth.

Divine Guidance in Every Moment

In the presence of His Holiness Sri Sri Sri Vidyanarayana Thirtha Swamiji, we are reminded of the timeless truth that leads us toward spiritual enlightenment. Swamiji's life of devotion, compassion, and wisdom shines brightly in a world that often feels lost in the complexities of material existence. His teachings inspire us to turn inward and seek the divine presence that resides within us all.

Let us walk the path of faith, surrendering our egos and embracing truth, love, and humility. With Swamiji as our guiding light, may we rise above the limitations of the material world and awaken to the divine potential within us. May we become vessels of compassion, light, and truth, carrying forward the legacy of Swamiji's teachings for generations to come.

A Tribute to Gurudev: Prayer of Reverence

O Gurudev, light of divine grace,
In your presence, we find our place.

With every step, your love we feel,
A light so bright, so pure, so real.

Through doubts and trials, your wisdom shines,
A beacon guiding hearts and minds.
Your words are rivers, flowing with peace,
In your love, all fears cease.

In your gaze, the cosmos is known,
The divine presence in every tone.
You heal with kindness, your heart so wide,
Embracing the world, with arms open wide.

You move among us, in love and light,
Turning darkness into sight.
Your compassion flows, unending and true,
Guiding us all with love anew.

O Gurudev, you are our guide,
With your wisdom, we walk with pride.
Through every prayer, in every breath,
We feel your presence, dispelling death.

In your embrace, we find our way,
With love and devotion, we walk each day.
O Gurudev, our hearts we lay,
In your sacred feet, forever to stay.

Chapter-4

The Divine Light of Sri Swamiji: A Path to Truth, Love, and Surrender

Sri Swamiji is not merely a spiritual guide but the living embodiment of **Sanatan Dharma**, the eternal truth that transcends time and space. His divine presence emanates love, compassion, and wisdom, leading souls toward liberation. Like the revered saints such as Sai Baba, Swamiji's love is boundless and all-encompassing. To his devotees, his teachings offer solace, inner peace, and a deep connection to the Divine, irrespective of worldly divisions. His guidance shows devotees the path to surrender, truth, and spiritual awakening.

The Divine Presence of Sri Swamiji

Sri Swamiji's transformative grace has touched countless lives, and his presence has been nothing short of miraculous. Devotees speak of profound healing, emotional relief, and spiritual awakening. His wisdom flows like a river of truth, offering answers that transcend the intellectual mind. His core teaching is surrender—a surrender of the ego, worldly desires, and the need for control. Through this surrender and selfless service (*Seva*), we align with the divine flow of the universe and receive blessings that transcend ordinary understanding.

As Lord Krishna says in the Bhagavad Gita (18:66):

"Surrender all your actions to Me, and I will liberate you from all sins. Do not grieve."

Swamiji's guidance mirrors this divine assurance. He encourages us to surrender to the Divine will, trust the process, and experience the liberation that comes from complete surrender.

The Purpose of His Sainthood

Sri Swamiji's sainthood is not for personal enlightenment but a divine call to all humanity. His life serves as a beacon, guiding souls back to their true essence. He reminds us to awaken the divinity within, teaching the importance of integrity, humility, and compassion. Swamiji's teachings are rooted in the understanding that true peace and joy are found not in external circumstances but within. His words echo the Srimad Bhagavatam, where it is said that aligning with divine timing leads to true fulfilment.

> *"When you trust in divine timing, all things come to you when you are ready,"*

Swamiji often reminds us, reinforcing the need to surrender to the flow of life and trust the Divine plan. In doing so, we align ourselves with the universe's natural rhythm and find peace.

Love, Compassion, and Faith: Pillars of Spiritual Growth

The essence of Swamiji's sainthood rests on the twin pillars of **love** and **compassion**. His unconditional love heals, transforms, and uplifts, offering peace to all who seek it.

As the Bhagavad Gita (12:13) teaches:

> *"Those who are free from ill will and pride, and devoted to the Divine, will be uplifted beyond the cycle of birth and death."*

Swamiji's love transcends boundaries—physical, emotional, and spiritual—offering healing to all who approach with faith. His divine healing is rooted in love and compassion, and through these qualities, one is able to overcome suffering and find peace.

Faith is also central to Swamiji's teachings. He encourages us to trust the divine process and have unshakable faith in God's timing. When we surrender to the Divine and trust its flow, we open ourselves to miracles and divine blessings. His message is clear: through unwavering faith, we experience a deeper connection to the divine, and our spiritual growth accelerates.

A Living Example of Surrender and Service

Swamiji's life exemplifies the power of **surrender** and **selfless service**. His every action reflects his commitment to the welfare of others, and his example shows us that true fulfilment does not come from material possessions, but from dedicating oneself to the betterment of others. He lives the principles of love, faith, patience, and humility—qualities that guide us toward spiritual growth.

As the Mahabharata teaches:

> *"The true servant of the Divine dedicates all actions to the Supreme, free from personal gain."*

Swamiji's life is a living testament to this teaching. His every moment of service, devotion, and surrender is an offering to the Divine and to the well-being of all beings.

Miracles and Healing: Divine Manifestations

Swamiji's miraculous healings are a testament to his divine grace. Many devotees have experienced profound changes—be it physical healing, emotional relief, or spiritual transformation—simply by coming into his presence with sincerity and faith. These miracles are not random occurrences; they are manifestations of Swamiji's deep connection with the Divine.

The **Vishnu Purana** affirms that the touch of the Divine purifies and transforms the soul. Through his healing presence, Swamiji embodies this truth, offering a powerful reminder that divine grace is not bound by time or space. Miracles are the tangible evidence of the divine's work, and Swamiji's life is an ongoing manifestation of this divine power.

A Call to Spiritual Awakening

Sri Swamiji's sainthood is a call for all humanity to awaken to the divine presence within. His life teaches us that true purpose is found in surrendering the ego, cultivating love, and aligning with the divine will. Swamiji's teachings are not just about individual enlightenment, but a collective awakening to the Divine truth that resides within each of us.

Sainthood, as Swamiji exemplifies, is not a title but a natural state of being—an expression of one who is in tune with the Divine. His life reminds us that divinity resides within all beings, and it is our true purpose to awaken to that truth and live from that space of divine understanding.

Spiritual Inferences: The Path to Divinity

Swamiji's life offers profound spiritual inferences, guiding us on our path toward divinity:

- **Surrender to the Divine:** The path to spiritual awakening begins with surrendering the ego and aligning with the divine will.

- **Service to Humanity:** Selfless service is the highest form of worship, a direct path to inner peace and spiritual growth.

- **Divine Timing:** Trusting in the divine flow and timing leads to spiritual maturity. The universe unfolds at the right moment.

- **Miracles of Grace:** Divine grace manifests in miraculous healings and transformations when we surrender with faith.

These inferences are not mere philosophical teachings but practical steps to live a life aligned with the divine, creating a harmonious relationship with the universe and experiencing true peace.

A Call to Embrace the Divine Within

Sri Swamiji's sainthood is a light that calls us to awaken to our own divine potential. His life and teachings remind us that divinity is not external but resides within each of us, waiting to be realized. Through surrender, faith, love, and selfless service, we can walk the path of self-realization and spiritual peace. Swamiji's example shows us that greatness lies not in the accumulation of worldly possessions but in the humble service to others and the Divine.

Through his teachings, we are called to live with purpose, love, and grace, spreading peace, love, and enlightenment throughout the world. His life is a beacon for all of humanity to awaken to the divine presence within.

Prayer to Invoke Divine Grace

O Divine Swamiji,
You are the embodiment of truth, love, and grace.
Through your light, we are guided from darkness to divine wisdom.
May we surrender our egos, embrace humility,
and live each moment in service to the Divine will.

Grant us the strength to trust in your divine timing,
and the courage to walk the path of selfless service,
knowing that through surrender, we find liberation.

May your love guide us, your wisdom illuminate our hearts,
and your grace heal our souls.
Bless us with the inner peace that comes from knowing our true essence,
and lead us to awaken to the divine presence within us all.

In your divine light, we seek refuge,
and through your teachings, we find our purpose.
Om Shanti, Om Shanti, Om Shanti.

Chapter-5

True Wealth: Purity Within

"Man's real wealth is his goodness, his inner purity, and the virtues he cultivates throughout his life."

In this insightful discourse, His Holiness Sri Vidyanarayana Theertha expounds on the profound truth that life's real treasure lies not in material possessions but in the virtues, we cultivate within ourselves. Qualities such as goodness, love, patience, endurance, forgiveness, charity, and sacrifice form the cornerstone of true wealth. These attributes not only define a person's character but also serve as the foundation for a peaceful and spiritually fulfilling life.

The practice of nurturing these qualities is known as **Samskara**—a continuous process of self-purification and spiritual discipline. His Holiness emphasizes that through regular practice, selfless actions, and a commitment to self-improvement, one can transform life into a reflection of divine principles.

The Path of Cultivating Virtue

"By keeping the heart pure, the entire life becomes sanctified. Therefore, it is essential to cultivate qualities such as goodness, purity, love, patience, and tolerance."

A pure heart is the foundation of a sanctified and harmonious life. His Holiness underscores that cultivating virtues such as love, patience, tolerance, and forgiveness enriches not only one's own life but also inspires others, creating a ripple effect of goodness in the world.

To achieve this, he advises steadfast dedication to spiritual practices and self-reflection. Every thought, word, and action must align with our higher goals. When an intention to perform a good deed arises, it is vital to act promptly, lest the inspiration fades. Over time, consistent practice engrains these virtues, transforming them into our very nature.

"A person is known by their actions, not by their external wealth." — Bhagavad Gita 17.20

The Essence of Self-Transformation

"Self-transformation is the key to realizing the divinity within. We can refine ourselves and realize our highest potential through constant effort."

His Holiness elucidates that spiritual growth is a gradual process of aligning our actions and thoughts with the divine will. It requires daily practices such as meditation, prayer, and acts of kindness. Transformation begins with small steps, guided by virtues like patience and humility, and blossoms into the realization of one's divine potential.

"Self-control and purity of thought and action lead one towards the Supreme." — Bhagavad Gita 6.5

The Role of Prayer in Spiritual Growth

"Prayer is not merely a ritual, but a means of expressing our deepest reverence and seeking divine guidance."

According to His Holiness, prayer is a bridge between the devotee and the Divine. It is not a mere tradition but a profound act of surrender, gratitude, and seeking divine guidance. He beautifully describes prayer as acknowledging the divine presence that permeates all creation.

In one such prayer, His Holiness offers a poetic depiction of our relationship with the Divine:

"The light that permeates this universe, the consciousness that flows through all creation, is You alone.

Everything, from the earth to the skies, is filled with Your divine presence.

My heart responds to You with compassion, and every movement of my body reflects Your influence.

We are nothing, and yet this entire creation moves through the threads of Your divine will. Through prayer, we remain connected to the eternal truth, drawing strength and guidance from the Divine.

"In prayer, the devotee surrenders completely to the Divine, seeking no reward but unity with the Supreme."
— Bhagavad Gita 9.22

The Power of Faith and Devotion

"Through unwavering faith and devotion, the disciple strengthens their connection with the divine and experiences divine grace."

Faith and devotion form the pillars of spiritual growth. His Holiness explains that true faith transcends blind belief; it is an intuitive trust in the divine order. Similarly, devotion involves surrendering to the divine will with complete acceptance. These qualities deepen our connection with the Divine and open us to experience the grace that guides our spiritual journey.

"Faith in the Divine and devotion to His will lead the soul to liberation." — Bhagavad Gita 9.22

A Life of Selflessness and Grace

"May we all strive to live lives filled with goodness, love, and compassion. Let our hearts remain pure, and our actions aligned with divine will, so that we may experience the ultimate grace of the divine."

His Holiness concludes with a heartfelt call to action: to live lives rooted in selflessness, guided by virtues, and devoted to spiritual growth. By purifying our hearts and aligning our actions with the divine will, we can transform our lives into expressions of grace and joy. The pursuit of goodness, faith, and devotion leads to lasting peace and spiritual fulfilment.

Reflection

"May the grace of the Divine be with us always, leading us toward spiritual awakening and liberation."

Inferences

1. **True Wealth is Inner Purity**: Genuine wealth lies in cultivating virtues such as goodness, love, and patience.

2. **Samskara (Self-Improvement)**: Regular spiritual discipline is vital for self-purification and transformation.

3. **Faith and Devotion**: Faith and devotion strengthen our bond with the Divine.

4. **Power of Prayer**: Prayer connects us with the Divine and fosters gratitude and guidance.

5. **Divine Grace**: Through devotion and faith, we experience the grace that leads to liberation.

6. **Selfless Service**: The ultimate goal of life is to serve others selflessly and align our actions with divine will.

Prayer

Divine light that fills the skies,
Your presence, in all things, lies.
In every breath, in every heart,
Your essence, never far apart.

The earth, the heavens, and the sea,
All move in Your divine decree.
In quiet prayer, I humbly bow,
Seeking Your grace in this very now.

Through every step, through every deed,
Guide me with wisdom, meet my need.
In Your vast love, I place my trust,
In Your will, I shall adjust.

Oh, Lord, Your light shines bright and true,
I surrender my heart to You.
Let all my actions, pure and wise,
Reflect Your grace that never dies.

Chapter-6

A Beacon of Divine Truth

(Message to Students by His Holiness Sri Vidyanarayana Theertha)

"A student's true education begins with self-examination and culminates in divine realization."

In this profound message, His Holiness Sri Vidyanarayana Theertha addresses students with timeless wisdom, emphasizing the importance of introspection, selflessness, and spiritual discipline. This discourse is a call to action for young minds to embrace the values of equality, humility, and dedication, which form the foundation of a meaningful and harmonious life. By aligning with higher truths and recognizing the divine essence within, students can become agents of positive transformation in their own lives and in the world.

Conquering Hatred Through Introspection

"To examine how close, we are to the Divine, we must ask ourselves: how much hatred have we distanced from our hearts?"

His Holiness encourages students to reflect on their inner state and strive to eliminate malice and hatred, which obstruct the path to peace. The Bhagavad Gita beautifully underscores this:

"He who is free from malice, who does not hate anyone, and who is free from pride, attains peace." —Bhagavad Gita 16.3

Cultivating a sense of universal brotherhood is paramount. As Sage Vyasa teaches in the Mahabharata:

"A person who sees the same soul in all beings and treats everyone equally attains true wisdom." — *Mahabharata, Anumarana Parva*

The ability to transcend ego, pride, and divisions is essential for harmony within oneself and the world. Self-reflection, therefore, becomes a crucial tool in this journey of transformation.

Understanding the Divine Force

The strength that governs the universe inspires awe, and we must seek to understand its source. The Bhagavad Gita reveals:

"The entire universe is pervaded by me in my unmanifest form. All beings are in me, but I am not in them." — *Bhagavad Gita 9.4*

Through disciplined minds and virtuous actions, students can connect with this universal force, realizing the oneness that exists in all creation. As the Mundaka Upanishad states:

"The whole world is in you, and you are in the whole world. There is no difference." — *Mundaka Upanishad 3.1.8*

This realization leads to true happiness and fulfilment, attainable here and now. The Ramayana echoes this sentiment:

"He who knows the truth and practices it lives in heaven, even if he is on earth." —*Ramayana, Yuddha Kanda*

The Path of Selfless Action

Selfless action is the cornerstone of a purposeful life. His Holiness calls upon students to rise above selfish motives and work for the greater good. As the Gita advises:

"Do your duty without attachment to the results." — *Bhagavad Gita 2.47*

The law of karma teaches us that the journey itself holds the essence of life. The Mahabharata warns:

> *"Pride, even in the face of success, leads to one's downfall."*
> — *Mahabharata, Shanti Parva*

The importance of serving a true Guru is also emphasized:

> *"A true Guru awakens the divine wisdom within us and guides us toward liberation."* — *Narada Bhakti Sutra 22*

Students can align their actions with divine will by surrendering to selfless service and the wisdom of the Guru.

Realizing the Oneness of Existence

This world is a divine temple, and the realization of oneness allows us to perceive the divine in all beings. The Mahabharata affirms:

> *"The entire world is the abode of the Divine; one who perceives this truth realizes oneness with the Supreme."* — *Mahabharata, Udyoga Parva*

Through prayer, meditation, and renunciation of selfish desires, students can transcend their limitations and experience divine grace. The Gita concludes with this ultimate assurance:

> *"Those who surrender to the Divine, free from desire and ego, achieve liberation and eternal peace."* — *Bhagavad Gita 18.66*

Reflections for Students

- Introspection and Selflessness: *Regularly examine your thoughts and actions, ensuring they serve the greater good.*
- Equality and Brotherhood: *See all beings as expressions of the same divine essence.*

- Guru's Guidance: *Seek wisdom from a true Guru to illuminate your spiritual path.*
- Self-Realization: *Recognize and embrace the divine within, fostering unity with all existence.*

Inspiring Conclusion

Life is a divine gift, filled with purpose and potential. His Holiness urges students to embody love, humility, and selflessness in every aspect of their lives. True education lies not in the accumulation of knowledge but in the realization of eternal truths.

"You are not the body; you are the soul that dwells within."
— Bhagavad Gita 2.13

By living in alignment with this realization, students can become beacons of peace and inspiration, spreading harmony in the world.

A Prayer for Wisdom and Peace

O Divine Light, guide our way,
Help us conquer hate today.
Let love bloom in every heart,
And see all souls as not apart.

Grant us strength to tame the mind,
In selfless action, truth we find.
Detach from fruits, yet strive with grace,
To serve the world, our rightful place.

Teach us stillness, pure and deep,
Where boundless peace and wisdom sleep.

Reveal the Oneness, vast and true,
The Self in all, and all in You.

O Guru's light, so ever bright,
Dispel our ignorance with Your sight.
May we walk the path You show,
In love and service, let us grow.

This world, O Lord, Your sacred shrine,
May our lives reflect the divine.
In thought, in deed, let goodness reign,
To bring us freedom from all pain.

Om Shanti, Shanti, Shanti.

Chapter-7

The Path to Inner Harmony: Wisdom for a Balanced Life

Timeless Wisdom:

In the fast-paced world we inhabit, where the pursuit of material success often overshadows spiritual growth, how can we find balance? How can we cultivate inner peace amidst external chaos? His Holiness Sri Vidyanarayana Theertha, a revered spiritual leader, offers us the timeless wisdom to lead a life of harmony—one that integrates both material responsibilities and spiritual aspirations.

In this illuminating conversation with Dr. Hari, Swamiji imparts profound teachings that encourage a life rooted in surrender, dharma, resilience, humility, and devotion. With insights drawn from sacred scriptures, epics, and the lives of legendary figures, Swamiji provides practical guidance for navigating life's challenges while remaining anchored in divine wisdom.

This chapter serves as a beacon for those seeking to harmonize their spiritual path with their day-to-day lives, offering tools to transform challenges into spiritual opportunities and live with greater purpose, peace, and fulfilment.

The Conversation

The Role of a Guru in Modern Life

Dr. Hari: Swamiji, how do you see your role in the lives of your devotees?

Swamiji: My role is to guide devotees toward realizing their divine potential.

As Krishna assures in the *Bhagavad Gita* (9.22):

> *"For those who worship Me with unwavering devotion,*
> *I carry what they lack and preserve what they have."*

My purpose is to remind them of their higher nature, helping them align with dharma and embrace the peace, love, and strength that come from surrendering to the divine. A Guru is like a lighthouse, showing the path through the stormy seas of life.

Inference: A Guru is a spiritual guide who helps the devotee discover their true essence, providing both guidance and protection along the path of righteousness. In the presence of the Guru, one can find both the strength and the clarity needed to navigate life's complexities.

The Meaning of Surrender

Dr. Hari: What does it mean to live a life of surrender to the divine?

Swamiji: Surrender is not a sign of weakness; it is the highest form of strength. Surrender means trusting the divine plan and letting go of ego and attachment. Look at Hanuman in the *Ramayana*: his immense strength and wisdom came from his complete surrender to Lord Rama.

Krishna teaches us in the *Bhagavad Gita* (18.66):

> *"Abandon all varieties of duties and simply surrender unto Me.*
> *I shall deliver you from all sinful reactions. Do not fear."*

This surrender is an active choice to align ourselves with divine will, accepting whatever life brings with faith and devotion.

Inference: Surrender does not mean renouncing action but rather acting with detachment and devotion. When we surrender our will to God, we open ourselves to divine guidance and protection, gaining peace and resilience even in the face of adversity.

Overcoming Life's Challenges

Dr. Hari: How do your teachings guide individuals through challenges in life?

Swamiji: Life's challenges are opportunities to grow spiritually. In the *Mahabharata*, when Draupadi was in distress, her faith in Krishna saved her. She trusted that no matter the obstacle, Krishna's guidance would always prevail. Similarly, life's difficulties are tests to strengthen our faith and resilience.

As Krishna says in the *Bhagavad Gita* (2.47):

> *"You have the right to perform your duty, but not to the fruits of your actions."*

Difficulties are divine opportunities that purify us and bring us closer to our true selves. By maintaining faith, we find strength and peace in the midst of life's tribulations.

Inference: Challenges are divine tests meant to purify us. By focusing on our duties and trusting in the divine, we can face any difficulty with resilience and spiritual growth. Each obstacle is an opportunity for deeper understanding and transformation.

Balancing Material and Spiritual Life

Dr. Hari: How can we balance material life with spiritual growth?

Swamiji: Material life is necessary for survival, but it should never overshadow spiritual pursuits. Detachment is key. Krishna says in the *Bhagavad Gita* (3.19):

"Perform your duties without attachment, and by doing so, you shall achieve the supreme."

Life should be lived like a lotus in the pond—engaged with the world but unaffected by it. Material pursuits should be tools for growth, not the ultimate goal. The pursuit of spiritual knowledge and peace should always be at the heart of our actions.

Inference: Balance comes from detaching from the fruits of our actions and focusing on the process itself. By living with spiritual awareness, we can lead a life that harmonizes both material success and spiritual fulfilment.

Cultivating Humility and Compassion

Dr. Hari: Swamiji, you emphasize humility and compassion. How can we nurture these qualities?

Swamiji: True humility arises when we understand our limitations and the interconnectedness of all beings. In the *Bhagavad Gita*, Krishna speaks of the person who is free of pride and ego, as one who is truly wise (13.8).

In this competitive world, rather than seeking to elevate ourselves above others, we should focus on elevating others. Serve with love, as every act of service is an act of worship.

Inference: Humility and compassion come from realizing the oneness of all beings. When we see ourselves as part of a greater whole, we naturally extend love and kindness to others, transcending competition and ego.

Deepening Divine Connection

Dr. Hari: How can we deepen our connection with the divine amidst life's challenges?

Swamiji: Prayer and devotion are the primary tools to deepen our connection with the divine. Krishna advises Arjuna in the *Bhagavad Gita* (9.22):

"To those who are constantly devoted and who meditate on Me with love,
I give the understanding by which they can come to Me."

Through prayer, meditation, and selfless service, we invite the divine into every aspect of our lives. Even in the midst of daily struggles, we can connect with the divine by performing each action with love and mindfulness.

Inference: Deepening our connection with the divine requires intentional practice—prayer, devotion, and service. These acts invite the divine into our hearts, transforming even mundane tasks into opportunities for spiritual growth.

Message from Swamiji:

May you walk the path of righteousness with unwavering faith. Let love, compassion, and humility be your guiding lights. Trust the divine plan, serve selflessly, and offer every action as an act of devotion."

Inferences:

On Surrender: Surrender is not passive; it is an active process of aligning with divine will. True surrender leads to freedom from ego and attachment, allowing divine grace to guide our actions and decisions. It is the key to peace and strength in life's turbulent moments.

On Challenges: Life's challenges are not to be feared but embraced as opportunities for spiritual growth. When faced with obstacles, we must focus on our duties, trust the divine plan, and see them as stepping stones to deeper wisdom and resilience.

On Material and Spiritual Balance: Material life should be seen as a means to an end, not the end itself. By maintaining detachment and focusing on spiritual growth, we can achieve a balance that enriches both our inner lives and our external realities.

On Humility and Compassion: Cultivating humility and compassion transforms our relationships and our sense of self. When we see the divine in others, we approach them with respect and empathy, fostering peace and understanding in our interactions.

On Divine Connection: Deepening our connection with the divine requires consistent effort—through prayer, meditation, and selfless service. By integrating these practices into our daily lives, we invite the divine to guide us, filling our hearts with love, peace, and clarity.

Divine Flow of Life:

His Holiness Sri Vidyanarayana Theertha's teachings offer profound guidance for leading a balanced life—one that integrates material success with spiritual fulfilment. By embracing surrender, humility, compassion, and devotion, we align ourselves with the divine flow of life. The challenges we face become opportunities to deepen our understanding, refine our character, and grow spiritually. Through these practices, we can find lasting peace and fulfilment in a world that often pulls us in multiple directions.

Living a life guided by spiritual wisdom transforms our everyday experiences into sacred moments. By aligning with divine principles, we discover a path that leads to both inner peace and outer harmony.

A Prayer for Inner Harmony

O Divine Mother and Father,
In Your boundless love, guide us to walk the righteous path.

Grant us the strength to rise above ego and attachment,
And the courage to face life's challenges with unwavering faith.
Fill our hearts with compassion for all beings,
And help us see Your divine presence in every living soul.

May our actions, words, and thoughts be offerings to You,
Transforming every moment into an opportunity for spiritual growth.
Bless us with the wisdom to serve selflessly,
And with the devotion to always trust in Your divine plan.

Om Shanti Shanti Shanti.

Chapter-8

A Journey of Grace and Light

Divine Experiences

The divine presence of a true Guru is often beyond comprehension, yet it guides us to self-realization, purity of heart, and connection with the divine. The experiences shared in this work reveal the profound wisdom and boundless grace of His Holiness Sri Vidyanarayana Theertha Swamiji, who has touched the lives of many with his celestial guidance. As Swamiji himself often states,

> *"The Guru is the light that dispels the darkness of ignorance. Through him, the soul finds its true essence and alignment with the Supreme."*

Swamiji, affectionately known as *"Doctor Dandy Swamy"* by his devotees, is not just a teacher but a divine presence who embodies the timeless wisdom of the Vedas, Upanishads, and epics. His teachings transcend the written word, offering the seeker an experience of divinity that resonates at the core of their being. His wisdom is rooted in the realization that the Guru is not just a physical figure, but a manifestation of the divine that guides us through life's journey.

As the Bhagavad Gita beautifully expresses, *"When the disciple is ready, the Guru appears."* This truth is evident in every encounter with Swamiji. His role as a spiritual guide is one of immense responsibility, but also of unparalleled grace. His divine words, actions, and presence open the gates of wisdom and truth, leading the seeker toward their highest purpose.

The power of the Guru lies not only in his teachings but in his ability to transform lives. A true Guru sees beyond the outer appearances, guiding the soul in its quest for divinity. Swamiji embodies this truth with every gesture, every word, and every act. His words are not mere instructions; they are divine whispers that awaken the seeker's latent potential, helping them realize their oneness with the universe.

A Guru's grace is described in the ancient scriptures as the ultimate force that removes obstacles and illuminates the path of spiritual awakening. Swamiji's divine energy acts as a bridge between the material and spiritual worlds, helping devotees cross over the turbulent waters of life with faith, devotion, and knowledge. As the revered philosopher Adi Shankaracharya said, *"In the Guru's presence, all doubts dissolve, and the soul shines with the light of truth."*

Through the experiences shared in this work, we come to understand the Guru's role as a compassionate guide, one who is not bound by time or space. Whether through miraculous occurrences, divine insights, or subtle acts of kindness, Swamiji's grace reaches beyond the ordinary and touches the divine core within every being. His influence extends far beyond the limits of the material world, leading devotees to experience profound transformations.

1. Shirdi Darshan Miracle: A Test of Faith and Divine Orchestration

One devotee, a long-time follower of Shirdi Sai Baba, had long wished to visit the sacred town of Shirdi but faced repeated obstacles in planning the pilgrimage. Upon meeting Swamiji, the devotee expressed the desire to visit Sai Baba's temple. Swamiji responded with a knowing smile, saying,

"Why suddenly now, after forgetting him for so long? Wait and see."

Two weeks later, the devotee and family embarked on the long-awaited trip to Shirdi. A curious incident unfolded near the temple queue: a man dressed like Sai Baba, surrounded by four dogs, sat quietly on a roadside platform. Strangely, other passers-by seemed unaware of his presence. The devotee offered him money, which was declined, though the man asked for coins in Marathi—words the devotee did not understand at the time. Inside the temple, despite having a quick-darshan ticket, their queue moved at an inexplicably slow pace. The devotee remembered Swamiji's words and prayed silently, asking for a resolution. Miraculously, the family was ushered to the front of the sanctum just in time for the evening Harati. Standing directly before Sai Baba during the holy ritual filled them with tears of joy. Upon returning to Bangalore, Swamiji asked, *"Why did you give so much money?"* This seemingly casual comment confirmed his divine connection to the events, leaving the devotee in awe of Swamiji's omniscience.

2. Harvard Business School Admission: A Leap Beyond Human Effort

After a successful corporate career spanning over two decades, the devotee found inspiration to pursue a Senior Executive MBA program at Harvard Business School (HBS). Despite the daunting application process, the devotee proceeded with faith, invoking Swamiji's blessings at every step.

Soon after submitting the application, Swamiji invited the devotee to visit his ashram in Malleshwaram, Bangalore. Two weeks later, an extraordinary confirmation arrived: the devotee was accepted into the program without the typical prerequisites of TOEFL and GRE scores. When the devotee shared the news, Swamiji simply smiled and said, *"I know."* This calm acknowledgment of what seemed like an extraordinary achievement reaffirmed the power of surrendering one's efforts to a Guru's grace.

3. The Kaarthika Deepam Procession: Carrying the Light of Lord Shiva

During the sacred Kaarthika month, the devotee visited a centuries-old Shiva temple in their native village. The morning was spent in devotion, participating in a special abhishekam for Lord Shiva. Throughout the day, thoughts of Swamiji persisted, as though his presence was subtly guiding the events.

That evening, during the Kaarthika Deepam procession, the temple trust unexpectedly asked the devotee to carry the sacred lamp (Deepam) and lead the grand parade of over 300 devotees. This honor, akin to carrying Lord Shiva himself, filled the devotee with an overwhelming sense of gratitude and divine connection. Later that night, Swamiji called during the auspicious Brahma Muhurta and spoke profoundly: *"Nene Deepam; Deepame Nenu"* (I am the lamp; the lamp is myself). Swamiji explained that the opportunity to lead the procession was a sign of Lord Shiva's grace and a call for greater seva. The devotee could not help but feel that Swamiji was the divine light guiding them to fulfil a higher purpose.

Peace and Tranquility:

- **Divine Communication:** The devotee often found that whenever they thought of Swamiji with sincerity, he would call or send a message as if sensing their thoughts.

- **A Sanctuary of Peace:** Visiting Swamiji's ashram always brought a profound sense of calm, akin to being in a temple.

- **Unspoken Care:** Swamiji's hospitality extended to anticipating the devotee's needs, whether it was offering food or water, even without any requests.

- **Boundless Patience:** Despite his busy life guiding devotees, Swamiji's demeanour remained serene and free of anger, exemplifying true spiritual equanimity.

Insights and Reflections

1. **The Guru as Divine Light:** Swamiji's presence in the devotee's life underscores the transformative power of a Guru who acts as a bridge between the mundane and the divine.

2. **Faith in the Unknown:** By surrendering to Swamiji's guidance, the devotee experienced seemingly impossible outcomes, showing the profound impact of unwavering faith.

3. **Grace Beyond Boundaries:** Whether it was a miraculous darshan, acceptance into a prestigious institution, or leading a sacred procession, Swamiji's blessings transcended worldly limitations, illuminating the devotee's life.

Ordinary Moments to Milestones:

The experiences of devotees are a testament to Sri Vidyanarayana Theertha Swamiji's divine grace. Through his blessings, ordinary moments have been transformed into milestones of spiritual growth and fulfilment. Swamiji's omniscience, compassion, and unwavering guidance continue to inspire countless devotees to lead lives of purpose and devotion. May these reflections inspire all who seek light on their spiritual path to find solace and strength in the boundless grace of a true Guru. Hari Om!

The Soul's Journey

Through trials and triumphs, many have learned,
In Sri Vidya Narayana Theertha Swamy's light, their souls discerned:
A Guru's grace is the divine thread,
That weaves through life where angels tread.

When doubts would rise, Swamiji would call,
A guiding hand through rise and fall.
In hunger or thirst, his care would flow,
A love unspoken, yet all would know.

His presence transforms, his blessings bestow,
A solace profound, where spirits glow.
For years and lifetimes, this bond has grown,
A flame of devotion, eternally known.

His ashram, a haven of peace divine,
Where hearts are healed, and souls align.
Each corner whispers sacred bliss,
A realm where earthly worries dismiss.

Sri Vidya Narayana Theertha Swamy, so wise, so kind,
Knows the thoughts of every heart and mind.
With a smile, he clears the paths of strife,
Infusing divinity into everyday life.

Through his grace, countless souls have seen:
The eternal truth, serene and keen.
The Guru, a father, a friend, a guide,
A divine flame that can never subside.

From mundane struggles to victories divine,
Swamiji transforms lives by design.
A reminder that faith, pure and true,
Brings miracles that renew and imbue.

In the tapestry of life, where mysteries dwell,
Swamiji's blessings weave stories to tell.
A teacher of truth, a harbinger of light,
Guiding all through the darkest night.

To Sri Vidya Narayana Theertha Swamy, the eternal flame,
We bow in gratitude and sing your name.

Chapter-9

Divine Harmony: Embracing Equality and Sacred Roles in Society

In a world where divisions based on caste, status, and roles have caused much conflict and confusion, the teachings of Sri Vidyanarayana Theertha stand as a beacon of divine wisdom. His profound insights into societal roles, dharma (*righteousness*), and the importance of inner harmony resonate deeply with those seeking a more compassionate, unified existence. Through the soul of Dr. Hari, we can delve into the teachings of Sri Vidyanarayana Theertha, embracing a modern understanding of ancient wisdom.

The Fourfold Path: Reinterpreting Ancient Roles

Sri Vidyanarayana Theertha emphasizes that the traditional divisions of society—Brahmins, Kshatriyas, Vaishyas, and Shudras—are often misunderstood. These roles, born from ancient times, are deeply tied to the inner nature and duties of individuals. However, as we move into the modern age, it is crucial to recognize that these divisions should not be seen as a source of superiority or inferiority, but rather as complementary functions within the greater tapestry of life. Each role contributes to society's overall well-being and spiritual harmony.

In the words of the Bhagavad Gita (4.13),

> *"Chaturvarnyam maya srishtham guna-karma-vibhagashah"* — *"The fourfold order has been created by Me, based on the three Gunas and the actions of individuals."*

Brahmins: Spiritual Guides

Brahmins, traditionally associated with the priestly and scholarly class, are now reimagined as Spiritual Guides. Their role is to teach, preserve, and impart sacred knowledge. It is their duty to guide others on their spiritual journey and provide wisdom that nurtures the soul. The true Brahmin embodies knowledge and wisdom, not by birth, but by deeds and spiritual awakening. This understanding reflects a more holistic view of their function in society—one that transcends rituals and focuses on guiding others toward enlightenment.

Kshatriyas: Guardians of Justice

The Kshatriyas, traditionally warriors and rulers, are now known as Guardians of Justice. This title reflects their role in protecting society, upholding law and order, and ensuring justice prevails. The Kshatriya's duty is to maintain dharma in society, stand as protectors of the people, and work to ensure that the rights and well-being of all individuals are preserved. Their role is not about dominance but about balance and fairness for all.

Vaishyas: Providers and Creators

Vaishyas, traditionally traders and merchants, are now Providers and Creators. They play a crucial role in economic growth, trade, and the creation of wealth. Their role is to foster prosperity through commerce, entrepreneurship, and agriculture, enriching society with resources needed for survival and development.

Supportive Builders: Honouring the Foundation of Society

Traditionally, these individuals were referred to as "*Shudras*," a term that, unfortunately, carries historical baggage and is no longer fitting in the modern, civilized world. It is unfair to continue using this label, as it diminishes their essential contributions to society. Instead, we can recognize them as Supportive Builders—those who, through their physical labour, craftsmanship, and service, play a vital role in sustaining the structure and function of society.

Their work is not to be overlooked but celebrated, for it is foundational. The labour and skills they offer ensure that all other roles can thrive, and their contributions deserve our deepest respect. By rethinking this role, we honour the dignity and importance of their efforts, acknowledging that every society is built upon the dedication of these essential workers.

On the Concept of Untouchability: An Anti-Divine and Unconstitutional Notion

Sri Vidyanarayana Theertha teaches that untouchability is a deviation from dharma and is neither divine nor constitutional. Every individual is sacred regardless of caste, birth, or social standing. The idea of labeling any group as untouchable is a misinterpretation of dharma and violates the principle of equality.

The Bhagavad Gita (5.18) teaches, *"The wise see the same divine essence in all beings, whether in a Brahmin, a cow, an elephant, a dog, or a dog-eater (Chandala)."* This verse clearly conveys that, in the eyes of the Divine, all beings are equal. There is no inferior or superior role in the divine order; each one is vital for the sustenance of the world. The real issue lies in our perception. Sri Vidyanarayana Theertha often says, *"We need to repair the chip in our minds that distorts our perception of others."*

Rebuilding Society: Harmonizing Mindsets

We must rise above notions of superiority and inferiority. The work we do, not our name or caste, defines our true value. Whether we are working in a palace or a field, our actions matter most. The pursuit of dharma—the righteous path—transcends all external labels. In a harmonious society, the collective effort of all ensures prosperity, peace, and justice.

Reflections for Contemplation

1. **Divine Equality:** Reflect on the understanding that in the eyes of the Divine, all beings are equal. How can this perception transform the way we interact with others?

2. **Sacred Roles:** Every role, whether a Spiritual Guide, Guardian of Justice, Provider and Creator, or Supportive Builder, is sacred. Consider the impact of your own work and how it contributes to the collective good of society.

3. **Overcoming Division:** Reflect on how societal labels like caste, class, or status can distort our perception of others. How can we actively dismantle these divisions in our lives?

4. **Inner Harmony:** True harmony begins within. Reflect on how aligning your thoughts, words, and actions with dharma can bring peace not only to you but also to the world around you.

5. **Justice and Compassion:** As we focus on justice, how can we ensure it is inclusive and compassionate, transcending biases based on birth or status?

Embracing the Divine in All

We must look beyond superficial divisions and embrace the divine essence present in all beings. Each role—whether that of a Spiritual Guide, Guardian of Justice, Provider and Creator, or Supportive Builder—is holy and essential to the flourishing of society. As we move forward, let us repair the chip in our minds that causes division and discord and, instead, celebrate the divine harmony that exists within us all. The wisdom of Sri Vidyanarayana Theertha invites us to embrace our shared humanity and work toward a world where equality, justice, and compassion reign supreme.

Prayer for Divine Harmony

O Divine Light,
You who pervade every being,
Guide us to see the sacredness in all,
Beyond the labels of caste, status, or birth.
May we embrace the unity of all,
In the wisdom of Dharma and the pursuit of Justice.

Help us to repair the distortions in our minds,
That cause division and disharmony.
May we, as Spiritual Guides, Guardians, Providers, and Builders,
Serve the greater good with humility and love.

Grant us the strength to rise above pride,
And to recognize the divinity in every soul,
So that we may live in harmony,
As one community, united in the Divine.

May compassion reign in our hearts,
And justice guide our actions.
With gratitude for the sacred roles we play,
We offer our lives in service to the Divine.

Chapter-10

Sanatana Dharma: The Eternal Light of Truth, Unity, and Divinity"

The Timeless Wisdom of Sanatana Dharma

Sanatana Dharma is not merely a set of rituals or customs; it is the eternal wisdom that has illuminated the path of humanity since time immemorial. Rooted in the Vedic teachings and the profound insights of countless sages, it is a living philosophy that transcends time and space. Sanatana Dharma encompasses a universal vision, guiding all souls to realize their higher selves and live in harmony with the cosmic order.

As Sri Sri Sri Vidyanarayana Thirtha Swamiji, the revered sage of Dwaraka Badarikashram, prays humbly at the divine feet of Lord Venkateshwara, he reflects on the eternal nature of Sanatana Dharma, stating, *"It is the universal truth, unchanging and eternal, guiding us all to find our divine essence and live with purpose, compassion, and unity."*

Sanatana Dharma is the soul's journey toward enlightenment, an invitation to explore the vastness of truth, to live with integrity, and to cultivate love and compassion. It is the foundation of universal unity, celebrating the divinity inherent in all beings. In this chapter, we will explore the core principles of Sanatana Dharma, address common misconceptions, and reflect on the teachings of Lord Venkateshwara, who stands as the epitome of compassion and divine protection.

False Notions Against Sanatana Dharma

Throughout history, Sanatana Dharma has often been misunderstood or misrepresented, leading to the propagation of several false notions. These misconceptions distort the true teachings of this ancient tradition, but the eternal wisdom of Sanatana Dharma stands undiminished. Let's address some of these misunderstandings:

1. **Sanatana Dharma is a Religion:** Many mistakenly categorize Sanatana Dharma as just another religion, akin to Western religious structures. However, Sanatana Dharma is a universal, eternal law that is not confined to any specific belief system. As Swamiji states, *"Sanatana Dharma is not just a religion; it is the very fabric of existence, the law that governs the universe, guiding all beings toward truth and enlightenment."*

2. **Sanatana Dharma Promotes Superstition:** Some argue that Sanatana Dharma is rooted in superstition or outdated rituals. In truth, it is a highly philosophical and spiritual system based on deep inquiry and the realization of higher truths. The rituals are symbolic acts that help align the mind with the divine, but the essence of Dharma is found in the wisdom of the scriptures and the inner experience of the self.

3. **Sanatana Dharma Encourages Inequality:** One of the most harmful misconceptions is the idea that Sanatana Dharma promotes caste-based discrimination. The original intent of the Varna system was to organize society based on qualities and duties, not birth. Over time, the misuse of this system has led to discrimination, which goes against the very principles of Sanatana Dharma, which promotes equality, justice, and respect for all.

4. **Sanatana Dharma is Against Modernity:** Another false belief is that Sanatana Dharma is incompatible with modern progress or science. However, the teachings of Sanatana Dharma encourage adaptation and growth, provided that

progress does not come at the cost of ethical values or spiritual wisdom. *"True progress is in spiritual evolution,"* Swamiji affirms, *"not in the accumulation of material wealth or power, but in realizing the divinity within and serving the world selflessly."*

5. **Sanatana Dharma is Exclusive:** Many think of Sanatana Dharma as being exclusionary, but it is deeply inclusive. It is not bound by national, cultural, or racial lines. As the *Rig Veda* says, *"Ekam Sat Vipra Bahudha Vadanti"*—*"Truth is one; the wise call it by many names."** Sanatana Dharma acknowledges the diversity of paths, honoring every individual's journey toward truth, whatever form it may take.

Core Principles of Sanatana Dharma

Sanatana Dharma is based on timeless principles that guide individuals toward a balanced, meaningful life. These principles, embodied in the four Purusharthas (goals of human life), are as relevant today as they were thousands of years ago:

- **Dharma (Righteousness)**: Dharma is the foundation of life. It represents truth, justice, and cosmic order. Swamiji reminds us, *"Living according to Dharma is living in harmony with the universe and our higher selves."*

- **Artha (Prosperity)**: Prosperity is essential, but it must be pursued with ethical integrity. It is not about amassing wealth for selfish gain, but using one's resources for the greater good. *"Artha must be pursued in harmony with Dharma,"* says Swamiji, quoting the *Mahabharata*, *"just as a charioteer and his steed must work together."*

- **Kama (Desire)**: Desires are part of human nature, but they must be moderated by wisdom. Unchecked desires lead to suffering, while balanced desires lead to fulfilment. As the

Bhagavad Gita teaches, *"Desires are like fire; they grow when fed but can be controlled by wisdom."*

- **Moksha (Liberation)**: The ultimate goal is Moksha—freedom from the cycle of birth and death. It is the realization of the oneness of the self with the Divine. Swamiji affirms, *"Moksha is the liberation of the soul, a return to the source from which we came."*

The Divine Incarnations and Exemplars

Sanatana Dharma teaches that the Divine descends to earth in the form of Avatars to restore Dharma. These incarnations serve as living examples of how to live virtuously and how to align oneself with the Divine will. As Lord Krishna says in the *Bhagavad Gita*, *"Whenever there is a decline in Dharma, and a rise in unrighteousness, I manifest myself."*

- **Lord Rama**: The embodiment of Dharma, Lord Rama's life exemplifies the triumph of righteousness and the importance of duty. His unwavering commitment to truth teaches us to honor our responsibilities, even in the face of adversity.

- **Lord Krishna**: In His divine discourse in the *Bhagavad Gita*, Lord Krishna expounds on the path of Nishkama Karma—selfless action. His teachings emphasize fulfilling one's duty without attachment to the fruits of labor.

- **Lord Buddha**: Lord Buddha's life is a testament to the power of compassion and mindfulness. He teaches us to let go of attachment and suffering, finding peace through non-violence and wisdom.

Inferences for Reflection

- **Sanatana Dharma is timeless** and transcends the limitations of any one culture or belief system. It offers a universal framework for spiritual growth, calling all beings to the realization of the Divine within.

- **True progress is spiritual** and is measured not by material wealth or social status, but by the cultivation of wisdom, compassion, and selfless action.

- **Dharma is the guiding force** that aligns all aspects of life with the cosmos. Living a life of Dharma leads to peace, harmony, and unity with the universe.

- **Sanatana Dharma embraces diversity**, celebrating the multiplicity of paths that lead to the one truth. It is not a closed system but an inclusive and expansive tradition that welcomes all seekers.

- **The ultimate aim of life is Moksha**, the liberation from the cycle of birth and death, achieved through self-realization and union with the Divine.

A Life of Dharma, A Life of Truth

In conclusion, Sanatana Dharma offers us not just a set of teachings but a way of life that guides us towards self-realization, harmony, and service to the world. As Sri Vidyanarayana Thirtha Swamiji reminds us, *"Let us walk this path of Dharma, not as a duty, but as a joy, honouring the wisdom of our ancestors and planting seeds of truth for future generations."*

Prayer to Lord Venkateshwara

Oh Divine Lord, Venkateshwara,
You who reside in the hearts of all,
Bless us with the wisdom to follow the eternal path of Dharma.
May Sanatana Dharma shine brightly within us,
Guiding us to live lives of righteousness, truth, and compassion.

Remove all falsehoods and misconceptions about the ancient wisdom,
And let the light of Sanatana Dharma dispel all darkness in our minds.
May we walk in unity with all beings,
Recognizing the Divine in every soul,
And serving the world with selfless love.
Oh Lord, grant us the strength to uphold your teachings,
And may we find liberation in the realization of the Divine within.
Om Shanti, Shanti, Shanti.

Chapter-11

Guru Purnima Message: The Divine Blessing of the Guru

The Sacred Guru Purnima

Guru Purnima is one of the most sacred occasions in the spiritual calendar, a day dedicated to honouring the Guru, the divine teacher. Celebrated on the full moon day of Ashada month, Guru Purnima is not just a ritual but a profound spiritual practice that acknowledges the Guru as the guiding force who leads us from ignorance to knowledge, from darkness to light. It is a day when we reflect on the invaluable teachings of our Gurus, who, like the moon in the night sky, illuminate the path of spiritual awakening for their disciples.

As His Holiness Sri Vidyanarayana Theertha Swamiji so beautifully reminds us, *"The Guru is the embodiment of divine knowledge, opening the doors to the sacred wisdom that connects us to the eternal truth."*

Guru Purnima honors not only the great spiritual masters of the past but also reinforces the eternal tradition of revering the Guru as the ultimate source of divine wisdom. This sacred day encourages us to offer our gratitude and seek the Guru's blessings for continued growth on the spiritual path.

Quote from the Bhagavad Gita:

"The Guru is the one who guides us through the darkness of ignorance to the light of knowledge." — (Bhagavad Gita 4.34)

The Role of the Guru in Spiritual Awakening

The Guru's role in the life of a disciple cannot be overstated. While parents give us physical life, it is the Guru who opens the door to spiritual life, helping us realize our true self. The Guru awakens the soul to its divine nature and directs the seeker on the path of self-realization. This awakening is not just intellectual but a deep inner transformation that aligns the disciple's consciousness with the higher realities.

As Swamiji emphasizes, *"The Guru does not just impart knowledge; the Guru reveals the divine truth that resides within each of us, guiding us to live in harmony with the universe."* The devotion to the Guru is a profound realization of the divine presence, a recognition that the Guru is not separate from the divine but is the living embodiment of that truth.

Quote from the Bhagavad Gita:

"A true Guru is one who leads you beyond the material world to the ultimate truth within." (Bhagavad Gita 4.34)

The Guru's Power: Spiritual Knowledge and Liberation

In the teachings of Sanatana Dharma, the Guru is the ultimate source of liberation. Through the Guru's blessings, the disciple transcends the ego and the limitations of the material world, moving towards moksha (spiritual liberation). The Guru's wisdom is the key that unlocks the door to eternal freedom, guiding the disciple toward the realization of their divine nature.

Swamiji explains, *"The Guru's grace is the gateway to liberation. Through surrender and devotion to the Guru's teachings, the disciple gains the wisdom that leads to the ultimate goal of life: freedom from the cycle of birth and death."*

Quote from the Bhagavad Gita:

"One who has received the true teachings from a Guru gains the wisdom that leads to liberation." (Bhagavad Gita 4.34)

The Path of Devotion and Compassion

True devotion is the essence of the spiritual path. As Swamiji teaches, *"Devotion is not a mere ritual; it is the sincere surrender of the heart to the Divine, manifesting as love, compassion, and selflessness in all aspects of life."* Devotion purifies the mind and heart, removing all barriers that create division. It is through devotion that one realizes the divine presence within every living being and fosters unity and compassion.

The Guru teaches us that devotion is not confined to temple rituals but is expressed in the way we interact with the world. True devotion leads to a deep sense of oneness with all beings, transcending the limitations of caste, creed, and race.

Quote from the Bhagavad Gita:

"Devotion to the divine leads to the realization that all beings are manifestations of the one supreme self." (Bhagavad Gita 9.22)

The Essential Qualities of a True Disciple

To receive the full grace and wisdom of the Guru, a disciple must cultivate two essential qualities: faith (Shraddha) and trust (Vishwasa). These qualities form the foundation of the disciple's spiritual journey, for without unwavering faith in the Guru's wisdom, the teachings cannot take root in the heart. A disciple with faith and trust in the Guru's guidance is open to receiving divine knowledge and undergoing the transformation that leads to spiritual liberation.

Swamiji underscores, *"Faith and trust in the Guru's teachings are the bedrock upon which all spiritual growth is built. Without these qualities, one cannot experience the divine grace that is essential for liberation."*

Quote from the Bhagavad Gita:

"With faith and trust in the Guru, one can achieve the highest wisdom and liberation." (Bhagavad Gita 4.34)

The Guru's Role in Uniting the Disciple with the Divine

The true Guru is a living embodiment of the highest wisdom. Free from ego and desire, the Guru guides the disciple to transcend worldly attachments and recognize the divine presence within. Through the Guru's teachings, the disciple learns to identify with the supreme self, realizing that the divine is not external but exists within their own being.

Swamiji reflects, *"The Guru is not just a teacher, but a bridge between the finite self and the infinite divine. Through the Guru's guidance, the disciple unites with the divine and attains spiritual freedom."*

Quote from the Bhagavad Gita:

"The Guru is the guide who leads the disciple beyond the ego to the ultimate realization of the divine." (Bhagavad Gita 9.22)

The Power of Words and Compassionate Speech

The spoken word holds immense power. Gentle, compassionate words can heal wounds and uplift the soul, while harsh words deepen suffering. Swamiji emphasizes that a true spiritual practitioner speaks with kindness, using words to spread peace, love, and compassion.

He teaches, *"Let our words be a reflection of our inner state of being. Just as the Guru's words uplift us, let us use our words to uplift others."* In our interactions, we must always choose words that nurture and heal, reflecting the divine wisdom imparted to us by the Guru.

Quote from the Bhagavad Gita:

"A wise person speaks with kindness, and through their words, they bring peace to all." (Bhagavad Gita 17.15)

Seeking the Blessing of the Guru

Guru Purnima is a day of reverence for the Guru, the divine teacher who leads us from ignorance to wisdom and from materialism to spirituality. By cultivating faith, devotion, and compassion, we can receive the Guru's divine grace and achieve the ultimate goal of self-realization and liberation.

On this sacred Guru Purnima, let us all seek the blessings of the Guru, humbling ourselves before the divine teacher who shows us the way to spiritual awakening and liberation. By embracing the Guru's wisdom and guidance, we can rise above the limitations of the material world and realize our highest potential. May the Guru's grace be with us always, lighting our path with wisdom, love, and compassion.

Reflection:

"May the Guru's grace shower upon us all, leading us toward spiritual awakening and eternal peace."

Inferences:

1. **Guru's Role in Spiritual Awakening**: The Guru opens the doors to spiritual realization, leading the disciple to self-awareness and divine knowledge.

2. **Devotion and Faith**: The essential qualities for a disciple are faith (Shraddha) and trust (Vishwasa) in the Guru's teachings.

3. **Overcoming Division**: True devotion involves shedding all barriers that cause division and recognizing the divine presence in all.

4. **Power of Compassionate Speech**: Speaking with kindness and compassion heals, while harsh words cause suffering.

5. **The Guru's Divine Role**: The Guru transcends ego and desires and unites the disciple with the divine presence within.

6. **The Path to Liberation**: Following the Guru's guidance leads to liberation from worldly attachments and self-realization.

The Guru's Light

In the darkness of ignorance, we roam,
The Guru's light, a guide to call home.
With wisdom vast and love so pure,
The Guru's grace makes the soul secure.

From the first breath to the last sigh,
The Guru's teachings lift us high.
Through devotion, faith, and trust,
We walk the path where spirits adjust.

No division, no walls to divide,
In the Guru's wisdom, we all reside.
With kind words and compassionate ways,
The Guru's grace shines through our days.

Transcending ego, desires cast aside,
The Guru's love is our spiritual guide.
To the divine, the Guru shows the key,
Uniting the soul with eternity.

So on this sacred Guru Purnima day,
We seek the blessings to light our way.
With faith and devotion, let our hearts unfold,
For the Guru's teachings make us whole.

Chapter-12

Living the Divine Path

(Wisdom from His Holiness Sri Vidyanarayana Theertha for Modern Seekers)

The Path to Transformation

In today's world, where the rapid advancements in science and technology dominate our lives, we find ourselves increasingly disconnected from our deeper, spiritual essence. Globalization has brought the world closer, yet, in many ways, it has led to a growing disconnect between human beings and their inner truths. While we are more technologically advanced than ever before, the real transformation that is needed—one that brings inner peace, compassion, and awareness—is often overlooked.

His Holiness Sri Vidyanarayana Theertha's teachings offer a much-needed remedy to this imbalance. His wisdom speaks to the heart of modern seekers, guiding them toward self-realization, inner harmony, and a deeper connection to the Divine. By returning to timeless spiritual values, we can overcome the challenges posed by modernity and find true fulfilment.

The Guru-Disciple Relationship

In the context of today's world, where external achievements often take precedence over internal growth, His Holiness Sri Vidyanarayana Theertha reminds us that the Guru-disciple relationship is the key to unlocking our true potential. The modern world might be busy with digital advancements and material pursuits, but true wisdom lies in looking inward and aligning with the Divine.

As His Holiness says,

> *"The Guru is not outside; the Guru is within. When the disciple's heart is open, the Guru reveals himself in the form of the Divine."*

This profound wisdom encourages seekers to understand that true transformation begins within. The Guru's guidance is not just external but is also a reflection of the Divine presence within every seeker.

Simplicity and Balance

In an age where the noise of technology, consumerism, and fast-paced living often drowns out the voice of the soul, Sri Vidyanarayana Theertha urges us to embrace simplicity. It is through simplicity that we achieve clarity and peace in our lives.

His Holiness teaches,

> *"Live simply, love generously, care deeply, speak kindly, and leave the rest to God."*

In our globalized world, where excess often prevails, simplicity offers a path back to balance. It is not about renouncing the world but learning to detach from the overwhelming distractions that cloud our perception of the Divine.

Time: The Teacher of Life's Lessons

In today's world, time is often measured in terms of productivity and efficiency. However, Sri Vidyanarayana Theertha teaches that time is a spiritual teacher, guiding us toward self-realization and inner peace.

> *"Time is God. Time is discipline. Time is a system. It is life and love. Time is your future, time is silence. Seek time to settle down, don't search to seek, but search to settle down."*

In a world where technology often tries to speed up time, His Holiness reminds us that true wisdom comes from respecting time and using it to reflect, grow, and align ourselves with the Divine.

Surrender and Self-Realization: A Path to Liberation

The modern world often encourages the pursuit of external success at the cost of inner peace. Sri Vidyanarayana Theertha teaches that true liberation comes from surrendering the ego and aligning with the Divine will.

> *"When you maintain yourself as Master, then you become yourself Master."*

This quote highlights that self-mastery is the gateway to true freedom. Only when we transcend the ego and embrace the Divine within can we experience liberation from the cycles of desire and attachment.

Maya and the Illusion of the Material World

In an era where materialism reigns supreme, Sri Vidyanarayana Theertha reminds us that the material world is but an illusion, shaped by our perceptions and desires. The real truth lies beyond the fleeting nature of worldly possessions and experiences.

> *"Maya is very powerful. Maya is multiple energy. Be with Maya, become one with Maya, bake in Maya, and benefit from Maya. Be away, but be near to Maya."*

While we must live in the world, His Holiness advises that we must not be consumed by it. By recognizing the world as an illusion, we free ourselves from attachment and begin to focus on the higher truth.

Karma and Dharma: The Path to Spiritual Growth

In the fast-paced, competitive world we live in, Sri Vidyanarayana Theertha teaches that every action has consequences. Living according to one's Dharma, or righteousness, leads to spiritual growth and fulfilment.

> *"Do your duty with full awareness, but do not get attached to the fruits of your actions. Karma is the path of self-realization; Dharma is the path of wisdom."*

By aligning our actions with Dharma, we cultivate purity of heart and mind, leading us toward self-realization and harmony with the universe.

A Path of Practical Spirituality: Living with Purpose

His Holiness Sri Vidyanarayana Theertha's teachings offer practical tools for living a balanced, spiritually aligned life. In today's material world, he reminds us that spirituality is not something separate but is interwoven into every aspect of life.

> *"Do all the good you can, by all the means you can, in all the ways you can, in all the places you can, at all the times you can, to all the people you can, as long as ever you can."*

This call to action encourages us to engage in selfless service, creating a life filled with purpose, compassion, and spiritual awareness.

Living with the Master's Grace

In conclusion, Sri Vidyanarayana Theertha's teachings offer a path to spiritual transformation that is both timeless and relevant to the challenges of the modern world. By embracing simplicity, surrender, self-awareness, and balance, we can transcend the distractions of science, technology, and globalization, and reconnect with the Divine within.

As Sri Vidyanarayana Theertha beautifully puts it,

"Master outside, Monk inside."

This reminds us that the journey of self-realization begins within. Only when we cultivate inner peace and discipline can we reflect that harmony in our external lives.

Key Inferences for Reflection:

- **Simplicity:** The key to clarity and peace in a chaotic world.

- **Time:** A spiritual teacher, guiding us to align with the Divine.

- **Surrender:** True liberation comes from aligning with the Divine will.

- **Maya:** The material world is an illusion; true fulfilment lies beyond it.

- **Karma and Dharma:** Act with awareness, aligning actions with righteousness.

- **Self-Realization:** The ultimate goal of life is to know one's true nature.

Prayer

In a world of endless noise and haste,
Where technology reigns, and time is misplaced,
We search for meaning in the things we see,
But true transformation begins within you and me.

Science may advance, and gadgets may grow,
Yet the heart still seeks a truth we must know.
In the rush to conquer, we often forget,
That peace is found in surrender, not in debt.

Globalization may bring us near,
But human connection is what we hold dear.
In the race for success, we lose our way,
But in stillness and prayer, we find the day.

So let us live simply, with love and grace,
Let the Divine's light shine on every face.
With every step, let compassion be our guide,
For in the heart of humanity, the Divine resides.

Chapter-13

The Path to Divine Knowledge and Inner Peace

The Dual Nature of the World and the Divine

"This world is dual in nature—one side represents light, joy, and peace, and the other side represents darkness, suffering, and hardship. Yet, in every situation, it is the Divine who is our true protector."

In His discourse, His Holiness Sri Vidyanarayana Theertha begins by explaining the dualistic nature of the world we experience—light and darkness, pleasure and pain, day and night. These opposites coexist in the fabric of life, yet the ultimate truth is that the Divine transcends both. The Divine is not bound by the duality of existence but is the unchanging force that guides and protects us through the ever-shifting circumstances of life. Recognizing the presence of the Divine in every situation is the first step toward attaining inner peace and security.

As the Bhagavad Gita states:

"In this world, there is duality, but the wise see beyond it, knowing that the Supreme Reality is present in all." (Bhagavad Gita 15.14)

The Role of Intelligence and Knowledge in Protecting Ourselves

"The truly wise are those who understand that only by trusting in the Divine can they truly protect themselves from the trials of life."

True wisdom, according to His Holiness, is not merely about acquiring worldly knowledge but recognizing the Divine presence in every aspect of existence. It is through this awareness that one can find true protection from the challenges of life. The material world is filled with uncertainties, but by trusting in the Divine, we find the ultimate security. The wise seek refuge in the Divine and find solace in the eternal truth.

The Upanishads teach us:

> *"The wise are those who understand the true nature of the world and seek refuge in the Divine for protection and guidance."*

The Nature of the Divine and the Power of the Elements

"Just as wind, fire, and the sea are bound by their natural limits, the Divine's power is expressed through the elements of nature."

His Holiness explains that nature functions according to intrinsic laws—the wind blows within its limits, fire burns within its boundaries, and the sea, though vast, does not overflow beyond its shores. In the same way, the Divine expresses Himself through the natural laws of the universe. By understanding this, we can begin to perceive the omnipresence and omnipotence of the Divine. Everything around us, from the elements to the living beings, is a manifestation of this divine presence.

As the Bhagavad Gita reveals:

> "All the elements of nature, from the wind to the ocean, operate within the parameters set by the Divine." *(Bhagavad Gita 10.20)*

The Importance of Labour and Dedication

"A labourer who works with dedication is embodying the qualities of the Divine, for it is through sincere effort that one experiences the blessings of God."

In His discourse, His Holiness emphasizes the significance of hard work and dedication. True devotion is expressed not through rituals alone, but through the sincerity with which we perform our duties. Whether we are laborers, craftsmen, or engaged in any work, when performed with devotion, every act becomes an offering to the Divine. This understanding transforms work from a mundane task into a spiritual practice.

The Bhagavad Gita teaches:

"A true worker, one who is dedicated to their work, is performing the highest form of devotion." (Bhagavad Gita 3.19)

The Transience of Life and the Unchanging Nature of the Soul

"Life passes through various stages—childhood, youth, old age. The body undergoes changes, but the soul remains eternal."

His Holiness reflects on the transient nature of life. From childhood to old age, the body undergoes numerous changes—growth, aging, and eventual decay. Yet, amidst this impermanence, the soul remains unchanged, eternal, and indestructible. Recognizing this truth allows one to transcend the fears and anxieties associated with the body's inevitable decline, and focus instead on the eternal journey of the soul.

As the Bhagavad Gita states:

"The soul is eternal and imperishable; it is never born and it never dies." (Bhagavad Gita 2.20)

The Need for Spiritual Awareness

"Most people fail to understand the true nature of life and the body. They become entangled in material pursuits, forgetting that the body is a temporary vessel."

His Holiness warns against becoming overly attached to the body or the material world. The body is like a chariot, while the soul is the driver. When the chariot reaches its end, the soul continues its journey. The true purpose of life is to recognize the soul's eternal nature and to focus on spiritual growth, rather than getting lost in the temporary distractions of the material world.

The Upanishads reveal:

> *"The body is like a chariot, and the soul is the driver. When the chariot breaks, the soul continues its journey."*

The Role of the Guru in Spiritual Awakening

> *"Only the Guru can lead us to the understanding of the true nature of the soul and the Divine. The Guru is the key to spiritual liberation."*

The Guru, according to His Holiness, plays a central role in our spiritual journey. It is the Guru who dispels the darkness of ignorance and illuminates the path to the Divine. Through the Guru's teachings, we come to understand the impermanence of the body, the eternal nature of the soul, and the omnipresent reality of the Divine. The Guru serves as the guiding light that leads us to the ultimate truth.

As the Upanishads teach:

> "The Guru's light dispels the darkness of ignorance and reveals the truth of the soul and the Divine."

The Ultimate Goal: Peace through Surrender to the Divine

"Through surrender to the Divine and the Guru's teachings, we find peace and liberation from the cycle of birth and death."

In the final part of His Holiness discourse, he emphasizes that the path to liberation is through surrendering the ego and following the teachings of the Divine and the Guru. Only through complete surrender can one transcend the cycle of birth and death, attaining eternal peace and bliss.

As the Bhagavad Gita beautifully says:

"Surrender all your actions to Me, and I will liberate you from all sins. Do not grieve." *(Bhagavad Gita 18.66)*

Inferences for Reflection

1. Wisdom and Protection: True protection comes from understanding that the Divine is the ultimate source of strength and security.

2. Divine in Nature: The natural elements operate under divine principles, and understanding these laws helps us see the Divine in everything.

3. Spiritual Work: Every act of sincere work is an offering to the Divine and should be approached with dedication and reverence.

4. Transience of the Body: While the body is temporary, the soul is eternal. Spiritual awareness helps transcend material limitations.

5. **Role of the Guru**: The Guru is essential for spiritual liberation, guiding us beyond ignorance to eternal truth.

6. **Surrender to the Divine**: True peace comes from surrendering to the Divine and trusting in the path shown by the Guru.

The Eternal Wisdom of the Divine

By understanding the impermanence of the world and surrendering to the Divine, we can live a life of peace and fulfilment. The world may be transient, but the Divine is eternal. By surrendering ourselves to the Divine and following the teachings of the Guru, we rise above suffering and find liberation.

Reflection:

Surrender to the Divine, trust in the Guru's guidance, and find peace in the eternal truth that transcends the illusions of the material world.

Invocation of Divine Grace".

O Divine Light, guide our way,
Through darkened night, to the bright day.
In Your shelter, may we find,
Peace and solace for the mind.

Ego surrendered, hearts aligned,
With Your grace, we are entwined.
Lead us beyond birth and death,
In Your eternal, boundless breath.

Grant us wisdom, pure and true,
To see Your presence in all we do.
In every step, in every prayer,
May we feel Your presence there.

With devotion deep, our hearts we lay,
In Your arms, forever to stay.

Chapter-14

Pearls of Wisdom

Crossing Dualities:

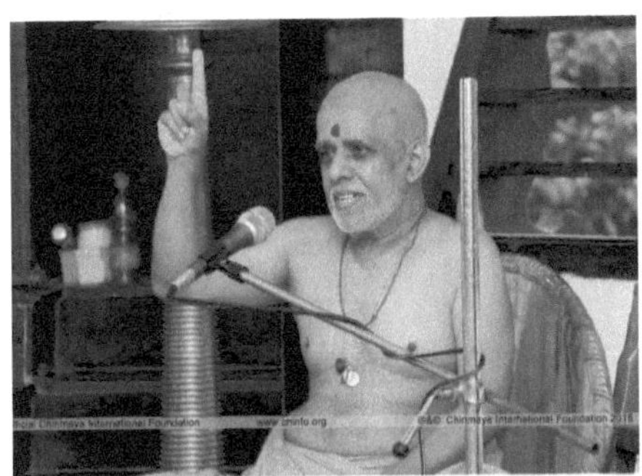

In a world defined by dualities—joy and sorrow, conflict and peace, belief and skepticism—His Holiness Sri Vidyanarayana Theertha, a revered doctor by profession, has shared timeless pearls of wisdom that transcend worldly divisions and point us toward the ultimate truth. His words, grounded in both spiritual insight and scientific understanding, offer a path to reconciliation between these seemingly opposing forces. Sri Vidyanarayana Theertha's teachings invite individuals from all walks of life to embrace unity, love, and peace, and to recognize that despite the varied paths we take, the divine essence remains one.

Where there is faith, there is love. Where love is, there is peace. Where peace exists, God or the supreme power dwells. And where the divine resides, there is no want or suffering. Through this beautiful cycle of faith, love, and peace, His Holiness reminds us that by prayer and surrender, we experience the true presence of the divine.

Sri Vidyanarayana Theertha, through his profound teachings, emphasizes that life itself is an intricate river that flows from an ancient source. The river of life winds through both serene and turbulent waters, reflecting the journey of the soul. Just like the river, our lives rise and fall, sing and dance, and face both struggles and moments of peace. Embracing this journey with wisdom, surrender, and steadfastness allows us to understand the deeper purpose of our existence.

In his teachings, he also speaks of the role of karma—our actions—as the cause of both happiness and sorrow. He encourages us to accept life's ups and downs with grace, surrendering our body, mind, and wealth to the divine. Through this surrender, we invite the transformative power of God and the guru to guide us, helping us transcend the effects of karma and find peace in every circumstance.

For those seeking spiritual wisdom, His Holiness Sri Vidyanarayana Theertha's message is clear: face life with devotion, patience, and wisdom. Like a mystic prince, we must adore, worship, and awaken to the truth, overcoming challenges through inner strength and the practice of self-control. By enduring life's trials, withdrawing from distractions, and remaining steadfast, we grow spiritually and realize our true nature.

Just as Sri Ramakrishna Paramahamsa beautifully stated, *"Religions are many, but they all lead to God,"* Sri Vidyanarayana Theertha's teachings encourage respect for all paths. Despite the many contradictions, conflicts, and beliefs that exist in the world, truth remains one, and the ultimate goal of all spiritual practices is the realization of oneness with the divine. Through wisdom, love, and the experience of divine grace, we find our way to the eternal truth.

1. The Nature of the Self

1. "The self is eternal and indestructible, beyond physical form."
2. "Understand the self as separate from the body; the true self is pure consciousness."
3. "The true self is beyond the limitations of material existence."
4. "Understanding the nature of the self is the key to spiritual awakening."
5. "The illusion of the ego must be transcended on the spiritual path."
6. "The self is not affected by birth or death; it is eternal."
7. "When you realize your true nature, you become free from all suffering."

2. The Importance of Discipline

8. "Discipline is essential for controlling the mind and senses."
9. "A disciplined life brings mental clarity and spiritual progress."
10. "Consistency in spiritual practices leads to transformation."
11. "Self-control is a virtue that accelerates growth on the path."
12. "Spiritual discipline requires perseverance and dedication."
13. "Without discipline, the mind remains scattered and distant from truth."
14. "Spiritual discipline purifies the mind, leading to inner peace."

3. Service to Others

15. "Service (Seva) is key to spiritual life and growth."
16. "Selfless service leads to inner peace and a connection with the divine."
17. "Helping others purifies the heart and mind."

18. "Compassion through acts of service is encouraged."

19. "Service to the community reflects divine love."

20. "True service is not for recognition but for the benefit of others."

4. Contemplation and Meditation

21. "Meditation is a tool to attain self-awareness and peace."

22. "Regular meditation purifies the mind and heart."

23. "Silent contemplation on the divine is essential for spiritual progress."

24. "In meditation, one experiences the true self."

25. "Meditation helps overcome distractions of the mind and senses."

26. "Through meditation, the heart connects with the divine presence."

5. The Role of Faith

27. "Faith in the divine is the foundation for spiritual progress."

28. "Trust in God is a source of strength in difficult times."

29. "Faith in one's spiritual path brings peace and clarity."

30. "Faith is an inner knowing, beyond mere belief."

31. "Devotion fueled by faith overcomes doubts and uncertainties."

32. "Unshakable faith in the divine dispels fear and confusion."

6. The Transience of Life

33. "The body is impermanent; focus on the eternal self."

34. "Detach from the temporary nature of the material world."

35. "Life's fleeting nature compels the seeker to seek spiritual enlightenment."

36. "Understanding the transience of life fosters wisdom and humility."

37. "Rise above the fear of death to live with purpose and clarity."

38. "True fulfilment lies beyond the ephemeral nature of worldly pleasures."

7. Unity of All Paths

39. "All paths lead to the same truth."

40. "Different spiritual practices are unique expressions of the same divine reality."

41. "Respect all spiritual approaches; each is valid in its own right."

42. "The unity of all religions reflects the universality of truth."

43. "Truth is the same, regardless of outward forms."

44. "Each path is a unique expression of the infinite divine."

8. The Role of Knowledge

45. "True knowledge is the understanding of the self and the divine."

46. "Intellectual knowledge must be complemented by experiential wisdom."

47. "Knowledge dispels ignorance and leads to liberation."

48. "The quest for knowledge brings realization of one's true nature."

49. "Knowledge that leads to humility and service is the highest form."

50. "Wisdom gained from experience is far superior to mere bookish knowledge."

9. The Practice of Patience

51. "Patience is essential for spiritual growth."

52. "Be patient with yourself as you walk the spiritual path."

53. "Patience is the ability to endure hardship without losing faith."

54. "Through patience, we learn to remain undisturbed by life's challenges."

55. "Patience in practice leads to greater understanding and inner peace."

56. "Patience is a sign of spiritual maturity."

10. The Power of Silence

57. "Silence is a powerful tool for inner reflection."

58. "Deep wisdom emerges in moments of silence."

59. "In silence, one hears the voice of the divine within."

60. "The practice of silence calms the restless mind."

61. "Silence is a means of connecting with the deeper aspects of reality."

62. "In stillness, the soul finds clarity."

11. The Importance of Gratitude

63. "Gratitude is a spiritual practice that fosters contentment."

64. "Expressing gratitude aligns us with the divine flow."

65. "Gratitude toward the guru, the divine, and creation is essential."

66. "A heart filled with gratitude is fertile ground for spiritual growth."

67. "Gratitude helps overcome negative emotions and cultivates a positive outlook."

68. "Thankfulness transforms ordinary experiences into profound spiritual practices."

12. The Vision of the Divine

69. "The divine is formless and beyond human comprehension."

70. "The divine is present in every aspect of existence."

71. "A true vision of the divine transcends physical appearances."

72. "The experience of the divine is personal and can take many forms."

73. "Devotion to the divine brings ultimate peace."

74. "Seeing the divine in all things reveals the oneness of existence."

13. Non-Attachment to Results

75. "Detach from the outcomes of your actions."

76. "Non-attachment allows you to act without ego or expectation."

77. "Focus on the purity of the action, not the rewards."

78. "Detachment from results brings peace and reduces suffering."

79. "True freedom comes from letting go of attachment to success or failure."

80. "Acting without attachment brings true peace of mind."

14. The Role of Meditation in Overcoming Ego

81. "Meditation helps transcend the ego and connect with the soul."

82. "Deep meditation reveals the illusory nature of the ego."

83. "The ego is a barrier between the individual and the divine."

84. "Meditation dissolves the false sense of separation from the divine."

85. "True meditation leads to the experience of oneness with all beings."

86. "Through meditation, ego is dissolved, and the soul experiences its divinity."

15. The Importance of Humility

87. "Humility is the foundation of all spiritual virtues."

88. "True humility comes from recognizing our dependence on the divine."

89. "A humble heart is open to divine wisdom."

90. "Humility allows us to learn from all experiences and beings."

91. "By embracing humility, we transcend ego and pride."

92. "Humility purifies the heart and attracts divine grace."

16. Detachment from Materialism

93. "Detachment from material possessions leads to freedom."

94. "True happiness comes from within, not from external acquisitions."

95. "The desire for material things creates bondage, while detachment brings liberation."

96. "Live with simplicity, and the soul will find peace."

97. "By detaching from the material, we can focus on spiritual wealth."

98. "Materialism distracts from the true purpose of life."

17. The Role of Devotion

99. "Devotion to the divine purifies the heart."

100. "Through devotion, one attains oneness with the divine."

101. "Devotion is the highest form of worship, transcending rituals."

102. "True devotion is not in words but in sincere action."

103. "Devotion transforms the mind and body into instruments of divine service."

104. "Surrendering to the divine through devotion leads to liberation."

18. The Power of Mantras

105. "Mantras are the sacred sounds that connect us with the divine."

106. "Chanting mantras purifies the mind and awakens spiritual energy."

107. "The power of mantras lies in their repetition and sincere invocation."

108. "By chanting mantras, we align ourselves with the divine frequency."

109. "Mantras are keys to unlocking spiritual insight and peace."

110. "Repetition of the divine name cleanses the heart."

19. The Transcendence of Suffering

111. "Suffering is a product of attachment; transcend it through detachment."

112. "Accepting suffering as part of the journey leads to peace."

113. "Through spiritual practice, we rise above the pain of worldly existence."

114. "Suffering purifies the soul and deepens understanding."

115. "Realizing the impermanence of suffering brings freedom from fear."

116. "Suffering, when accepted, leads to spiritual awakening."

20. The Illusion of the Material World

117. "The world is an illusion, a temporary manifestation of the divine."

118. "The material world appears real but is ultimately transient."

119. "Understanding the illusory nature of the world brings detachment."

120. "The senses deceive us; true reality is found beyond them."

121. "One who perceives the world as an illusion is free from attachment."

122. "The material world is a reflection of divine consciousness, not its essence."

21. The Importance of Self-Reflection

123. "Self-reflection leads to greater self-awareness and spiritual insight."

124. "Through introspection, one can discern the truth of one's nature."

125. "Regular self-reflection helps one stay on the path of righteousness."

126. "Self-awareness is the first step toward spiritual freedom."

127. "Self-reflection reveals the mind's true condition and its potential for growth."

128. "The journey of self-reflection leads to self-realization."

22. The Path to Liberation

129. "The path to liberation is through self-awareness and devotion."

130. "By transcending ego and attachment, one achieves liberation."

131. "Liberation comes from the realization of the self's oneness with the divine."

132. "The ultimate goal is to be free from the cycle of birth and death."

133. "Through wisdom, compassion, and devotion, the soul attains liberation."

23. The Significance of the Guru

134. "The Guru is the guiding light on the spiritual path."

135. "The Guru imparts wisdom that removes the darkness of ignorance."

136. "Devotion to the Guru brings the disciple closer to the divine."

137. "The Guru's presence is a blessing that leads to spiritual elevation."

138. "A true Guru does not seek followers, but transforms lives."

139. "Trusting the Guru's guidance opens the path to realization."

140. "The Guru is the bridge between the seeker and the divine."

24. The Power of Compassion

141. "Compassion is the essence of all spiritual practice."

142. "True compassion is rooted in understanding the interconnectedness of all beings."

143. "Compassionate actions purify the heart and mind."

144. "To be compassionate is to live in harmony with the divine will."

145. "When you act with compassion, you become a channel of divine love."

146. "Compassion heals the wounds of the soul and uplifts humanity."

147. "Through compassion, one transcends the limitations of the ego."

25. The Importance of Silence

148. "In silence, the divine speaks to the soul."

149. "Silent contemplation leads to deeper understanding."

150. "Through silence, we remove distractions and focus on the divine."

151. "Silence is the gateway to the inner peace that resides within."

152. "True wisdom emerges when we embrace silence and stillness."

153. "By cultivating silence, the mind becomes a mirror for divine truth."

154. "In silence, we find the answers to life's deepest questions."

26. Embracing the Present Moment

155. "Live in the present, for the present is all we truly have."

156. "To embrace the present moment is to connect with the divine."

157. "Attachment to the past or future brings suffering; embrace the now."

158. "The present moment is the eternal now, where the divine resides."

159. "Focus on the present, and the future will unfold as it should."

160. "Living in the present moment frees us from the chains of worry and regret."

161. "The divine manifests in the present, so do not dwell in the past or future."

27. The Importance of Humility

162. "Humility is the foundation of all spiritual practices."

163. "True humility arises from the understanding that everything is a gift from the divine."

164. "A humble heart is open to the wisdom of the divine."

165. "By embracing humility, we transcend ego and approach the divine with purity."

166. "Humility is the doorway to the highest spiritual wisdom."

167. "The humble soul is at peace, for it is free from pride and arrogance."

168. "Through humility, one becomes worthy of divine grace."

28. The Role of Devotion in Overcoming Obstacles

169. "Devotion to the divine removes all obstacles from the path."

170. "True devotion is not swayed by difficulties, for it is rooted in faith."

171. "When faced with challenges, deepen your devotion and trust in the divine."

172. "Obstacles on the spiritual path are opportunities for growth in devotion."

173. "The more we surrender to divine will, the fewer obstacles we face."

174. "Through devotion, even the toughest challenges become stepping stones."

175. "Surrendering all to the divine through devotion dissolves all barriers."

29. The Transformative Power of Love

176. "Love is the highest form of spiritual practice."

177. "True love is unconditional and transcends all boundaries."

178. "Love for the divine transforms the heart and mind."

179. "In loving others, we express the divine love within."

180. "Love is the key to overcoming hatred and ignorance."

181. "Love purifies the heart and leads to spiritual liberation."

182. "Through love, we experience the oneness of all creation."

30. The Practice of Equanimity

183. "Equanimity is the ability to remain calm amidst life's storms."

184. "Practice equanimity by remaining unaffected by praise or criticism."

185. "Equanimity arises from the understanding that all experiences are transient."

186. "Through equanimity, we gain control over our emotions and desires."

187. "Cultivating equanimity allows the mind to remain steady and focused."

188. "The balanced mind is unaffected by external circumstances."

189. "Equanimity is the hallmark of a spiritually awakened soul."

31. The Path of Renunciation

190. "Renunciation is not the abandonment of life, but the abandonment of attachment."

191. "True renunciation comes from within, through detachment from desires."

192. "Renounce desires, but not the duties given to you by the divine."

193. "Renunciation is not withdrawal from the world but non-attachment to it."

194. "Renunciation is the ultimate freedom, for it frees us from the bonds of the material world."

195. "True renunciation is living in the world without being attached to it."

196. "Through renunciation, we align ourselves with the divine purpose of life."

32. The Role of Mindfulness

197. "Mindfulness is the practice of being fully present in each moment."

198. "Through mindfulness, we cultivate awareness of the divine in all things."

199. "Mindfulness allows us to control the wandering mind and focus on the divine."

200. "The practice of mindfulness purifies the mind and enhances spiritual perception."

201. "In every action, be mindful of the divine presence that guides you."

202. "Mindfulness helps us align our thoughts, words, and actions with the divine will."

33. The Divine Presence in All Things

203. "The divine is present in every atom of creation."

204. "Recognizing the divine in all beings leads to peace and harmony."

205. "When we see the divine in everything, we transcend duality."

206. "The divine presence is not separate from us, it is within and around us."

207. "By recognizing the divine in all, we overcome the illusion of separation."

208. "All creation is a manifestation of the divine, and through this understanding, we experience unity."

34. The Unity of All Paths

209. "All spiritual paths lead to the same truth."

210. "Each path is a unique approach to the infinite divine."

211. "Though the forms may differ, the essence of all paths is the same."

212. "Respect and honour all spiritual traditions, for they all guide toward the one truth."

213. "The diversity of spiritual paths reflects the infinite ways the divine manifests."

214. "The goal of all paths is to awaken the soul to its divine nature."

A Sacred Journey:

In the profound teachings of Sri Vidyanarayana Theertha, we find a timeless guide to navigating the complexities of life. His wisdom encourages us to transcend the dualities and contradictions of our existence, to embrace love and peace as pathways to the divine, and to recognize that, at the core of all religions, there is but one truth—a truth that binds us all in unity and purpose. Just as the river of life flows with its twists and turns, so too does the soul journey through moments of joy and sorrow, growth and struggle. By surrendering to the divine, practising selfless devotion, and cultivating inner strength, we come to understand that life itself is a sacred journey, a dance between the finite and the infinite, between worldly existence and spiritual realization.

In this journey, faith becomes the foundation, love is the bridge, and peace is the ultimate destination. As we walk the path illuminated by the pearls of wisdom shared by Sri Vidyanarayana Theertha, we move ever closer to the divine presence, discovering that where there is faith, there is no want, and where there is love, there is eternal peace. May we all seek this peace and, through prayer, surrender, and wisdom, experience the grace of the divine in every moment of our lives.

"In Gratitude to the Divine Wisdom"

O Gurudev, whose wisdom shines,
Like pearly drops through sacred lines,
You've gifted us the truth so pure,
A light that guides, a love so sure.

Through words divine and teachings deep,
You've woken us from restless sleep.
In every pearl, a world untold,
A treasure more than silver or gold.

With steady hands and heart so kind,
You've freed the soul, enlightened the mind.
In your embrace, we find our way,
A brighter path to walk each day.

For every truth you've shown our hearts,
For every lesson that imparts
The strength to rise, the peace to live,
We thank you, Gurudev, for all you give.

You've taught us love, beyond all fear,
To see the Divine, both far and near.

In every word, a flame was lit,
To burn away all doubts that sit.

O Gurudev, we humbly bow,
For in your wisdom, we know now—
That all paths lead to God's embrace,
And peace resides in truth and grace.

Thank you, Gurudev, for guiding light,
For making our hearts pure and bright.
In your pearls of wisdom, we find our way,
Now and forever, we live in your sway.

Chapter-15

Youth: The Architects of Unity and Harmony

A Special Message from His Holiness Swamy Vidyanarayana Theertha

Dear Youth,

You are the torchbearers of tomorrow, the hope of humanity in a world yearning for harmony. Amidst the turbulence and challenges that shape our world today, it is you who carry the responsibility and the potential to build bridges, heal divides, and foster peace. Your voices, actions, and dreams will echo through generations, leaving an indelible mark on the fabric of society.

The Infinite Potential of a Single Cell: Inspiring Icons of India

Every human being, regardless of race, religion, or background, originates from a single cell—a divine spark carrying infinite potential. From this singular foundation, many great souls have emerged, leaving behind legacies that continue to guide and inspire us today. These iconic figures, whose lives were filled with wisdom, compassion, and courage, demonstrate the power of purpose-driven action to shape not just a nation but the entire world.

Here are a few exemplary figures whose lives serve as guiding lights for all:

Dr. A.P.J. Abdul Kalam: The Missile Man of India

A visionary scientist, Dr. Kalam transformed India's defense capabilities and inspired millions through his humility and dedication. He urged the youth to dream big, work relentlessly, and integrate spirituality with scientific progress.

Specialty: His life teaches us the importance of blending knowledge with wisdom and fostering a self-reliant, harmonious India.

Swami Vivekananda: The Spiritual Leader Who Bridged East and West

Swami Vivekananda's message of universal brotherhood illuminated the spiritual essence of India for the world. His call to the youth of India to embrace fearlessness, discipline, and self-realization is a beacon for the future.

Specialty: Vivekananda inspired inclusivity and unity, urging the youth to celebrate India's spiritual heritage while embracing the interconnectedness of all people.

Adi Shankaracharya: The Philosopher of Oneness

As a philosopher, Adi Shankaracharya re-established the spiritual unity of India through his teachings on Advaita Vedanta, emphasizing that all of creation is interconnected and part of a singular truth.

Specialty: His philosophy transcended religious and social boundaries, reminding us of the oneness of existence.

Rani Lakshmibai: The Warrior Queen of Jhansi

A symbol of courage and patriotism, Rani Lakshmibai's resistance against British colonial rule exemplifies the power of resilience, determination, and the fight for justice.

Specialty: Her life reminds us that courage can ignite revolutionary change even in the face of overwhelming odds.

Rabindranath Tagore: The Bard of Bengal

Tagore's contributions in poetry, music, and philosophy celebrated humanity's connection to nature and the universal spirit. His vision of education at Shantiniketan emphasized creativity, freedom, and holistic growth.

Specialty: Tagore's work transcended barriers of language and culture, offering a vision of global unity and coexistence.

B.R. Ambedkar: The Champion of Social Justice

Dr. Ambedkar, the architect of India's Constitution, dedicated his life to fighting for the rights of the marginalized and establishing a just society.

Speciality: His life inspires us to pursue equality, justice, and the dignity of all individuals.

Mother Teresa: The Saint of the Gutters

With her boundless compassion, Mother Teresa's service to the poorest and the suffering in society left an indelible legacy of love and care.

Speciality: She showed us the transformative power of small, selfless acts of kindness, proving that love is a force for social change.

C.V. Raman: The Light of Indian Science

Dr. C.V. Raman's groundbreaking discovery of the Raman Effect not only revolutionized science but also placed India at the forefront of global intellectual achievement.

Speciality: His relentless curiosity and scientific inquiry remind us of the importance of knowledge, discovery, and innovation.

Lessons from the Cell for Your Journey

As you, the youth of today, embark on your own journey of growth and learning, draw inspiration from the fundamental truths of existence. Just as the parts of a cell work together in perfect harmony to form life, you too must embrace these key principles for a meaningful life:

1. Unity in Diversity

Like the cell's many parts working together, embrace diversity as a strength. Respect differences and foster unity in families, communities, and beyond. Every person you meet is an essential piece of the greater whole.

2. Nurture Holistic Growth

Just as a cell thrives in balance, you, too, must care for your body, nurture your mind, and connect to your inner spirit. Seek knowledge, but also practice mindfulness, compassion, and wisdom in all that you do.

3. Wisdom and Responsibility

You have been gifted with intelligence and discernment. Use this gift to uplift yourself and others with kindness, purpose, and integrity. Your wisdom holds the power to shape not just your destiny but that of the world around you.

4. Overcome Divisions

Remember that God resides not in temples, churches, or mosques but in acts of love, truth, and compassion. Rise above societal divides to see the oneness in all people. Embrace every individual as a reflection of the divine.

5. Patience and Purpose

Challenges are opportunities to grow. "Wait, watch, and win," as I always say. Observe the world with clarity, act with purpose, and success will follow in due time. Stay grounded in your purpose, and let patience guide your actions.

The Call to Peace in a Conflicted World

In a world plagued by division, misunderstanding, and fear, the youth have a unique role to play. You hold the energy, courage, and potential to become champions of peace, justice, and unity. Let your actions speak louder than words. Be the voice of love and the agents of change. Let your life be an example of choosing unity over division, love over hatred, and understanding over judgment.

Your ability to look beyond superficial differences and understand the deeper essence of humanity will shape the future of our world. The world looks to you to heal the wounds of the past and create a world where every individual is valued and respected.

Discover Your Divine Potential

Within you lies the same divine energy that created the universe. Recognize it. Nurture it. Seek Amma—the universal mother, your guiding force. As I have said: *"Amma sees, Amma is Amma. Amma accepted the cell."* You are her creation, chosen for greatness and destined to make a difference in this world.

Embrace the infinite potential within you. You are a divine spark with the power to heal, unite, and transform. Trust in this truth, and let it be your guiding light in every step you take.

My Blessing to You

May you shine as a beacon of hope in a divided world. Transform hatred into love, conflict into understanding, and fear into courage. Your path is not just yours—it will uplift humanity. Walk with wisdom, act with compassion, and live with purpose. The future of the world rests in your hands, and I have unwavering faith in your ability to create a world of peace and harmony.

Prayer

O Divine Lord,
You, the eternal source of wisdom and compassion,
Bless these young souls with clarity of mind and purity of heart.
Grant them the strength to embrace unity in diversity,
To nurture holistic growth, and to serve others with love and selflessness.
May they rise above all divisions,
Seeing the divine presence in every individual,
And may they be the architects of a world rooted in peace, harmony, and
understanding.

Guide them in their journey to discover their divine potential,
And may their lives be a reflection of Your infinite grace.

Om Shanti, Shanti, Shanti.

Chapter-16

The Divine Path of Devotion

The Universal Power of Devotion

"Divine is the power of devotion that binds all creation."

Devotion is not just a human experience; it is an omnipresent divine force that transcends the boundaries of species, forms, and time. As His Holiness Sri Vidyanarayana Theertha beautifully explains, devotion exists everywhere, whether in the devotion of animals to their instinctual paths, or the unwavering dedication of plants and flowers to the natural cycle. This powerful energy, like a needle drawn to a magnet, pulls the soul toward God, awakening a deeper understanding of life's divine purpose.

Devotion is thus a universal thread that connects all beings to the Divine, an inherent part of creation itself.

Quote from the Bhagavad Gita:

"The love of the devotee for God is so pure and selfless that it elevates them to the highest spiritual plane, where they become one with the Divine." — Bhagavad Gita 9.22

The Path of Devotion: The Binding Force

"Devotion is the force that connects the soul to God."

Through the lives of great devotees like Ramadasu and Tukaram, His Holiness illustrates how pure love for God transcends worldly desires and creates an eternal bond between the devotee and the Divine. Their devotion was not ordinary—it was beyond human affection, reaching the realm of the divine. Through their unwavering love, they experienced God as their very reflection, their very mirror.

Quote from the Ramayana:

"When Sita's devotion to Rama was unshakable, no trial could ever separate her from him. The love between the devotee and the Divine is eternal and impervious to obstacles."

Quote from the Bhagavad Gita:

"To those who are constantly devoted and who always remember Me with love, I give the understanding by which they can come to Me."
— Bhagavad Gita 10.10

Four Types of Human Behavior: A Reflection on the Self

His Holiness further outlines four distinct categories of human behavior, each reflecting a different approach to devotion and self-awareness:

1. **The First Type**: Those who recognize their faults and the goodness in others. They embrace spiritual growth through humility and introspection.

2. **The Second Type**: Those who see both their own goodness and the goodness in others. These individuals radiate compassion and embody virtue.

3. **The Third Type**: Individuals who fail to recognize their flaws, living in self-deception and hypocrisy.

4. **The Fourth Type**: Those who distort the truth, projecting their own faults onto others and pretending to be virtuous.

Quote from the Bhagavad Gita:

"A person who is hypocritical and acts in a manner contrary to their true nature is an obstacle to themselves and others."
— Bhagavad Gita 16.16

The Role of Faith and Suffering in Devotion

"Through devotion, suffering becomes a means of spiritual cleansing."

His Holiness teaches that faith in God and the Guru is essential for navigating life's trials. Suffering, when viewed through the lens of devotion, becomes a tool for spiritual purification. Just as a patient trusts their doctor for healing, the devotee must trust God to overcome life's difficulties. Trials are not punishments—they are opportunities to shed the layers of ignorance and attachment, leading to a more enlightened state.

Quote from the Bhagavad Gita:

"Suffering is a part of the spiritual journey. Just as a seed must break open to grow into a tree, a devotee's soul must undergo trials to reach spiritual maturity."

The Guru: The Divine Healer

"The Guru is the spiritual physician who cures the ailments of the soul."

The Guru, much like a physician who heals the body, guides the devotee through spiritual practices and teachings to cleanse the soul. It is only through the Guru's grace that one can overcome the diseases of ignorance, attachment, and ego. Through the Guru's guidance, the soul is led from darkness to light, from ignorance to wisdom.

Quote from the Upanishads:

"The Guru is the supreme healer who removes the ignorance that clouds the soul, guiding the seeker from darkness to light."

Spiritual Suffering: A Tool for Purification

"The challenges and suffering a devotee faces are a part of the divine purification process."

His Holiness uses the metaphor of washing a dirty cloth to explain how suffering purifies the soul. Just as a cloth must undergo multiple stages of washing to become clean, the soul, too, is purified through suffering and spiritual discipline. Each challenge the devotee faces becomes a step toward liberation, an opportunity to cleanse the mind and heart.

Quote from the Bhagavad Gita:

"The purification of the mind through suffering is essential for spiritual progress. The devotee must learn to embrace every trial as a step toward liberation."

Inferences:

1. **Devotion Transcends All**: Devotion is not merely a ritual—it is a powerful force that binds the devotee to God and purifies the soul. True devotion transforms the individual and brings about spiritual awakening.

2. **Faith as the Pillar**: Faith is the foundation of spiritual growth. It turns every trial into an opportunity for progress and helps the devotee navigate life's challenges.

3. **The Guru's Grace**: The Guru's guidance is indispensable for overcoming obstacles and attaining spiritual liberation.

Through the Guru's grace, the devotee gains the wisdom and strength to progress on the divine path.

4. **Devotion Overcomes All Trials**: Devotion to God and the Guru is the key to transcending all obstacles. Challenges and sufferings faced by the devotee are not signs of punishment, but steps toward divine purification and spiritual growth.

5. **Surrender and Liberation**: The highest form of devotion is complete surrender. In surrendering to the Divine and the Guru, the devotee reaches the ultimate goal of liberation, where the soul is united with the Divine in eternal peace and bliss.

The Ultimate Goal of Devotion

"Devotion is the only path to true happiness, peace, and liberation."

His Holiness Sri Vidyanarayana Theertha concludes by emphasizing that devotion is the highest path to spiritual enlightenment in this Kali Yuga. No power is greater than the power of devotion, as it leads the devotee to eternal peace, joy, and union with the Divine. The Guru's grace and guidance are essential for navigating this path. Through unwavering faith and complete surrender, the devotee can reach the ultimate goal of liberation.

Quote from the Bhagavad Gita:

"The highest form of devotion is surrendering everything to the Divine and remaining in the eternal embrace of love."
— Bhagavad Gita 18.66

Prayer

O Divine Lord, so pure and bright,

Guide us on this sacred flight.
With faith unwavering, hearts aglow,
In Your divine love, let us grow.

May we see You in all we meet,
In every soul, Your presence greet.
Surrendered fully, hearts unbound,
In Your eternal grace, we're found.

Grant us strength to walk the way,
With love and truth in every day.
Purify our hearts through each test,
Lead us to Your eternal rest.

In the light of the Guru, guide,
Through trials, with You by our side.
May we unite with You, above,
In endless peace, eternal love.

Om Shanti Shanti Shanti.

Chapter-17

The Divine Principle of Radha-Krishna Tattva

The Essence of Radha and Krishna

"Radha signifies the Mother, the Earth, the Divine Power, while Krishna represents the Father, the Life Force, the Soul Power. Without the soul, the body cannot exist, and without the body, the soul is not realized. Therefore, both the soul and the body are essential and interdependent."

The divine relationship between Radha and Krishna reflects a profound spiritual truth: both are inseparable, with Radha embodying the divine feminine energy (Shakti), and Krishna representing the divine masculine consciousness (Purusha). This divine union cannot be separated by anyone or anything. Radha is nature in its purest form, and Krishna is the soul, eternal and transcendent. Together, they form the foundation of creation, and their unity is not just symbolic but an essential and inseparable truth of the universe. Wherever Radha exists, Krishna also exists, and vice versa. Their divine bond teaches us that the spirit and energy must work together in perfect harmony.

Quote from the Bhagavad Gita:

"Krishna, the divine consciousness, pervades everything, and Radha, the divine energy, brings it to life." — Bhagavad Gita 10.20

Radha-Krishna as the Eternal Divine Dance

"In every individual, we find the essence of Radha and Krishna. Just as a seed cannot grow without the earth, the universe cannot exist without the divine principle of Radha-Krishna. This divine principle is the very foundation of creation."

The union of Radha and Krishna represents the divine principle that governs all creation. Radha, as energy, and Krishna, as consciousness, are inseparable; they work together in divine harmony to create and sustain the universe. Without the divine energy of Radha and the consciousness of Krishna, nothing would exist. Together, they manifest the entire cosmos, making creation a divine play—a cosmic dance of the universe where both energies are in constant motion. The divine couple's union is the source of life and creation.

Quote from the Bhagavad Gita:

"The soul is eternal, and the divine energy that brings it to life is equally eternal. Together, they create the world in which we live."

The Path to Alleviating Suffering in the World

"How can we alleviate the suffering and pain in the world? Is it within the power of humans to do so?"

Human suffering, while an inevitable part of life, can be alleviated through compassion and empathy. It is not enough to feel pity for those who suffer—we must take active steps to ease their pain through kindness, understanding, and support. Radha and Krishna's divine love exemplifies the power of selfless compassion. Their love is not just about emotional affection but about active service to the world and to those in need. By following their example and expressing love in our everyday actions, we can reduce suffering in the world.

Quote from the Bhagavad Gita:

"Be merciful, for mercy brings peace, and peace brings spiritual fulfilment."
— Bhagavad Gita 16.3

Realizing the Divine Instrument Within Us

"Every individual must recognize that they are an instrument of the Divine. When one understands that all thoughts, actions, and feelings belong to the Divine, peace naturally arises within."

Recognizing that we are instruments of the Divine brings peace and humility. When we truly understand that all our actions and thoughts are guided by the Divine, we free ourselves from ego and selfish desires. This realization leads to a sense of tranquillity and fulfilment, as we begin to live not for ourselves, but as servants of the Divine. Krishna resides in everything, every moment, and every being. Only by remembering Him in our hearts can we begin to experience peace, love, and true fulfilment.

Quote from the Bhagavad Gita:

"I am present in all things. There is nothing that exists without Me."
— Bhagavad Gita 9.4

The Importance of Humility and Self-Reflection

"Before criticizing others or indulging in harmful speech, reflect on your own actions and thoughts. Recognize the greatness of the Divine and strive to act in accordance with it."

Humility is the foundation of spiritual growth. Before we judge or criticize others, we must first reflect on our own actions and thoughts. Radha and Krishna exemplify the highest form of humility. They show us that true spiritual growth comes from recognizing the Divine in ourselves and others. When we act in humility, we align ourselves with the Divine will and bring about harmony in the world.

Quote from the Bhagavad Gita:

"Let your actions be guided by wisdom, not by ego. When you act with humility, you act in harmony with the Divine." — Bhagavad Gita 3.35

The Power of Love, Faith, and Devotion

*"If we act with love, faith, and sincerity,
the Divine will bless us with the ultimate goal — liberation."*

Radha and Krishna's love for each other is an eternal example of devotion, pure and unconditional. To follow their example, we must act with love, faith, and sincerity in our everyday lives. It is through these qualities that we attain spiritual fulfilment and liberation. By offering our devotion with purity of heart, we are graced by the Divine, just as Radha and Krishna were forever united through their devotion to each other. This devotion is the path to liberation, to freedom from the cycles of birth and death.

Quote from the Bhagavad Gita:

"Devotion to Me, performed with sincerity and love, leads to liberation. It is the highest form of spiritual practice." — Bhagavad Gita 18.66

Inferences:

- **Radha and Krishna as the Divine Principle**: Radha and Krishna represent the inseparable energies of the Divine, with Radha as the energy (Shakti) and Krishna as the consciousness (Purusha). They form the basis of all creation and are eternally intertwined, symbolizing the unity of the masculine and feminine energies of the universe.

- **The Spiritual Bond Between Radha and Krishna**: The divine bond between Radha and Krishna is eternal and inseparable. Together, they embody the complete union of the Divine Feminine and Masculine, symbolizing the unity of Shakti and Purusha. This union is often referred to as *"Radhakrishna,"* representing their undivided and eternal connection.

- **Alleviating Suffering**: Compassion and empathy are key to alleviating suffering in the world. By embodying love and kindness, we can ease the pain of others.

- **Recognizing the Divine Within**: Understanding that we are instruments of the Divine brings peace and fulfilment, leading us to a life of service.

- **Humility and Self-Reflection**: True spiritual growth comes from humility, self-reflection, and alignment with the Divine will.

- **Love, Faith, and Devotion**: These qualities are the foundation of spiritual practice, leading to liberation and peace.

The Path to Spiritual Liberation

"By remembering the Divine and acting with love and compassion, we can experience the ultimate peace and liberation."

In conclusion, the Radha-Krishna principle teaches us the inseparable nature of the Divine energies of love and consciousness. Radha and Krishna represent the union of the divine masculine and feminine forces, guiding us toward spiritual liberation. By embracing the teachings of Radha and Krishna—acting with humility, love, and devotion—we can experience true inner peace and eventually attain liberation. Their union is not just a story—it is the eternal truth, the cosmic dance of life that reflects the divine harmony within all of us.

Quote from the Bhagavad Gita:

"The highest form of devotion is surrendering everything to the Divine and remaining in the eternal embrace of love." — *Bhagavad Gita 18.66*

Prayer

O Divine Radha, O Krishna bright,
Guide us through the darkest night.
With hearts full of love, with minds so pure,
May we your grace and blessings secure.
In every breath, in every word,
Let your presence be felt, heard.
Teach us humility, love, and grace,
To reflect your truth in every place.
May our actions be filled with devotion,
Flowing like an endless ocean.
Surrender we must, to your will divine,
In your light, let our souls shine.
O Krishna, with Radha by your side,
In your love, may we always abide.
Grant us peace, compassion, and bliss,
To dwell in your eternal embrace, in endless bliss.

Chapter-18

The Eternal Path to Fearlessness and Self-Realization

Spiritual Alignment:

The monsoon season, with its serene and tranquil atmosphere, reminds us of the divine cycles of nature. It invites us to introspect on the deeper truths of existence. Through spirituality, we align ourselves with the divine, embracing wisdom that leads to peace, fearlessness, and liberation from ignorance. As the Bhagavad Gita beautifully states, "He who has no attachment can really love others, for his love is pure and selfless" (Bhagavad Gita 12.13). True spiritual love is fearless, detached, and untainted by worldly attachments. It is this love, free of ego and desire, that forms the foundation of self-realization.

The Nature of Divine Will and Time

The Supreme Being governs all aspects of life and nature. The alignment of divine will with time determines the success of any endeavor. This is why ancient practices emphasize consulting auspicious timings (Panchangam) before beginning any task. When our actions align with the cosmic order and divine grace, harmony prevails. Life's uncertainties—whether natural calamities or personal trials—must be faced with unwavering faith, surrender, and gratitude. As the Bhagavad Gita reminds us, "Whenever there is a decline in righteousness and an increase in unrighteousness, O Arjuna, at that time I manifest myself on earth" (Bhagavad Gita 4.7).

This divine intervention ensures the restoration of cosmic order when righteousness wanes.

Understanding Fear and Its Roots

Fear arises from ignorance—the lack of true knowledge of oneself and the divine. It traps individuals in webs of desires, possessions, and ego, perpetuating restlessness and dissatisfaction. Recognizing that there is no "other" beyond the self removes the basis for fear. Aligning with the eternal principles of Sanatana Dharma leads to fearlessness, replacing anxiety with inner strength and divine peace. The Bhagavad Gita teaches us, "There is neither this world nor the world beyond. How can there be happiness without peace?" (Bhagavad Gita 2.66). The peace of mind attained through self-realization dissolves all fears, for true peace is the antidote to fear.

The Role of Meditation in Self-Purification

Meditation, particularly in the early morning, has the power to calm the mind and reveal the divine spark within. Through daily practice, we begin to recognize our flaws, working to overcome them gradually. As spiritual progress deepens, we begin to perceive divinity in all beings and circumstances, ultimately uniting with Sachidananda Paramatma—the ultimate blissful reality. The Bhagavad Gita highlights, "The mind is restless, O Krishna, and difficult to control; but it can be controlled by constant practice and detachment" (Bhagavad Gita 6.34). Through persistent practice and detachment, the mind aligns with the higher self, enabling spiritual growth.

The Burden of Forgetfulness

Forgetfulness, often a by-product of fear, leads to confusion and inefficiency. It clouds judgment, perpetuates ignorance, and binds the soul to cycles of desire and attachment. True liberation begins when the mind is freed from distractions and focused on the eternal truth of the self—the Atma. The Bhagavad Gita reminds us, *"The soul is neither born, nor does it die"* (Bhagavad Gita 2.20). The true essence of the self is eternal and unaffected by the fleeting experiences of the world. Fear and forgetfulness, therefore, are illusions, and recognizing the eternal self brings lasting peace.

The Divine Feminine: Lakshmi and Parvati

The Supreme Energy, or Parashakti, manifests as both wealth (Lakshmi) and wisdom (Parvati), governing the natural elements. By revering this divine energy, we honor the source of all creation. Worshipping the Divine Mother is a pure and transformative practice that grants both peace and prosperity. As the Bhagavad Gita states, *"The Earth, Air, Fire, Water, and Ether, are the five elements which make up this material world, governed by my eternal power"* (Bhagavad Gita 7.4). The divine feminine sustains and governs the universe, reminding us to revere the source of all existence.

Surrender and Truth as the Path to Liberation

Truth is the eternal foundation of life, unchanging across the physical, mental, and spiritual realms. When we live in alignment with truth, we liberate the soul from worldly attachments, achieving the realization of the Supreme Brahman. Surrendering the ego and embracing the truth leads to insight into the infinite divine power within us. As the Bhagavad Gita expresses, *"The one who has surrendered all actions to me, who is free from desires and attachments, I will protect from all dangers"* (Bhagavad Gita 18.66). Through complete surrender, we are freed from the entanglements of fear and worldly desires, guided by divine protection.

Inferences

- **Fear and Ignorance**: Fear arises from ignorance and can be transcended by self-awareness and surrender to the divine.

- **Meditation**: Regular meditation reveals the divine within, offering clarity, peace, and spiritual progress.

- **Forgetfulness**: Forgetfulness distracts the soul from its eternal purpose, highlighting the need for mindful living.

- **Divine Energy**: Reverence for Parashakti aligns us with the natural order of existence.

- **Truth**: Truth is the key to spiritual liberation, guiding one to live harmoniously with the divine.

Surrendering EGO:

Through devotion, meditation, and the practice of truth, we can overcome fear, ignorance, and the attachments that bind us. The divine presence we often seek outside is already within us, waiting to be realized. By surrendering the ego and embracing truth, we unlock this infinite source of divine energy, connecting us to the eternal bliss of Sachidananda Paramatma.

Let us dedicate ourselves to living truthfully, fearlessly, and with unwavering faith in the divine, knowing that this path leads to ultimate peace, grace, and liberation.

Om Tat Sat

Prayer

O Divine Presence,
Grant us the courage to walk the path of truth,
Free us from the shadows of fear and ignorance,

May our hearts remain open to love and compassion,
And may we always seek Your light,
In every moment, in every breath.

Lead us to the realization of the eternal Self,
That we may live with peace, grace, and fearlessness,
In alignment with Your will.

Om Shanti Shanti Shanti

Chapter-19

The Path of Transformation

(From Human to Divine)

The Journey of Transformation

Dear devotees, you are blessed to have the opportunity to remember the divine name and live with a heart full of devotion is the highest blessing. Just as birds and animals come into this world and leave it, so too does every human being. However, unlike them, humans are bestowed with a higher purpose. We are not bound to just live and die; we are meant to attain divinity and transform our human nature into a divine one. This is the opportunity given to humanity—let us utilize it wisely!

As the Bhagavad Gita teaches, *"You have a right to perform your prescribed duties, but you are not entitled to the fruits of your actions"* (Bhagavad Gita 2.47). This verse encourages us to focus on our duties without attachment to outcomes, which is the essence of spiritual transformation. When we let go of the fruits of our labor, we open ourselves to the true joy of service rather than being bound by the results.

The Chains of Desire and Attachment

Animals roam freely, unburdened by attachments, but human beings often find themselves chained by desires, ego, and material possessions. These desires bind us and make us believe that true happiness lies in wealth, comfort, or status. However, this endless pursuit leads to greed, and overindulgence can destroy our peace, health, and sanctity of life.

The Bhagavad Gita reminds us, *"The man who is free from desire, who is content with what he has, and who has conquered his senses, is a true yogi"* (Bhagavad Gita 6.12). True peace comes not from fulfilling our desires, but from freeing ourselves from them. When we embrace contentment, our inner peace flourishes, and we move closer to the divine.

The Importance of Proper Living and Self-Realization

To begin our spiritual journey, we must first learn how to live properly. The way we eat, act, and engage in righteous deeds must reflect our higher purpose. We must understand our true nature: Who am I? What is my duty in this world? Once we realize our purpose, we can then focus on cultivating the intellect. When the mind, intellect, and heart are aligned, wisdom arises. This wisdom enables us to discern the truth and to see beyond the illusions of the material world.

The Bhagavad Gita teaches, *"When meditation is mastered, the mind is unwavering like the flame of a lamp in a windless place"* (Bhagavad Gita 6.19). This verse emphasizes the importance of disciplined living and meditation in attaining inner peace. A steady mind leads to clarity, helping us to align ourselves with our divine purpose and realize our true selves.

Purification of the Mind and Spirit

A true yogi purifies his actions, speech, and mind. Through this purification, his nature transforms. Like gold purified in fire, the soul becomes radiant with divine knowledge. As we purify our hearts and minds, we attune ourselves to the divine presence within. This purity enables us to live in harmony with the world, acting as instruments of divine will.

The Bhagavad Gita reminds us, *"He who has conquered his mind, has conquered the world"* (Bhagavad Gita 6.5). Mastery over the mind leads to victory, not only over external circumstances but also over our own desires and attachments. When the mind is disciplined and purified, we gain the power to transcend worldly limitations and live in alignment with divine wisdom.

The Power of Purity and Self-Discipline

Just as the great saints, yogis, and sages purify their hearts and minds through meditation and surrender to the divine, we, too, can purify ourselves. Purification leads to transformation. The more pure we become, the more we align ourselves with divine light. With purity of heart, we gain control over our senses, desires, and actions.

The Bhagavad Gita teaches, *"A person is said to be in pure consciousness when his actions are in harmony with the divine will"* (Bhagavad Gita 18.16). Purity of consciousness allows us to align our actions with divine purpose. When we live according to this harmony, we move closer to spiritual fulfilment, embodying the qualities of truth, love, and peace.

The Role of Self-Discipline and Service to Society

We must be self-disciplined and work for the benefit of society. Our actions should be in harmony with the greater good, and we must always strive to maintain peace, humility, and compassion. A true spiritual seeker refrains from causing harm or discord. We must cultivate virtues of kindness, respect, and humility, and live as examples for others to follow. In this way, we uplift society and contribute to the greater good.

The Bhagavad Gita reminds us, *"Serve all beings as if they were the divine"* (Bhagavad Gita 9.22). Through selfless service to others, we serve the divine presence in them. Every act of kindness, every gesture of compassion, becomes a step toward spiritual growth. By serving others, we elevate our own consciousness, aligning it with the divine.

The Power of Divine Guidance and Surrender

Surrendering to a spiritual guide or guru is the highest form of humility. The guru's wisdom illuminates the path, leading us toward self-realization. When we surrender our ego and desires, we experience the true essence of the self. In the presence of a true sage, even wild animals become docile, and the guru's grace transforms the most fearful creatures. This is the power of divine knowledge and purity.

The Bhagavad Gita emphasizes, *"When the mind is purified by meditation, the yogi becomes free from desires and attachments, and attains supreme peace"* (Bhagavad Gita 6.47). Surrendering to divine guidance purifies the mind, freeing it from worldly desires and attachments, and leading to ultimate peace and spiritual freedom. The grace of a true teacher leads us beyond the limits of the ego, allowing us to experience the divine presence within.

Psychological Insights on Transformation

From a psychological perspective, the transformation from human to divine is akin to a process of inner self-realization and overcoming conditioned behaviors. Desires, attachments, and ego are closely linked to our psychological need for control, security, and approval. These are rooted in fear—fear of not being enough, of losing control, and of facing the unknown.

Modern psychology validates the teachings of spiritual traditions through concepts such as mindfulness, cognitive reframing, and emotional regulation. Meditation practices, for instance, help in rewiring the brain by enhancing neuroplasticity, which enables individuals to break free from habitual thoughts and emotional patterns. When we let go of our ego and desires, we are more aligned with our true self, and this transformation is reflected in greater emotional resilience, mental peace, and the ability to face life's challenges without fear.

Scientific Perspectives on Purification and Transformation

Studies in neuroscience show that meditation and spiritual practices can physically alter the structure of the brain, especially areas related to stress, decision-making, and emotional regulation. For example, regular meditation has been shown to increase the size of the prefrontal cortex, which is responsible for higher cognitive functions such as decision-making and self-control. This scientific backing reinforces the spiritual idea that purification of the mind leads to transformation—both spiritually and psychologically.

Additionally, research into the effects of gratitude and mindfulness, which are central to many spiritual practices, demonstrates their power in promoting emotional well-being. Regular practice of gratitude has been shown to reduce stress, increase happiness, and even improve immune function, suggesting that spiritual practices align with both mental and physical health.

Personal Development and Leadership Insights

Spiritual practices such as discipline, selflessness, and humility are not only beneficial for personal growth but also for leadership development. Leaders who practice these qualities are more likely to inspire trust, foster cooperation, and lead with compassion. The principles of surrendering the ego, embracing truth, and serving others are foundational to creating a work environment where individuals thrive.

By adopting these principles, leaders can elevate their leadership to divine levels by focusing on service rather than self-interest, fostering a culture of empathy, and making decisions that benefit the collective good. This transformation aligns not just with personal well-being but also with the creation of harmonious communities.

Inferences

- **Self-Realization**: The path to divinity requires self-realization and understanding our true purpose in life. By aligning ourselves with divine will, we discover the deeper meaning behind our existence.

- **Purification**: Purification of the mind and heart is essential for spiritual transformation and achieving true wisdom. Meditation and mindfulness are key tools in this process.

- **Service to Society**: Living a life of service and humility benefits others and accelerates spiritual progress. Acts of kindness elevate our consciousness.

- **Surrender and Guidance**: Surrendering to a spiritual guide and following their wisdom is the quickest path to liberation. It leads to true peace and freedom from the ego.

- **Psychological Transformation**: Transformation from human to divine also involves psychological change, including emotional regulation, mindfulness, and letting go of attachment and ego.

- **Scientific Validation**: Practices like meditation and mindfulness have tangible benefits on mental and physical health, supporting the principles of spiritual transformation.

Living as Divine Beings

Let us strive to live with purity of heart and mind, free from desires and attachments. Practicing meditation, self-discipline, and service to society can elevate us to the divine state. Through constant practice, the true self emerges, and we attain spiritual peace and enlightenment. Let us surrender our egos, trust in the divine guidance of our gurus, and live a life that reflects the divine purpose. By embracing these teachings, we can transform from ordinary human beings to divine embodiments of love, wisdom, and compassion.

Prayer

O Divine Source of all,
Guide us on the path of transformation,
Purify our minds and hearts,
And lead us towards self-realization.
May we serve all beings with love and humility,
And surrender our ego to Your divine will.
Grant us the strength to live as divine beings,
In service to the greater good.
Om Shanti Shanti Shanti

Chapter-20

The Path to Divine Harmony: Wisdom, Love, and Devotion

The Depth of Vedanta

"Vedanta is like a vast ocean; one can find the precious gems only by diving deep into it. To explore its depths, the help of an experienced guide, someone who has already discovered the treasure within, is essential. This guide, the guru, is indispensable for understanding the true essence of Vedanta."

The Swamy compares Vedanta to a vast ocean, where the true jewels are found only through deep exploration. This deep understanding can only be attained with the help of a knowledgeable guide who has already experienced the truth. The guidance of a realized teacher is crucial, as the ocean of worldly life is filled with waves of desires, distractions, and attachments. To gain true wisdom, one must not get lost in these illusions but focus on the deeper truths that can be revealed only with the guru's help.

Research Insight: Research on spiritual guidance shows that mentorship or guidance from experienced individuals plays a key role in personal growth. A study published in the *Journal of Positive Psychology* highlights the importance of mentorship in spiritual development, noting that individuals who receive guidance from experienced spiritual leaders tend to exhibit higher emotional well-being and a deeper sense of purpose in life. Additionally, spiritual mentorship has been associated with enhanced resilience, suggesting that guidance not only enriches spiritual understanding but also supports mental health and coping mechanisms in the face of life's challenges.

The Role of the Guru

The Guru, like a physician, diagnoses the spiritual ailments of the mind and heart and prescribes the proper remedies. Just as one would rush to a doctor when ill, the individual must seek a spiritual doctor when suffering from the afflictions of life. The guru helps align one's thoughts, actions, and mind with the divine will, leading the disciple toward spiritual health and well-being. Only by following the guidance of the guru with complete faith can one achieve spiritual success.

Quote from the Bhagavad Gita:

"When the disciple surrenders to the guru with full trust, the guru reveals the truth and removes ignorance." — (Bhagavad Gita 4.34)

Research Insight: Modern psychology supports the concept of mentorship and guidance, emphasizing the role of a trusted advisor in personal transformation. According to research by the *Harvard Business Review*, mentoring relationships enhance emotional intelligence, self-awareness, and the ability to cope with stress. This is crucial in the spiritual realm as well, where guidance leads to a higher state of self-awareness and spiritual growth. The trust in a mentor, akin to surrendering to a guru, has been shown to enhance personal development by providing clarity, confidence, and wisdom.

The Power of Love as the Weapon Against Hatred

"There is only one weapon that can destroy all troubles and obstacles, and it is love. Love is a sharp weapon that can cut through all hatred,

jealousy, and ignorance. True love, unlike bargaining or selfish desire, has the power to transform the world."

The Swamy emphasizes that love is the most powerful weapon available to humanity. This love is not selfish or transactional, but pure and divine. When cultivated, love can vanquish all negative forces such as hatred, jealousy, and greed. True love is divine, and through this love, one can align with the divine will. The power of divine love is beyond comprehension, as it reflects the supreme energy of the Divine.

Quote from the Bhagavad Gita:

"Love is the highest form of devotion. It transcends all other qualities and leads to the divine." — (Bhagavad Gita 9.22)

Research Insight: Scientific studies support the transformative power of love. Research in the field of positive psychology, including studies by Dr. Barbara Fredrickson, shows that love and compassion increase personal well-being, strengthen social bonds, and improve mental health. The practice of love activates the brain's reward system, fostering a sense of connection and fulfilment. Moreover, acts of compassion have been shown to reduce stress, improve cardiovascular health, and increase longevity, further illustrating how love, when practiced selflessly, not only elevates the soul but also contributes to physical and mental harmony.

Reflection on Our Inner Divinity

"The divinity within us must be recognized and nurtured. Our inner conscience is a reflection of the Supreme Being. By recognizing this, we can engage in actions that reflect this inner divinity and live a life of harmony."

The Swamy urges us to look within and recognize the divinity that resides in each of us. Our inner conscience is a reflection of the

Divine, guiding us toward righteous actions. By understanding and embracing this inner divinity, we can live a life of peace, purity, and spiritual fulfilment. True fulfilment comes from recognizing and acting in harmony with the divinity within.

Quote from the Bhagavad Gita:

"You are not the body; you are the eternal soul, which is a reflection of the Divine." — *(Bhagavad Gita 2.30)*

Research Insight: Psychological studies in self-actualization, particularly those related to Maslow's hierarchy of needs, show that self-awareness and self-recognition of one's potential are critical to achieving personal fulfilment. The recognition of inner divinity aligns with these findings, suggesting that when individuals connect with their higher self, they experience greater life satisfaction, purpose, and mental well-being. Researchers have also found that spiritual practices, such as meditation and introspection, enhance self-awareness and promote a deeper understanding of one's true nature.

Guidance on Virtuous Living

The Swamy provides practical advice on how to live a virtuous and fulfilling life:

1. **Self-Reflection on Criticism:** *"Before criticizing others, reflect on whether we are making the same mistakes. Approach situations with impartiality and humility."*

   This suggests that before judging others, we must examine ourselves and our actions, realizing that no one is perfect. Self-awareness and humility are keys to personal growth and compassion.

2. **Using Time and Energy to Help Others:** *"Instead of selfishly using our time and resources, we must use them to serve others. Time and energy should be spent helping those in need."*

   The Swamy stresses that selflessness is the core of spiritual life. Our resources—time, energy, and effort—should be used for the welfare of others, as this fosters goodwill and spiritual progress.

3. **Sharing in the Joy and Suffering of Others:** *"The true sign of a virtuous person is one who can share in the suffering of others and find joy in their happiness."*

   True compassion is about empathy—sharing in the sorrows and joys of others. This interconnectedness creates a bond of unity and love, strengthening our spiritual growth.

4. **Gratitude in Adversity:** *"Instead of lamenting our own troubles, we should remember how much more fortunate we are compared to others. Cultivate an attitude of gratitude and joy."*

Gratitude is a transformative attitude. In times of hardship, focusing on the blessings we have rather than the challenges we face brings peace and contentment.

Quote from the Bhagavad Gita:

"Gratitude and humility bring divine favour and peace."
— *(Bhagavad Gita 9.22)*

Research Insight: The psychological benefits of gratitude have been extensively researched. Dr. Robert Emmons, a leading expert on gratitude, shows that regularly practicing gratitude increases happiness, improves relationships, reduces depression, and enhances overall well-being. Research in the field of positive psychology reveals that gratitude practices foster resilience and help individuals cope with stress, making it an essential virtue for personal and spiritual growth.

Realizing the Divine Through Practice and Devotion

"By recognizing and honoring the Divine within ourselves, we live a life of pure devotion. The more we surrender to the Divine, the more we align ourselves with its eternal truth."

Living a life of devotion to the Divine is the key to spiritual liberation. By recognizing the Divine presence within and aligning our actions with divine will, we transform our lives into a pure expression of love, service, and truth. This process leads us toward peace, joy, and the ultimate realization of the divine truth.

Quote from the Bhagavad Gita:

"Those who dedicate their actions to Me, with devotion and purity, are liberated from the cycle of birth and death." — (Bhagavad Gita 9.22)

Inferences

- **The Role of the Guru:** The guru is essential for guiding one through the spiritual journey, offering wisdom and correcting the course.

- **Power of Love:** Love is the strongest force against hatred and jealousy, leading to spiritual transformation.

- **Recognizing Divinity Within:** Our inner divinity reflects the Supreme Being, guiding us toward righteous living.

- **Virtuous Living:** Self-reflection, helping others, sharing joy and sorrow, and gratitude are crucial virtues for spiritual growth.

- **Surrendering to the Divine:** True devotion and surrender to the Divine lead to peace, liberation, and fulfilment.

Living a Life of Divine Harmony

"Let us dedicate our lives to the Divine, acting with love, humility, and devotion. By doing so, we not only uplift ourselves but also contribute to the welfare of the world."

The Swamy concludes by urging us to dedicate our lives to the Divine. We can achieve peace, joy, and ultimately spiritual liberation through love, service, and devotion. Recognizing the Divine within and aligning with divine principles is the essence of a virtuous life. By living in this way, we experience true fulfilment and contribute positively to the world around us.

Prayer

O Boundless Ocean of Truth Divine,
Guide our hearts and make them Thine.
With love unselfish, pure, and great,
Help us conquer envy, anger, and hate.
Teach us to see Your light in all,
And humbly heed Your gentle call.
With gratitude in trials we stand,
Led by the touch of Your guiding hand.
O Guru bright, O Wisdom's ray,
Lead us through life's uncertain way.
May love and virtue light our path,
And cleanse our souls from worldly wrath.
To Thee, O Lord, we bow in prayer,
In Your grace, we place our care.
With devotion pure, let our spirits rise,
To dwell forever in the Eternal skies.

Chapter-21

The Path to Spiritual Wisdom and Inner Peace

The Experience of the Divine Within

"Though we may not be able to see God with our physical eyes, we can certainly experience His divine power in every particle around us. Experience is the highest form of knowledge."

His Holiness emphasises that true knowledge transcends mere intellectual understanding and is found through direct experience. This experience is not limited to any one field but extends into the deepest parts of the human heart. In contemporary science, particularly in quantum physics, there is growing recognition of the interconnectedness of all things. Every particle in the universe is intertwined, much like the spiritual truth that the Divine pervades all aspects of creation. This profound experiential knowledge, or *"anubhuti,"* is the highest form of wisdom (*"jnana"*) and illuminates the heart, bringing us closer to God. The Bhagavad Gita states, *"The best knowledge is that which leads to the experience of the Divine within. It is this experience that enlightens the heart and brings us closer to God."* This sacred knowing is accessible to all who seek it, not as a distant intellectual pursuit, but as an intimate, internal realization.

The Heart as the Laboratory of Divine Science

"The heart is the laboratory where the science of devotion is researched."

In modern scientific endeavours, we often speak of research conducted in controlled environments, where hypotheses are tested and results meticulously analyzed. Similarly, His Holiness points out that the heart is the true research laboratory for spiritual exploration. Here, the tools of devotion (bhakti) and knowledge (jnana) intersect to form a deeper understanding of the Divine. Neuroplasticity research has shown that the brain's pathways can be rewired through practices like meditation and devotion, suggesting that the heart, both as a spiritual and physiological centre, plays a critical role in shaping our consciousness and connecting us with a higher reality. The bond between God and the soul is not temporary like human relationships but eternal, spanning across lifetimes. This connection is echoed in the Upanishads, which describe the heart as the sacred space where the Divine dwells.

The Unbroken Bond with the Divine

"No human being, no matter how atheist they may seem, can ever break their bond with God. This bond transcends lifetimes and is eternal."

His Holiness affirms that the connection between the soul and the Divine is unbreakable, regardless of one's personal beliefs or doubts. Even those who deny God's existence are still intrinsically linked to the Divine—this is not an abstract idea, but a spiritual truth deeply rooted in human nature. Recent studies in epigenetics and the concept of ancestral memory suggest that our deepest traits and inclinations are passed down through generations, and likewise, our spiritual bond with the Divine may be inherited or cultivated through various lifetimes. This eternal relationship is beyond intellectual reasoning or material conditions, and can only be fully realized through devotion and spiritual practice. As the Bhagavad Gita affirms, *"Even if a person is entirely disillusioned and does not believe in the Divine, their bond with God remains unbroken."*

The Role of Faith and Belief

"The Guru and the scriptures serve as guides, helping us believe in what we cannot see or understand."

In the same way that scientific discoveries often begin with a hypothesis, belief is the starting point in the spiritual journey. Faith does not negate reason; rather, it complements it, offering a direction to seek deeper truths. In scientific inquiry, we trust models and theories even before they are empirically proven. Similarly, the Guru and scriptures offer a framework for belief that helps us navigate the unseen aspects of existence. Research in cognitive science shows that the brain responds to the cultivation of positive beliefs and intentions, which align with the idea that faith can guide and shape our spiritual experiences. The Bhagavad Gita teaches, *"Those who have faith in the scriptures and trust the teachings of the Guru will come to understand what is beyond the limitations of the senses."* This trust builds a foundation for deeper spiritual practice, transforming belief into lived experience.

Overcoming Suffering through Devotion

"The experience of God's presence in our lives can transform suffering into peace."

Suffering is an inevitable aspect of the human condition, but it also serves as a path for spiritual awakening. His Holiness teaches that by cultivating devotion, suffering can be transformed into a powerful tool for inner peace. Neuroscience has long studied the relationship between stress and the human body, and recent findings show that meditation and mindfulness significantly reduce the negative impact of stress, allowing individuals to maintain peace even in the face of hardship. This is the essence of devotion: it reorients our perception of suffering, helping us view it not as a burden but as an opportunity for growth. As the Bhagavad Gita notes, *"Those who take refuge in the Divine experience peace even in the midst of suffering, for their hearts are steadfast in devotion."*

The Guru's Guidance: A Light in Darkness

"The Guru is the beacon that lights the path toward spiritual awakening."

In a world often filled with confusion and uncertainty, the role of the Guru is to serve as a guiding light. This concept finds resonance in modern psychology, where mentorship and guidance are considered essential for personal and professional development. Just as a mentor helps a student navigate the complexities of life, the Guru's wisdom illuminates the path to spiritual awakening. This wisdom is not simply theoretical knowledge but the practical application of divine truth. The Bhagavad Gita highlights, *"The Guru is the one who dispels the darkness of ignorance, showing the way to the light of knowledge and divine realization."* Through the Guru's guidance, one can shed the layers of ignorance that obscure the true nature of the self.

Living in Harmony with the Divine Will

"By surrendering our will to the Divine, we find peace and purpose in every moment."

When we live in alignment with the Divine will, we experience peace, purpose, and fulfilment. This aligns with recent studies in positive psychology, which show that individuals who engage in selfless acts and live according to a higher purpose report greater life satisfaction and psychological well-being. Surrendering to a higher will, whether divine or philosophical, allows us to let go of the burdens of the ego and the mind, which often lead to anxiety and stress. As the Bhagavad Gita teaches, "When a person surrenders all actions to God and lives in accordance with His will, they are free from fear and doubt." This surrender is not about submission, but about aligning oneself with a higher order that brings ultimate peace.

Inferences:

1. **Divine Knowledge Through Experience:** True wisdom arises from direct, experiential knowledge of the Divine, which transforms the heart and leads to deep spiritual insight.

2. **The Eternal Bond with God:** Our connection with the Divine is unbreakable, existing beyond intellectual understanding and transcending lifetimes.

3. **The Role of the Guru:** The Guru serves as the guiding light that dispels ignorance, offering practical wisdom for spiritual realization.

4. **Surrendering to the Divine Will:** Aligning our will with the Divine brings peace, fulfilment, and liberation from the anxieties of life.

The Divine is Always With Us

"God's presence is with us every moment, in every thought, in every action."

His Holiness concludes with a reminder that the Divine is not a distant or abstract entity but a present, living force within every thought, action, and moment of our lives. This perspective is supported by the findings in quantum physics, where it is suggested that everything in the universe is interconnected at a fundamental level. The Divine is not separate from us; it is the very fabric of existence. By turning our hearts toward God and living in alignment with divine principles, we experience peace, joy, and the realization of our true self. As the Bhagavad Gita encapsulates, *"In surrendering to the Divine, we are not losing ourselves; rather, we are discovering our true self in the eternal embrace of God."*

Prayer

O Divine Lord,
We humbly bow before You, seeking Your divine grace.
Guide us with the light of Your wisdom and love.
May our hearts always be filled with devotion,
And our actions aligned with Your will.
Grant us the strength to surrender our ego and desires,
That we may find peace in Your eternal embrace.
Lead us on the path of divine knowledge,
That through Your grace, we may experience the ultimate truth and bliss.

Om Shanti, Om Shanti, Om Shanti.

Chapter-22

"Journey to Divine Wisdom and Eternal Peace

The Dual Nature of the World and the Divine

"This world is dual in nature—one side represents light, joy, and peace, and the other side represents darkness, suffering, and hardship. Yet, in every situation, it is the Divine who is our true protector."

His Holiness begins by explaining the dualistic nature of the world around us—light and darkness, pleasure and pain, day and night. These opposites exist side by side, but the ultimate truth is that God transcends both. He is the one who leads us through every circumstance, providing us with the strength and guidance to navigate life's challenges. Understanding this divine presence is the first step toward attaining peace and security.

Research insights into duality in nature resonate with the understanding that opposites often exist to balance each other in the universal order. Many spiritual traditions, including Advaita Vedanta, suggest that both light and darkness are manifestations of the same Divine, emphasizing a holistic perception of reality. As the Bhagavad Gita says:

"In this world, there is duality, but the wise see beyond it, knowing that the Supreme Reality is present in all." — (Bhagavad Gita 15.14)

The Role of Intelligence and Knowledge in Protecting Ourselves

"The truly wise are those who understand that only by trusting in the Divine can they truly protect themselves from the trials of life."

His Holiness emphasizes the importance of wisdom and intellect in life. True wisdom is not just about understanding worldly knowledge but also about recognizing the hand of the Divine in every aspect of existence. The intelligent person is one who acknowledges the Divine as their ultimate protector and seeks refuge in Him. This is the only true security, for the material world is fraught with uncertainties.

This notion is closely aligned with modern research in psychology and existential philosophy, which suggests that trust in something greater than oneself—whether that be God, the universe, or universal laws—can provide a profound sense of inner peace and stability. The Upanishads teach us:

"The wise are those who understand the true nature of the world and seek refuge in the Divine for protection and guidance."

The Nature of the Divine and the Power of the Elements

"Just as wind, fire, and the sea are bound by their natural limits, the Divine's power is expressed through the elements of nature."

His Holiness illustrates that everything in nature follows its own intrinsic laws. The wind blows within its limits, the fire burns within its boundaries, and the sea, despite its vastness, does not overflow beyond its shores. Similarly, the Divine expresses Himself through the natural laws of the universe. Understanding this divine presence in nature is essential for realizing His omnipresence and omnipotence.

The research into the laws of nature—whether in physics, biology, or environmental science—reveals that everything in existence operates within natural limits and balances. These laws are not arbitrary but governed by deeper forces, which many spiritual traditions interpret as expressions of the Divine. The Bhagavad Gita reveals:

> *"All the elements of nature, from the wind to the ocean, operate within the parameters set by the Divine."* — *(Bhagavad Gita 10.20)*

The Importance of Labour and Dedication

> *"A labourer who works with dedication is embodying the qualities of the Divine, for it is through sincere effort that one experiences the blessings of God."*

His Holiness highlights the significance of hard work and dedication in every aspect of life. When we perform our duties with focus and devotion, we align ourselves with the divine principles that govern the universe. The labourer, the craftsman, and every person who works with sincerity are, in essence, engaging in a spiritual act. This is an important lesson for us to value work not as a burden but as a divine offering.

From a research perspective, the concept of work as devotion can be explored through the lens of mindfulness and intrinsic motivation. Studies in positive psychology show that when work is approached with mindfulness and dedication, it leads to greater fulfilment and a deeper sense of purpose. The Bhagavad Gita emphasizes:

> *"A true worker, one who is dedicated to their work, is performing the highest form of devotion."* — *(Bhagavad Gita 3.19)*

The Transience of Life and the Unchanging Nature of the Soul

"Life passes through various stages—childhood, youth, old age. The body undergoes changes, but the soul remains eternal."

His Holiness reflects on the impermanence of life and the body. From childhood to old age, the body experiences growth, decay, and transformation. Yet, despite these changes, the soul remains unchanged and eternal. Understanding this truth allows one to transcend the fears and anxieties that come with the aging process and to focus on spiritual progress.

This idea resonates with research in the field of consciousness studies, which suggests that there is a distinct separation between the mind (consciousness) and the body. Many neuroscientists and philosophers have pondered the nature of consciousness, often pointing to the possibility of an eternal soul or self. As the Bhagavad Gita states:

"The soul is eternal and imperishable; it is never born and it never dies."
— (Bhagavad Gita 2.20)

The Need for Spiritual Awareness

"Most people fail to understand the true nature of life and the body. They become entangled in material pursuits, forgetting that the body is a temporary vessel."

His Holiness warns against becoming too attached to the body and the material world. The body is like a ship navigating through the sea of life. When the ship (the body) reaches the end of its journey, it is no longer needed. But the soul, which has been on this journey, continues its eternal path across lifetimes. Therefore, it is essential to focus on the eternal nature of the soul rather than the temporary nature of the body.

This aligns with the research in the field of existential psychology, which explores how the awareness of our mortality leads to greater meaning in life. Spiritual practices often focus on helping individuals transcend material concerns and connect with the eternal aspect of themselves.

The Upanishads reveal:

"The body is like a chariot, and the soul is the driver. When the chariot breaks, the soul continues its journey."

The Role of the Guru in Spiritual Awakening

"Only the Guru can lead us to the understanding of the true nature of the soul and the Divine. The Guru is the key to spiritual liberation."

His Holiness explains that the Guru plays an indispensable role in our spiritual journey. The Guru is the one who removes the darkness of ignorance and illuminates the path to the Divine. Through the Guru's guidance, one comes to understand the impermanence of the body, the eternal nature of the soul, and the presence of the Divine in every aspect of life.

The concept of a Guru is closely related to the role of mentors in modern psychology. Mentors are recognized for their capacity to help individuals transcend their limitations and reach their potential. The Upanishads teach:

"The Guru's light dispels the darkness of ignorance and reveals the truth of the soul and the Divine."

The Ultimate Goal: Peace through Surrender to the Divine

"Through surrender to the Divine and the Guru's teachings, we find peace and liberation from the cycle of birth and death."

In the final part of His Holiness' discourse, he emphasizes that surrender to the Divine and following the Guru's guidance is the path to liberation. By surrendering the ego and embracing the teachings of the Guru, we transcend the cycle of birth and death and attain eternal peace and bliss.

Research on mindfulness and surrender in spiritual practices suggests that letting go of the ego and accepting the present moment can lead to profound peace and a sense of liberation. As the Bhagavad Gita beautifully says:

"Surrender all your actions to Me, and I will liberate you from all sins. Do not grieve." — (Bhagavad Gita 18.66)

Inferences:

1. **Wisdom and Protection**: True protection comes from understanding the Divine as the ultimate source of strength and security.

2. **Divine in Nature**: The natural elements are governed by divine principles, and understanding these laws helps us perceive the Divine in the world around us.

3. **Spiritual Work**: Every act of sincere work is an offering to the Divine and should be approached with dedication and reverence.

4. **Transience of the Body**: The body is temporary, but the soul is eternal, and spiritual awareness helps transcend material limitations.

5. **Role of the Guru**: The Guru is essential for spiritual liberation, guiding us beyond ignorance to eternal truth.

6. **Surrender to the Divine**: True peace comes from surrendering to the Divine and trusting in the path shown by the Guru.

The Eternal Wisdom of the Divine

"By understanding the impermanence of the world and surrendering to the Divine, we can live a life of peace and fulfilment."

His Holiness concludes with the profound truth that the world is transient, but the Divine is eternal. By understanding this, we can rise above the suffering and difficulties of life. By surrendering ourselves to the Divine and following the teachings of the Guru, we attain true peace and liberation.

Reflection:

"Surrender to the Divine, trust in the Guru's guidance, and find peace in the eternal truth that transcends the illusions of the material world."

Prayer

O Divine Light, guide our way,
Through darkened night, to the bright day.
In Your shelter, may we find,
Peace and solace for the mind.
Ego surrendered, hearts aligned,
With Your grace, we are entwined.
Lead us beyond birth and death,
In Your eternal, boundless breath.
Grant us wisdom, pure and true,
To see Your presence in all we do.
In every step, in every prayer,
May we feel Your presence there.
With devotion deep, our hearts we lay,
In Your arms, forever to stay.

Chapter-23

The Path to Divine Realization: Teachings on Faith, Peace, and Self-Discovery

Self-Realization and Spiritual Growth:

The journey of self-realization and spiritual growth is an inward path that leads us to the truth of our divine nature. As we navigate the challenges of life, it is common to experience fear, doubt, and suffering, which cloud our minds and distract us from our higher purpose. The teachings of great spiritual guides, such as Swamiji, offer timeless wisdom to help us overcome these obstacles and find peace, love, and inner fulfilment.

In this chapter, we delve into the core teachings of Swamiji, who addresses key questions that are relevant to our daily lives—questions about fear, forgetfulness, suffering, and the role of devotion. These teachings provide us with the tools necessary to transcend our limitations and connect with the divine presence within us. Through meditation, prayer, faith, and the guidance of a Guru, we are shown how to navigate the complexities of life with clarity and peace. This path leads us to the realization that the divine is not separate from us, but is the very essence of our being, waiting to be discovered and embraced.

Let us explore the profound wisdom shared by Swamiji, which encourages us to awaken to our true nature, dispel fear, and experience the peace that comes from deep faith and devotion.

Theme 1: The Root Cause of Fear and Forgetfulness

Question: *What is the root cause of fear and forgetfulness, and how can one overcome them to attain inner peace?*

Answer:

Fear and forgetfulness arise from ignorance of the true Self. Fear is born when we perceive something as separate from ourselves, which creates a sense of isolation and turmoil. The root cause of fear is the attachment to the ego, driven by external desires and ambitions. When we are identified with the ego, we become disconnected from our true nature, resulting in fear. Forgetfulness stems from this fear, leading to distraction and loss of focus on our divine purpose.

To overcome these challenges, practice silence through meditation. Meditate for 10-20 minutes each morning, ideally at dawn, to quiet the mind and reconnect with the Self, the Atman.

Living in truth is the key to liberation. Truth is unchanging across body, mind, and intellect. By reflecting on this truth, we naturally detach from worldly attachments and experience Sat-Chit-Ananda— the eternal bliss of unity with the Supreme. May we follow the path of truth to dispel fear and forgetfulness, realizing our true Self.

Theme 2: The Essence of Chaturmasa and Connecting with God

Question: *What is the essence of Chaturmasa, and how can we connect with God during this time?*

Answer:

Chaturmasa is a sacred period in the spiritual calendar that offers an opportunity for deepening our connection with God. God, in essence, is the life force within us, inseparable from nature. By surrendering our ego, we realize that the Divine is not separate from us but is the limitless force within.

During Chaturmasa, engage in sincere prayer, asking for the strength to fulfill the duties God has entrusted to you. Prayer nourishes the soul, just as food nourishes the body. A true prayer involves surrendering to God's will, trusting in His guidance. Remain anchored in the remembrance of God's name, "Hari Om," and let this sacred vibration fill your heart with divine peace.

Theme 3: The Nature of Bhakti

Question: *What is the nature of Bhakti, and how can it help us in life?*

Answer:

Bhakti is a divine force present in all of creation, drawing us closer to God. It is through devotion that the soul becomes bound to the divine. In Kali Yuga, the path of Bhakti is particularly potent for strengthening our faith and receiving God's grace.

Bhakti purifies the heart and mind, cultivating peace and joy. It is not confined to rituals but involves surrendering the heart to God in all actions. The mind aligns with the Divine through sincere devotion, leading to liberation and eternal bliss.

Theme 4: Facing Hardships and the Role of Faith

Question: *Why do some people experience tests and hardships despite being devoted to God?*

Answer:

Hardships are part of God's divine plan to purify us. Just as a cloth must be cleaned of dirt, we need to shed ego, attachments, and negativity to progress spiritually. Suffering, whether in the form of poverty, health issues, or disrespect, is an opportunity to detach from materialism and elevate our consciousness.

In times of hardship, trust God's guidance and the Sadguru. These trials, though difficult, are opportunities for spiritual growth. Just as a patient trusts a doctor for healing, trust in God's plan and emerge purified and free from illusion. With faith, resilience, and patience, we find peace and strength.

Theme 5: The Role of the Guru in Our Spiritual Journey

Question: *What is the role of the Guru in our spiritual journey?*

Answer:

The Guru is the doctor of the soul, diagnosing spiritual ailments and offering the right path for healing. The Guru's teachings help us cleanse ourselves of ego, selfishness, and negativity. By surrendering to the Guru's guidance with trust, we free ourselves from attachments and dualities.

A pure mind, filled with compassion and equanimity, is the true heaven. The Guru reveals our divinity and leads us to eternal peace and bliss. May we surrender fully to the Sadguru and follow His path toward spiritual fulfilment.

Theme 6: Faith, Love, and Peace

Question: *What is the connection between faith, love, and peace?*

Answer:

Where there is faith, love flourishes, and where love exists, peace follows. Faith in God removes all desires and worries. When we have unwavering faith, we surrender anxieties and fears, allowing love to bloom. This love cultivates inner peace and brings us closer to the divine.

Faith transforms how we perceive the world, enabling us to accept life's challenges gracefully. With love and faith, peace naturally arises, drawing us nearer to the Divine Presence.

Theme 7: Handling Mental Pain and Suffering

Question: *How should we handle mental pain and suffering?*

Answer:

Mental pain and suffering are a part of life, like *"rent payments"* for the body. They are temporary and can be faced with faith and patience. The key is to count our blessings, forgive others, and let go of negativity.

Even good people experience suffering, but through these trials, we grow spiritually. Trust God's plan, and peace will follow, even in the midst of adversity.

Inferences:

- **The Root of Fear**: Fear arises from the illusion of separation from the Divine. Understanding our oneness with God is the antidote.

- **The Power of Prayer**: Prayer nourishes the soul and strengthens our connection with God, especially during sacred times like Chaturmasa.

- **The Transformative Power of Bhakti**: Devotion purifies the heart and mind, aligning them with divine will, leading to peace and liberation.

- **Faith in Adversity**: Hardships are divine opportunities for growth and purification. Faith in God's plan transforms suffering into spiritual progress.

- **The Guru's Guidance**: The Guru is essential for spiritual awakening, helping us overcome ego and attachments, leading to peace and fulfilment.

- **Faith, Love, and Peace**: Faith creates the foundation for love and peace, and these qualities bring us closer to the Divine.

- **Embracing Suffering with Faith**: Mental pain and suffering are part of life's journey. By embracing them with faith, we can find inner peace and growth.

The Divine Path to Peace and Self-Realization

By following the teachings of faith, devotion, and surrender, we can transcend the fears and distractions of the material world. Through our connection with the Guru and the Divine, we purify the heart and mind, gaining access to eternal peace and spiritual fulfilment. May we walk this path with unwavering faith, surrendering to God's will and discovering the true nature of the Self.

Prayer

Prayer for Divine Grace and Peace"
O Divine Light, guide our way,
Through darkened night, to the bright day.
In Your shelter, may we find,
Peace and solace for the mind.
Ego surrendered, hearts aligned,
With Your grace, we are entwined.
Lead us beyond birth and death,
In Your eternal, boundless breath.
Grant us wisdom, pure and true,
To see Your presence in all we do.
In every step, in every prayer,
May we feel Your presence there.
With devotion deep, our hearts we lay,
In Your arms, forever to stay.

Chapter-24

Divine Wisdom for a Fulfilled Life

Spiritual Principles and Modern Challenges:

In today's rapidly changing world, where the pursuit of material success often overshadows our spiritual growth, the teachings of Swamy Sri Vidyanarayana Theertha offer a much-needed balance. His timeless wisdom integrates the importance of both spiritual and worldly pursuits, showing us how to live harmoniously while deepening our connection with the divine. This compilation of core teachings delves into life's most essential questions, providing profound insights on how we can navigate our path with clarity and purpose. By exploring ancient spiritual principles alongside modern-day challenges, we can learn to foster inner peace, embrace humility, and awaken to the deeper truths of our existence.

Recent research into spirituality and well-being consistently highlights the importance of integrating both material and spiritual aspects of life for overall happiness. Studies suggest that spiritual practices, such as meditation, prayer, and acts of service, can significantly improve mental health, reduce stress, and enhance overall life satisfaction. Swamiji's teachings resonate with these findings, offering a path that leads to both material fulfilment and spiritual liberation.

Core Teachings and Questions:

1. **Why is worshipping Kamadhenu important?**

   - *Answer*: Worshiping Kamadhenu, the divine cow, brings humanity both material and spiritual benefits. The cow symbolizes nourishment, purity, and life's sustenance. As revered saints have taught, the cow is not only a source of material support but also a spiritual guide, leading us closer to the divine. Through devotion to Kamadhenu, one receives blessings on both physical and spiritual planes.

2. **What is the connection between the cow and the soul's journey?**

   - *Answer*: The cow represents the sacred journey of the soul. Before incarnating, the soul is symbolically nurtured in the cow's womb, emphasizing the connection between life and spirituality. After death, the soul merges with the divine, symbolized by the return to the "*Mother*" of all existence. This highlights the eternal cycle of life, death, and rebirth, wherein the cow plays a key role in the spiritual evolution of the soul.

3. **How does life resemble an exam?**

   - *Answer*: Life, much like an exam, assesses our spiritual and ethical progress. Our actions determine our path forward. Just as an exam tests knowledge and preparation, life evaluates how well we uphold dharma, our duties, and our spiritual awareness. Success in life comes from fulfilling our duties with integrity and devotion.

4. **How can we divide our life's responsibilities or duties into four main areas to live a balanced and purposeful life?**

   o *Answer*: Life's duties can be categorized into four guiding principles:

     - **Pray**: Dedicate time to spiritual practices and seek divine guidance.
     - **Protect**: Care for life, health, relationships, and resources.
     - **Help**: Engage in service to uplift others.
     - **Uphold**: Maintain ethical integrity and fulfil duties. By focusing on these four principles, we align our efforts with a higher purpose, ensuring balance and fulfilment.

5. **What does "Life is a game" mean?**

   o *Answer*: Life is a game of growth, learning, and self-mastery. Success is not just about material gains but about how we face challenges and grow from them. The true victory in life lies in personal transformation and spiritual enlightenment, not in external achievements. In this game, the goal is to master oneself and transcend the fleeting pursuits of the material world.

6. **What does "Prince, Pauper, Prince" mean?**

   o *Answer*: The phrase symbolizes the soul's eternal journey. The soul begins as a *"prince"* in its pure, divine state. Through earthly experiences, it may face struggles, symbolized by becoming a "pauper." Ultimately, through spiritual awakening, the soul returns to its true, divine nature—the *"prince."* This cyclical journey reflects the soul's quest for self-realization, where worldly struggles are seen as stepping stones towards spiritual evolution.

7. **What is the importance of mystic energy returning to zero?**

   ○ *Answer*: Mystic energy returning to zero represents the return to a state of pure potential. This state, symbolized by "*zero*," is where dualities such as joy and sorrow, success and failure, merge into unity. The journey of spiritual realization is not about accumulating external experiences but about shedding distractions and returning to a state of simplicity, stillness, and union with the divine.

8. **What lessons come from Swamiji's encounter with two saints?**

   ○ *Answer*: Swamiji's encounters with saints such as Sri Sivananda of Rishikesh and Dr. Nagaraj of Anantapur taught humility, devotion, and spiritual healing. Sri Sivananda taught Swamiji the importance of surrendering the ego, while Dr Nagaraj emphasized the integration of physical healing with spiritual wisdom. These teachings continue to inspire those on the path of self-realization.

9. **How should one approach old age and physical challenges?**

   ○ *Answer*: Approaching old age with grace involves accepting life's natural limitations while focusing on spiritual growth. Practices such as meditation, prayer, and contemplation can help redirect energy toward divine realization, turning challenges into opportunities for deeper wisdom and understanding.

Inferences:

- **The Power of Humility and Devotion**: Swamiji's teachings emphasize that humility and devotion are the keys to spiritual growth. By surrendering to the divine and following the teachings of saints, one can purify the heart and experience peace.

- **Life as an Ethical Exam**: Just as an exam tests knowledge, life tests our actions, our adherence to dharma, and our spiritual progress. Success is defined not by material achievements but by how well we align our actions with divine principles.

- **Life's Balance**: The four key duties—pray, protect, help, and uphold—provide a practical framework for achieving a balanced and purposeful life. By prioritizing spiritual growth alongside our worldly responsibilities, we can live in harmony with both ourselves and the world.

- **Spiritual Awakening Through Struggles**: The challenges of life are part of the soul's journey toward enlightenment. By embracing these struggles with faith and patience, we purify ourselves and move closer to divine realization.

Opportunities for Growth:

Swamiji's teachings provide profound insights into how we can lead a fulfilling, purposeful life. By embracing devotion, spiritual discipline, and ethical integrity, we align ourselves with our higher purpose. Life's challenges are not obstacles but opportunities for growth, and through each experience, we are drawn closer to the divine truth that resides within us. Let us walk this path with faith, humility, and a deep commitment to serving the greater good, knowing that the ultimate goal is to realize the divinity within and to live in harmony with the cosmos.

Prayer for Divine Guidance and Inner Peace

O Divine Source of All Life,
We seek Your guidance on this sacred path,
Bless us with the strength to live with humility and devotion,
To uphold our duties with integrity and wisdom.
Grant us the clarity to see beyond the illusions of the material world,
And the courage to embrace our higher purpose,
In service to others, in love, and in truth.
May we find peace in the stillness of our hearts,
And may our actions always reflect Your divine light,
Guiding us through the challenges of life,
Toward the ultimate realization of our true selves.
We offer this prayer with gratitude,
Trusting in Your grace and protection.
May we walk this journey with faith,
And return to the Source with purity and love.

Om Shanti, Shanti, Shanti.

Chapter-25

The Path to Self-Realization and Service to Humanity

(A Journey of Love, Humility, and Service)

The Nature of Human Birth and the Path to Selflessness

"Just as a child is born and immediately begins to accept everything around it, we too are born into this world with a nature that wants to receive everything."

In this opening reflection, His Holiness emphasizes the innate nature of human beings to receive. From the moment of birth, a child is dependent on the world around it, accepting nourishment, love, and care without question. However, as we grow, the true challenge lies in transitioning from a mindset of being a receiver to that of a giver.

Actionable Takeaway: Reflect on how much you've received in your life—love, resources, education—and consider how you can give back. Can you offer your time, kindness, or wisdom to someone in need today?

This is a vital teaching in a world often fixated on self-gain. As adults, we must learn to give with the same joy and generosity as we once received. Society thrives on mutual care, yet imbalance occurs when individuals prioritize their own desires at the expense of others. The world faces challenges such as poverty, hunger, and suffering not simply because we take without giving, but due to our reluctance to return what we have received.

Quote from the Bhagavad Gita:

"True happiness lies in giving, not in receiving." — (Bhagavad Gita 9.22)

Human Nature and the Desire for Love: A Call to Reciprocity

"We expect everyone to love us, but do we love and care for others in the same way?"

His Holiness draws attention to the paradox of human relationships. We long to be loved, but how often do we ask ourselves whether we are showing the same love to others? This imbalance breeds selfishness, leading to violence, hatred, and societal conflict. When love is not reciprocated, humanity turns self-destructive.

Actionable Takeaway: Evaluate your relationships. How can you demonstrate love in a more selfless way, especially in the face of conflict or difference?

The call to nurture love, compassion, and understanding in our hearts is essential. Love is not merely an emotion, but the foundation of peace and a tool to heal a broken world.

Quote from the Bhagavad Gita:

"Those who live in harmony with all beings are blessed with peace." — (Bhagavad Gita 16.3)

The Ills of a Self-Centered World: The Dangers of Ego

"The world is filled with destruction because of the absence of love and the dominance of ego."

Ego is the root cause of much conflict, division, and suffering in the world. His Holiness explores how self-centeredness leads to wars, environmental degradation, and social unrest. When we allow our ego to dominate, we sow seeds of conflict. But when we act from a place of humility and selflessness, unity and peace emerge.

Actionable Takeaway: Reflect on your ego's role in your actions. When you feel anger or frustration, pause and ask: Is this coming from my ego, or is it driven by love and understanding?

By surrendering the ego, we become more connected with others and open ourselves to greater love and wisdom.

Quote from the Bhagavad Gita:

"Where there is ego, there is conflict; where there is selflessness, there is peace." — (Bhagavad Gita 16.4)

The Call to Serve Society: Beyond Personal Desires

"The time has come to actively contribute to the betterment of society and remove the veils of ignorance from our hearts."

His Holiness urges us to rise above personal desires and embrace a life of selfless service. Service is the highest form of devotion, and through it, we cleanse our hearts. To help others is to serve God within them. Service is not just charity but a sacred path to spiritual growth.

Actionable Takeaway: Start with small acts of service—whether it's helping a neighbor, volunteering, or simply listening to someone in need. How can you be a beacon of light in someone else's life today?

In helping others, we purify our own souls and experience the joy that comes with selfless service.

Quote from the Bhagavad Gita:

"Service to others is the greatest form of devotion." — *(Bhagavad Gita 12.4)*

The Unity of All Creation: Seeing the Divine in All Things

"All of nature is connected, and we are all part of the same divine whole."

One of the central teachings of His Holiness is the interconnectedness of all beings. We are not isolated entities but part of a larger cosmic unity. The ego creates the illusion of separation. When we recognize the divine essence in all beings, we begin to see the world through compassionate eyes.

Research Insight: Modern neuroscience and psychology reveal that acts of compassion and mindfulness activate neural pathways associated with happiness and emotional well-being. When we practice recognizing the divine in others, we nurture both our inner peace and outer harmony.

Actionable Takeaway: Practice mindfulness in your daily life— whether it's through meditation, a few moments of gratitude, or simply being present with others. Recognize the divine in the world around you.

Quote from the Bhagavad Gita:

"All beings are a part of Me, and I am the essence of all beings."
— *(Bhagavad Gita 9.4)*

The Path to Purity and Divine Connection

"To leave behind a legacy of love and service, we must first purify our hearts and minds."

The true purpose of life is to cultivate love, selflessness, and devotion. As we surrender our ego and desires, we begin to see the Divine in all aspects of life, purifying our hearts and minds. This alignment with the Divine will enables us to act in harmony with the universe.

Actionable Takeaway: Commit to a daily practice of reflection, service, and gratitude. This will help purify your heart and align you with divine purpose.

Through service, love, and humility, we find our connection with the Divine and realize our ultimate purpose—to love, to give, and to serve.

Inferences:

- **Human Nature and Selfishness**: The desire to take without giving leads to societal decay and personal dissatisfaction.
- **The Power of Love and Service**: True fulfilment comes from loving others and serving humanity selflessly.
- **The Role of Ego**: Ego creates division and conflict, while selflessness brings peace and unity.
- **Unity of Creation**: We are all interconnected, and recognizing this truth leads to spiritual awakening and wisdom.
- **The Path to Purity**: Purifying the mind and heart through service and devotion is the path to true spiritual fulfilment.

A Call for Selfless Service and Divine Unity

Let us walk the path of light,
Guided by love, with hearts so bright.
May service to others be our creed,
In every moment, fulfilling a need.
With humility and grace we stand,

Offering kindness, hand in hand.
May our hearts be pure, our minds aligned,
With the Divine presence in all we find.
Let us surrender ego, let it go,
In selfless love, let our spirits grow.
Through service, wisdom, and devotion's song,
May we find peace, where we belong.
With every step, may we rise above,
Spreading kindness, sharing love.
May our lives be filled with the Divine's glow,
And in every heart, may compassion flow.

Chapter-26

The Path to Spiritual Wholeness

The Quest for Oneness

Swami Vidyanarayana's teachings offer a profound journey into the heart of spiritual awakening, rooted in the core philosophy of Advaita Vedanta—the oneness of the individual soul (Atman) with the universal consciousness (Brahman). This realization is not only an intellectual understanding but a transformative experience that transcends the illusion of separateness. In his discourse, Swami Vidyanarayana delves into several key concepts and spiritual practices that guide the aspirant toward this divine unity. These teachings not only emphasize the importance of the Guru and mental mastery but also draw from the deep symbolism of ancient practices such as the Dandi and the influences of the cosmic forces.

Non-Duality: "Aham Brahmasmi" and "Tat Tvam Asi"

At the core of their conversation lies the essence of non-duality (Advaita), embodied in the famous Mahavakyas: *"Aham Brahmasmi"* (*"I am Brahman"*) and *"Tat Tvam Asi"* (*"Thou art That"*). These declarations encapsulate the truth of the non-separateness between the individual soul and the universal consciousness. Swami Vidyanarayana stresses that these sayings are not merely philosophical concepts, but a call to experience oneness with the divine, beyond all distinctions. *"The realization of Aham Brahmasmi is not of individual pride,"* he explains, *"but of recognizing the true self as the ultimate reality."* In this light, these teachings help dissolve the ego's sense of individuality, encouraging a recognition of the unity that binds all of existence.

The Role of the Guru and the Three Shaktis

A significant part of the spiritual journey is the role of the Guru, who serves as the guide to enlightenment. According to Swami Vidyanarayana, the Guru embodies the balance of the three Shaktis, which are the fundamental forces of creation: Ichasakti (*will*), Gnanasakti (*knowledge*), and Kriyasakti (*action*). These forces are symbolized in the father, mother, and Guru, respectively:

- **Ichasakti**: The father represents the will, which kindles the desire for spiritual awakening.

- **Gnanasakti**: The mother symbolizes knowledge, offering wisdom and clarity to guide the seeker.

- **Kriyasakti**: The Guru, as the embodiment of Kriyasakti, translates wisdom into transformative action, guiding the aspirant to apply the knowledge in real-life practice.

Swami Vidyanarayana affirms, *"The Guru is the embodiment of Kriyasakti, helping the disciple not only acquire wisdom but also turn it into action."* The dynamic interplay of these energies shapes the seeker's path and leads them toward spiritual realization.

The Dandi: A Symbol of Renunciation and Spiritual Discipline

The Dandi, or staff, is a key symbol in the life of ascetics. While it may seem like a simple physical aid, it holds a much deeper spiritual meaning. The Dandi represents renunciation and the discipline of self-control, integral to the ascetic path. More importantly, it symbolizes the spinal column, the core channel of spiritual energy in yogic traditions. *"The Dandi is not just a stick but a symbol of the disciplined spine,"* Swami Vidyanarayana explains, *"which channels spiritual energy. When the spine is aligned, so too is the spiritual aspirant."*

The straight posture maintained by ascetics mirrors the alignment of the spine during meditation, facilitating the flow of spiritual energy and promoting inner harmony. This alignment allows the practitioner to access higher states of consciousness, aligning the individual's will with the cosmic forces.

Mastering the Mind: The Influence of the Nine Planets (Nava Grahas)

Swami Vidyanarayana also explores the cosmic influence of the Nava Grahas—the nine planets in Vedic astrology. According to ancient teachings, the planets significantly influence the mental and emotional states of individuals. Mastery over the mind is essential for spiritual growth, and part of this mastery involves understanding the planetary forces at work.

"The planets influence not only the external world but also the inner world of the mind," he shares. *"To control the planets is to master the mind."* Swami Vidyanarayana teaches that by harmonizing one's thoughts and emotions with the cosmic rhythms, the seeker can transcend distractions and attain spiritual clarity. This mental discipline is critical for maintaining focus on the ultimate goal: union with the divine.

Subramanya: Commander of Mental Discipline and Self-Mastery

Subramanya, a revered deity in Indian spiritual traditions, is central to the ascetic life. He is considered the commander of divine forces that govern mental discipline and control. Swami Vidyanarayana highlights Subramanya's role in the practice of Sapatha Matrikasa, a technique for mental purification. This method is designed to help the practitioner maintain focus, clarity, and a sense of inner peace. By controlling the mind and emotions, Subramanya's teachings guide the seeker toward spiritual mastery.

The Cosmic Alignment: Ashtadik Pariparilaka and the Nine Planets

The concept of Ashtadik Pariparilaka, being influenced by the eight directions and the nine planets, emphasizes the interconnectedness of the individual with the cosmos. Aligning oneself with these forces through mental discipline and self-awareness allows the seeker to move in harmony with the universe. *"Mastery over the nine planets and their influence on the mind is essential for spiritual growth,"* says Swami Vidyanarayana. Through disciplined practice, the seeker can align their inner world with the cosmic order, achieving a state of spiritual wholeness.

Transition from Maya to Realization: The Significance of 11 and 12

Swami Vidyanarayana delves into the symbolic significance of numbers, particularly the transition from 11 to 12. The number 11 represents Maya, the illusion of separation and duality that creates a sense of individuality and disconnection from the divine. The number 12, however, marks the completion of the spiritual journey, signifying unity with the divine and the transcendence of the illusion of separateness.

"In the transition from 11 to 12, we move from the illusion of separateness to the realization of divine unity," explains Swami Vidyanarayana. This shift is key to spiritual enlightenment and symbolizes the aspirant's journey toward self-realization and oneness with all creation.

The Threefold Path: Ichasakti, Lokabandhu, and Lokaraksha

The threefold path outlined by Swami Vidyanarayana is crucial to achieving spiritual wholeness. It consists of:

1. **Ichasakti**: Will—awakening the desire for spiritual truth.

2. **Lokabandhu**: Connection with the world—understanding that we are interconnected with all beings.

3. **Lokaraksha**: Protection of the world—acting to safeguard and uplift the world around us.

Swami Vidyanarayana asserts, *"To surrender to the divine will is to understand the interconnectedness of all beings. It is through surrender, devotion, and right action that one achieves liberation."* The seeker must balance personal transformation with active participation in the world, contributing to the well-being of all.

Insights for Reflection

1. **Unity with the Divine**: The teachings of non-duality encourage us to see beyond the surface distinctions that divide us and recognize our essential oneness with all existence. Realizing the unity between the self and the divine is central to spiritual awakening.

2. **Discipline and Alignment**: The Dandi symbolizes the importance of discipline and alignment—not only of the body but also of the mind and spirit. Just as the spine supports the physical body, spiritual discipline supports the seeker on their journey toward divine realization.

3. **Mental Mastery**: The influence of the Nava Grahas serves as a reminder of the importance of mental discipline. By mastering our thoughts, we can free ourselves from the distractions of the external world and achieve inner peace.

4. **The Journey from Illusion to Truth**: The transition from 11 to 12 represents the shift from the illusion of separateness (Maya) to the realization of divine unity. This transformation is at the heart of spiritual awakening.

5. **Balance in Action**: The threefold path of Ichasakti, Lokabandhu, and Lokaraksha emphasizes the importance of balancing spiritual growth with active participation in the world. True spiritual growth involves both personal transformation and compassionate action.

Integration of Cosmic Forces and Personal Transformation

Swami Vidyanarayana's teachings offer a profound and holistic approach to spiritual growth. By integrating will, knowledge, and action, the aspirant aligns with the divine forces that govern the universe, moving toward oneness with the cosmos. This path allows the dissolution of the illusion of separateness and fosters a deep connection with the divine truth that underlies all existence.

The essence of this journey is not about seeking something outside of ourselves, but about recognizing the divine presence within— our true nature, the boundless potential for transformation and unity with the divine. As we move forward on this path, may we embody the qualities of love, care, trust, and surrender, which form the foundation of spiritual advancement.

A Prayer for Unity and Divine Light

O God, we bow before Your grace,
Guide our hearts, show us Your face.
In Your light, we seek to rise,
Help us see through worldly disguise.

Beyond all names, beyond all form,
In Your love, we are reborn.
Teach us to love, teach us to serve,
In every soul, Your truth we observe.

Grant us peace, grant us sight,
To walk Your path, to do what's right.
Help us act with open hands,
In Your service, as You command.

From every path, from every place,
Let kindness reign, in Your embrace.
Through unity, may we be one,
In Your love, the journey's done.

With wisdom deep and hearts so pure,
Guide us, God, to love and endure.
May we rise with strength and grace,
In Your light, we find our place.

Chapter-27

The Power of Divine Grace: A Journey Through Surrender and Spiritual Love

Swamy's grace, a light so pure,
In every heart, His love endures.
With trust we walk, through joy and pain,
Surrendering to Him, we rise again.
His life a model, kind and true,
Serving others, as He knew.
Through devotion, love, and care,
He taught us peace beyond compare.
In every prayer, His grace we feel,
Guiding us to hearts that heal.
With every step, we find our way,
Living His truth, both night and day.

The Essence of Divine Grace

Life, in its beautiful complexity, unfolds as a mixture of highs and lows, joy and sorrow, success and failure. In the midst of this flux, humanity has long searched for deeper meaning—seeking answers to questions of purpose, identity, and the mysteries of existence. Central to this quest is the concept of divine grace, a force that transcends human understanding, yet offers profound solace, guidance, and inner peace.

Divine grace is not merely an abstract or religious concept but a practical, transformative force that can shape the way we experience life's challenges and triumphs. To surrender to this grace is not a passive act of helplessness; rather, it is an active choice to trust in something greater than ourselves. Through this trust, we open ourselves to a higher power's guidance, which leads to clarity, peace, and deeper spiritual fulfilment.

The simple and powerful invocation *"I love you, Krishna. I trust you, Krishna. I surrender to your holy feet,"* offers an entry into this powerful state of surrender. These words encapsulate deep devotion and unconditional trust, embodying the essence of grace in a way that resonates deeply with the seeker.

Divine Grace: A Universal Concept Across Spiritual Traditions

Grace, or the act of surrendering to the divine, is central to many of the world's spiritual traditions. In Hinduism, the principle of **Bhakti** (devotion) emphasizes the relationship between the devotee and the divine, surrendering one's ego to the higher will of God. This resonates deeply with the **Bhakti movement**, which celebrated the surrender of one's heart and soul to God as the highest form of spiritual practice.

Similarly, Christianity speaks of divine grace as a free and unearned gift from God. The act of surrender in Christian faith—placing trust in God's will and love—provides believers with the peace that surpasses understanding. In **Buddhism**, the practice of non-attachment and surrender to the flow of life reflects the understanding that suffering arises from clinging to the transient, and true peace comes through letting go.

In every tradition, the common thread is the belief that surrendering to a higher power is not an act of weakness but one of strength and wisdom. By surrendering, we align ourselves with the divine will, which is inherently good, loving, and compassionate. It is through this alignment that we gain clarity and spiritual strength, helping us navigate the complexities of life with grace.

Swami Vidyanarayana: A Living Example of Divine Grace and Surrender

The teachings of **Swami Vidyanarayana** offer a profound example of how divine grace works in action. Known for his unwavering devotion, deep compassion, and selfless service, Swami Vidyanarayana's life was a testament to the transformative power of grace. His surrender to the divine was not limited to rituals or formal prayers but was reflected in every aspect of his life. Through acts of service, love, and kindness, he demonstrated the true essence of spirituality: surrendering to the divine will and serving humanity selflessly.

Swami Vidyanarayana's teachings emphasize that spirituality is not confined to the temple or sacred texts but is something that must be lived in daily interactions and in our approach to others. His life reminds us that true devotion is manifested through love, compassion, and humility in every moment. This lesson is especially relevant in today's world, where the demands of modern life often lead to stress, isolation, and a sense of disconnection from our spiritual roots.

Swami's message encourages us to embrace a life of purpose, service, and trust in the divine presence. His surrender to God was not about renouncing the world, but about finding God in all aspects of life—through loving actions, compassionate service, and deep devotion. His example continues to inspire individuals around the world to live in accordance with divine will, bringing peace and joy to all those they encounter.

Research and Psychological Insights on Surrender and Divine Grace

From a psychological perspective, surrendering to divine grace can be seen as a form of **emotional resilience**. Studies have shown that individuals who trust in something greater than themselves tend to experience lower levels of stress and anxiety. This is because surrender involves letting go of the need to control every aspect of life, allowing individuals to release the burden of perfectionism and embrace life as it is. Research in **positive psychology** has also shown that individuals who practice mindfulness and trust in life's unfolding tend to experience greater well-being and emotional stability.

The **neuroscience of surrender** also supports the idea that faith and trust can promote mental health. Studies on meditation and mindfulness practices suggest that surrendering to the present moment activates areas of the brain associated with emotional regulation, peace, and calmness. By learning to surrender, individuals can rewire their brains to respond to stress more effectively, cultivating a greater sense of balance and inner peace.

Practical Tools for Cultivating Divine Grace and Surrender

Living with divine grace involves more than understanding its concept—it requires practical steps to bring it into our lives. Here are some actionable tools:

1. **Mindfulness and Meditation**: Practices that help individuals stay present and cultivate trust in the divine flow of life. By focusing on the present moment, we learn to release anxiety and control, trusting that everything unfolds as it should.

2. **Daily Reflection and Prayer**: Dedicate time each day to connect with God through prayer or silent reflection. This

practice fosters a sense of gratitude and reinforces the trust that divine grace is always available to us.

3. **Acts of Service and Compassion**: Swami Vidyanarayana's teachings underscore that spiritual surrender is expressed through selfless acts of love and kindness. By helping others, we practice humility and divine love, living in alignment with grace.

4. **Letting Go of Attachment**: Learning to detach from the need for external validation or control over outcomes. Surrender is about accepting what comes, trusting that it is part of a larger divine plan.

Global Perspectives on Surrender: Surrender as a Path to Peace and Transformation

In a world filled with challenges—be it global crises, social injustice, or environmental concerns—spiritual surrender offers a path to inner peace. As the pressures of modern life mount, the practice of surrender provides solace and strength, reminding us that we are part of a larger, interconnected whole.

The global appeal of surrender can be seen in movements advocating for **non-violent resistance** and **compassionate service**. Figures like **Mahatma Gandhi** and **Martin Luther King Jr.**, who embraced spiritual principles of surrender and service, demonstrated how faith and trust in a higher power can inspire global movements for justice, equality, and peace. Their lives are testimonies to the transformative power of grace—not only for personal peace but for social and global change.

Conclusion: A Life Transformed by Divine Grace

Incorporating the practice of surrender and divine grace into our daily lives allows us to live with greater peace, resilience, and compassion. As we embrace this spiritual path, we begin to see the world through a new lens—one that acknowledges the interconnectedness of all beings and trusts in the higher wisdom that guides us.

Whether through Swami Vidyanarayana's life of devotion, the teachings of world spiritual leaders, or the inner peace found in surrendering to the divine, the message is clear: surrender is not an act of weakness, but one of strength. It is a path that leads to greater wisdom, deeper connection, and the transformative power of unconditional love.

Swamy's Message

Surrender to grace, let your heart be light,
Trust in the journey, walk in the light.
Live with love, serve with care,
In every moment, God is there.
Let kindness bloom like flowers in the spring,
With every action, let your heart sing.
Peace will follow, joy will flow,
When you trust in the grace that helps you grow.
"Live in love, surrender to me,
In my grace, you are truly free."

Chapter-28

The Path of Purity: Cultivating Goodness, Faith, and Divine Friendship

The Power of Goodness

"Good thoughts, good intentions, and good actions reflect a person's true character and spiritual cultivation."

In this discourse, His Holiness emphasizes that our true nature is revealed through our thoughts, actions, and intentions. A virtuous heart leads to pure thoughts and actions, and this purity is the foundation of spiritual growth. Society celebrates those who walk the path of righteousness and reject evil. Individuals who live with love and truth are seen as divine, comparable to the great sages. His Holiness stresses that society always supports good over evil, and therefore, when we live with a pure heart and mind, good results naturally follow.

In the modern world, where distractions such as technology, consumerism, and social pressures abound, living with goodness is a deliberate choice. It requires a conscious effort to act from a place of integrity, to resist the temptations of the ego, and to cultivate virtuous habits such as mindfulness, compassion, and self-discipline. The foundation of this purity lies in consistent self-reflection and the daily practice of good thoughts, good words, and good deeds.

Practical Tip: Start your day with gratitude and intention. Reflect on your values, and ask yourself how you can act in alignment with your highest self throughout the day. This simple practice sets the tone for a day filled with purpose and spiritual growth.

Quote from the Bhagavad Gita:

"Goodness, purity, and kindness are the ultimate virtues that define a soul's connection to the Divine." — (Bhagavad Gita 16.3)

Friendship with the Divine

"True friendship with God is built on selflessness, mutual understanding, and guidance along the righteous path."

His Holiness refers to Lord Krishna's declaration in the Bhagavad Gita that He is the "Sakha" (friend) of all beings. A true friend is one who helps, guides, and leads us towards righteousness. Lord Krishna, as the ultimate guide, demonstrates that friendship with the Divine is not about asking for favours but about receiving wisdom and direction in life.

True friendship with God is rooted in selfless love. It's not about seeking personal benefits or desires but about connecting with the Divine out of reverence and love. This is similar to how a friend guides us with sincere advice, encouraging us to stay true to our path even when it's difficult.

The story of the thief who listens to his conscience illustrates the importance of recognizing the Divine's voice guiding us in the right direction. His conscience, that inner divine friend, stopped him from committing the act of theft. This teaches us that our conscience is not only a moral compass but also the voice of the Divine, always calling us toward righteousness.

Practical Tip: Dedicate a moment each day to converse with the Divine—whether through prayer, meditation, or reflection. Cultivate a relationship with God where you seek wisdom and guidance, and listen for the inner prompts that lead you toward your highest good.

Quote from the Bhagavad Gita:

"I am the friend of all beings, guiding them toward righteousness and light."
— *(Bhagavad Gita 9.22)*

The Importance of Self-Reflection and Conscience

"Man's inner peace is found through self-reflection and the adherence to conscience."

In His Holiness' teachings, listening to the conscience is crucial for spiritual growth. When we ignore our conscience, we step away from our true selves and towards spiritual decline. However, when we heed the conscience, we align with the Divine will and walk the path of righteousness.

In today's fast-paced world, people often make decisions based on external pressures, such as societal expectations or material desires. Yet, true peace comes from turning inward and listening to our conscience, which connects us to our higher self.

The life of a wealthy man who, despite his material comforts, faces the limitations of time, serves as a reminder that no external possession can provide eternal satisfaction. True fulfilment lies not in external wealth but in internal wisdom. The key to a peaceful life is knowing what truly matters—spiritual values over material success.

Practical Tip: Take a few minutes every evening to reflect on your actions of the day. Ask yourself if you have lived in alignment with your values and if your actions were guided by your higher self. This simple practice of self-reflection will help you course-correct and stay connected to your spiritual path.

Quote from the Bhagavad Gita:

"True wealth is found in spiritual abundance, not material accumulation."
— *(Bhagavad Gita 13.31)*

The Fleeting Nature of Life

"Life is transient, and only the eternal joy of the Divine remains."

In the discourse, His Holiness addresses the impermanence of life. Everything in the material world is fleeting, but the only thing that is eternal is joy found in the Divine. True happiness comes not from external sources but from within, through a steady and unwavering connection to God.

In the modern world, the chase for external validation, wealth, and pleasure often clouds the deeper truth of existence. Yet, as His Holiness points out, all these are temporary. The key to a fulfilling life is to seek the lasting joy of spiritual awakening, knowing that the soul's connection with the Divine is the ultimate source of peace.

Practical Tip: Embrace the practice of detachment. While it's natural to enjoy the pleasures of the world, do not become attached to them. Recognize that the source of true joy lies in your relationship with the Divine, not in material possessions or fleeting experiences.

Quote from the Bhagavad Gita:

"The soul is eternal; all else is impermanent and transient."
— *(Bhagavad Gita 2.14)*

Spiritual Practice and Purity of Mind

"Purity of the mind leads to purity of thought, speech, and action."

Purity of the mind is the cornerstone of spiritual practice. A pure mind is free of distractions, desires, and ego, allowing us to align every action with divine will. When the mind is pure, the body follows suit, and every word, action, and thought becomes a reflection of our connection with the Divine.

In our daily lives, we are constantly bombarded by distractions and temptations. Yet, as His Holiness teaches, we don't need extreme practices to achieve purity. Simple practices like mindfulness, meditation, and keeping good company help maintain the purity of mind.

Practical Tip: Incorporate mindfulness into your daily routine. Whether you are eating, working, or interacting with others, practice being fully present. This practice helps cultivate a pure mind and ensures that your actions are aligned with your highest self.

Quote from the Bhagavad Gita:

"Purity of heart is the foundation of all spiritual practices."
— *(Bhagavad Gita 9.22)*

The Power of Faith and Humility

"Humility and faith are essential for spiritual progress."

To experience the Divine fully, one must release the ego and approach life with humility and faith. As we let go of our pride, we become more open to divine guidance. Faith and humility are the means through which the Divine grace flows into our lives, transforming us from within.

Humility dissolves the ego, while faith in God's wisdom and timing brings peace in every circumstance. The more we surrender to God with faith and humility, the more we open ourselves to spiritual wisdom and blessings.

Practical Tip: Practice humility by offering service without expecting recognition or reward. Serve others, not for personal gain, but as an expression of love and devotion to the Divine. This practice helps dissolve ego and strengthen your faith.

Quote from the Bhagavad Gita:

Those who surrender their ego to me are blessed with eternal peace."
— (Bhagavad Gita 18.66)

Inferences:

- **True Friendship with God**: True friendship with the Divine is rooted in love, guidance, and the pursuit of righteousness.

- **Self-Reflection and Conscience**: Listening to one's conscience and acting in accordance with it leads to spiritual growth.

- **The Impermanence of Life**: Life is fleeting, and true happiness comes from spiritual awakening, not material wealth.

- **Purity of Mind and Action**: Spiritual progress depends on maintaining purity of thought, speech, and action.

- **Faith and Humility**: Devotion, humility, and surrender to God are essential for experiencing divine grace and achieving liberation.

- **The Path to Liberation**: The spiritual journey is one of selflessness, devotion, and detachment from the material world.

The Path to Spiritual Liberation

"The journey to liberation is through selflessness, devotion, and detachment from the material world."

His Holiness concludes by urging everyone to follow the path of selflessness, devotion, and humility. The pursuit of spiritual growth is not an external journey but an internal one, marked by the cultivation of virtues and the purification of the heart. Those who remain steadfast in their devotion to God, surrendering the ego and embracing humility, will ultimately experience spiritual liberation.

As the world around us continues to evolve, His Holiness reminds us that spiritual fulfilment comes not from external achievements but from inner transformation. The ultimate goal is to align ourselves with the Divine through faith and self-reflection, allowing us to experience true joy and liberation.

Prayer

O Divine, our hearts do seek,
A path of virtue pure and meek.
In every thought, in every deed,
Let love and truth be all we need.

Guide us on this sacred way,
With faith and light, show us the way.
With humility, our hearts align,
In grace, we surrender, O Divine.

Bless us with wisdom, strength, and peace,
And let our souls find true release.

Chapter-29

Spiritual Liberation

The Role of Prayer in Spiritual Illumination

"Prayer has the power to illuminate the mind and elevate the heart, guiding the soul towards divine consciousness." In this profound discourse, His Holiness Sri Vidyanarayana Theertha emphasizes that prayer is not merely a ritualistic action, but a means to purify the mind, enhance spiritual energy, and establish a deep connection with the divine. As the Bhagavad Gita beautifully states, *"Whosoever remembers Me with a devoted heart, I am always with them"* (Bhagavad Gita 9.22). Through prayer, we align our consciousness with the Divine, fostering peace and guiding us towards spiritual awakening.

By sincerely engaging in prayer, the seeker can transcend feelings of fatigue and sorrow, bringing mental peace and joy. Prayer, in its truest sense, purifies the mind, aligning it with the Divine purpose, and opens the heart to the infinite grace of the Guru. In today's world, amidst chaos and distraction, the practice of prayer acts as a stabilizing force, helping one reconnect with the Divine.

The Sacred Practice of Chanting Mantras: A Gateway to Divine Presence

His Holiness further elaborates on the significance of chanting sacred mantras, especially the Vishnu Sahasranama. These practices, when done consistently, are not just ritual acts but an invaluable treasure that taps into a divine power, cleansing the mind and removing obstacles. The Bhagavad Gita asserts, *"With sincere devotion, chant the holy names of God, and they will purify you"* (Bhagavad Gita 9.14). This repetition carries the essence of the Divine and brings us closer to spiritual enlightenment.

In today's fast-paced world, the spiritual power of chanting can provide an anchor, offering inner peace and a sense of purpose. Studies on the psychological and physiological effects of chanting, such as stress reduction and improved emotional well-being, highlight its importance in modern life. Just as mantras were practiced by ancient sages, their relevance in contemporary times is profound.

The Allegory of the Tiger and the Goat: Awakening to One's True Nature

His Holiness compares the human condition to a tiger raised among goats. A tiger that forgets its true nature and lives as a goat symbolizes how humans may live in ignorance, unaware of their divine essence. When the tiger meets another tiger, it recognizes its strength and inherent nature, much like how, under the guidance of a Guru, individuals can awaken to their spiritual truth.

The Bhagavad Gita states, *"A person who is ignorant of their true self is like a blind man walking in the dark, unaware of the truth that lies before them"* (Bhagavad Gita 5.15). The Guru's guidance lifts the veil of ignorance, revealing the divine essence within, and helping the disciple discover their inherent strength and divinity. In today's world, where people often get lost in material pursuits, the Guru's wisdom is crucial for reawakening our true nature.

The Power of Guru's Guidance: Illuminating the Path to Liberation

The Guru's wisdom is the light that leads us out of ignorance and towards spiritual liberation. Just as the tiger needed another tiger to recognize its true nature, humans require the guidance of a Guru to discover their divine essence. As the Bhagavad Gita teaches, "*A true Guru dispels the darkness of ignorance and illuminates the path to liberation*" (Bhagavad Gita 4.34). Through the Guru's teachings, the disciple transcends ignorance and is guided toward the ultimate goal of spiritual fulfilment.

The Guru's role extends beyond mere intellectual instruction; it is an embodiment of divine grace. Modern-day challenges, such as the distractions of the digital age, often obscure our spiritual essence. In these times, the Guru's guidance offers clarity and direction, helping us navigate through life's complexities with wisdom.

The Importance of Self-Realization: Liberation Through Knowledge

His Holiness stresses that "*realizing one's true nature is the key to overcoming the cycle of birth and death.*" Without this realization, we remain trapped in the illusion of worldly attachments. Self-realization is the key to transcending the cycle of samsara (birth and death), and the Guru's teachings help uncover the truth of our existence. As the Chandogya Upanishad declares, "*Realize the Self within you, for through this realization, you shall transcend the world of birth and death*" (Chandogya Upanishad 6.14.2).

In today's world, where materialism often dominates our lives, the journey of self-realization becomes all the more important. By uncovering our true nature, we are freed from the cycle of samsara and attain liberation. The process of self-realization is a form of inner awakening that can profoundly transform not only an individual's life but also society at large.

Guru's Role in Transcending Ignorance: The Mirror of Truth

His Holiness compares the Guru to a mirror that reflects the disciple's true form. The Guru's teachings act as a mirror, helping the disciple see their divine nature and transcending ignorance. As the Bhagavad Gita affirms, *"The Guru is the one who reveals the divine truth and shows the way to liberation"* (Bhagavad Gita 4.34). Through the Guru's wisdom, the disciple awakens to their true self and moves towards spiritual freedom.

The modern world's emphasis on external achievements and appearance often obscures the internal truth. The Guru's role is to guide us back to this inner truth, helping us see beyond worldly illusions and discover the eternal light within.

The Significance of Surrendering to the Guru: Trusting Divine Will

Surrendering to the Guru is the highest form of devotion, notes His Holiness. It is not about submission, but about trusting the Guru fully and allowing them to guide us towards spiritual progress. As the Bhagavad Gita beautifully states, *"Surrender all your actions to Me, with full faith, and I will liberate you from all sin"* (Bhagavad Gita 18.66). In this surrender, the disciple finds peace, liberation, and eternal wisdom.

In today's world, surrender is often misunderstood. It is not passive submission but an active process of trust and devotion. Surrender to the Guru helps transcend ego and invites the divine grace that leads to spiritual enlightenment. The act of surrender becomes a powerful tool for personal transformation.

Guru as the Source of Liberation: Grace and Guidance in Difficult Times

The Guru's grace is compared to the Kalpavriksha, the wish-fulfilling tree, offering peace and spiritual growth. His Holiness elaborates on the comfort and strength that come from the Guru's shelter, especially in times of difficulty. The Guru's teachings fulfill the disciple's spiritual needs, offering the peace and wisdom required for spiritual growth.

As the Bhagavad Gita suggests,

> *"In the shelter of the Guru's grace, one finds peace, wisdom, and liberation"*
> *— (Bhagavad Gita 10.10).*

In today's world, where individuals face countless challenges—whether emotional, psychological, or physical—the Guru's guidance provides solace, offering a roadmap to overcome these obstacles and attain inner peace. The Guru, through their grace, serves as the steady anchor amidst the storms of life.

Insights:

1. **Psychological Benefits of Chanting and Meditation**

   Modern research shows that chanting and meditation significantly reduce stress, improve emotional health, and increase clarity, helping individuals maintain peace amidst external turbulence. These practices have been scientifically linked to enhanced emotional regulation and resilience, supporting a peaceful and balanced state of mind even during challenging circumstances.

2. **Self-Realization and Mental Health**

   The journey of self-realization is increasingly recognized for its profound impact on mental health. Practices of self-awareness and spiritual contemplation contribute significantly to emotional stability, providing clarity, a sense of purpose, and enhanced well-being. By integrating self-realization into one's life, individuals find a path toward personal balance and mental equilibrium.

3. **The Timeless Guru-Disciple Relationship**

Throughout history, the Guru-disciple relationship has been considered an eternal bond, transcending time and culture. From ancient Upanishadic wisdom to modern spiritual practices, the Guru's guidance remains a constant force in empowering individuals to transcend worldly distractions and attain spiritual liberation. This timeless connection continues to offer profound value in guiding the seeker on the path of truth and wisdom.

Embracing the Guru's Guidance for Spiritual Awakening

His Holiness concludes by urging devotees to embrace the Guru's teachings with full devotion. Through surrender, prayer, mantra chanting, and self-realization, the disciple can transcend the limitations of the material world and attain liberation. The Guru's grace and wisdom are the guiding forces on this path of spiritual awakening.

In the fast-paced and often chaotic world we live in, the Guru's teachings offer us a sense of grounding, purpose, and direction. By practicing devotion and trust, one can realize the eternal truth that resides within. As the Bhagavad Gita teaches, "Surrender to the Guru with love and devotion, for through their grace, you will find liberation from all worldly suffering."

A Prayer for Divine Illumination

O Divine Guru, source of endless grace,
You who guide us from ignorance's dark place,
In your light, let our hearts awake,
From the slumber of samsara, for liberation's sake.
With every prayer, may our minds be clear,
Purified by mantras, dispelling all fear.
Let the sacred syllables rise from our soul,
Bringing us closer to the eternal goal.
Through your wisdom, O Guru, we find our way,
In your shelter, let us ever stay.
Grant us the courage to trust and surrender,
In your grace, let us grow and remember,
The divine truth that lies deep within,
The eternal light that frees us from sin.

Chapter-30

The True Essence of Swadharma

Understanding Swadharma and Its Importance in Spiritual Life

"Swadharma is not merely the fulfilment of daily tasks for survival, but the path through which one progresses spiritually, aligning the individual with their divine nature."

– His Holiness Sri Vidyanarayana Theertha

Swadharma, as described in the teachings of His Holiness Sri Vidyanarayana Theertha, is a fundamental concept in spiritual life. It goes beyond the performance of everyday duties—it is the embodiment of one's true nature and the fulfilment of responsibilities that arise from the innermost self. Swadharma is not merely a set of actions, but a divine law that governs the heart and mind, leading one towards spiritual evolution. It calls for living with purity, integrity, and selflessness while fulfilling one's role in society, family, and the universe.

At the heart of Swadharma lies the **purity of heart**—the true wealth of life. According to His Holiness, this purity is not something external but an inner state of clarity, compassion, and divine alignment. A heart free from ego, desires, and worldly attachments is a heart that can serve others selflessly and reflect the divine in every action. It is when the heart is untainted by selfish motives that it becomes a pure vessel, channeling divine grace and wisdom.

This purity forms the very foundation of Swadharma. Only with a heart devoid of impurities can one genuinely align with their highest purpose—selfless service to others. A pure heart becomes a mirror of divine light, acting as a conduit for the spiritual principles that guide us. By practicing Swadharma in this manner, an individual contributes to the collective good while attaining inner peace and spiritual growth.

In the context of today's fast-paced world, where the boundaries between personal, professional, and spiritual lives often blur, understanding and practicing Swadharma becomes even more crucial. It offers a path to not only spiritual fulfilment but also to lasting peace. Swadharma teaches us to integrate our spiritual values into every aspect of our lives, creating harmony and balance amid the chaos of modern existence.

Quote from Bhagavad Gita:

"It is better to fail in one's own dharma than to succeed in another's dharma."
— *(Bhagavad Gita 3.35)*

Swadharma in the Modern World

In today's interconnected, fast-paced world, Swadharma transcends traditional rituals and offers a deeper meaning. Many people, caught in the whirlwind of modern life, often lose sight of their true purpose. Swadharma offers a timeless solution—by reconnecting individuals with their deeper spiritual duties.

Selfless service today takes many forms—from volunteering at local charities to advocating for environmental sustainability, to dedicating oneself to the well-being of others in personal or professional settings. Swadharma, therefore, becomes an expression of compassion and care, where each individual's actions are rooted in the desire to contribute to the collective good. In a world increasingly driven by material pursuits, the practice of Swadharma serves as a reminder to align our personal actions with our highest values.

This ancient principle teaches us that fulfilment comes not from seeking personal gain but from serving others and offering ourselves selflessly to the welfare of the world.

The Path of Selfless Service: Karma as Swadharma

"Swadharma involves doing one's duty with love, compassion, and without selfish desires. It is not about seeking fame or wealth but about nurturing others and contributing to their happiness."

– His Holiness Sri Vidyanarayana Theertha

At the heart of Swadharma lies the principle of Karma, or action. Swadharma is not merely about following set rituals or fulfilling basic responsibilities; it is about performing every action with the awareness of its divine purpose. True service is selfless and driven by compassion. The Bhagavad Gita teaches that fulfilling one's duty (Karma) without attachment to the fruits of the action is the highest form of spiritual practice.

Selfless service is a powerful expression of Swadharma. It frees the practitioner from ego and material attachments, directing their energy towards the welfare of others. Whether in the form of everyday acts of kindness or larger efforts to contribute to societal well-being, each selfless act becomes a part of the spiritual journey.

Quote from Bhagavad Gita:

"Perform your prescribed duties, for action is better than inaction."
— (Bhagavad Gita 3.8)

Self-Realization and Mental Health

Swadharma is not only a spiritual practice but also a powerful tool for mental well-being. Modern psychology recognizes the benefits of mindfulness, self-awareness, and compassion in improving mental health. In a world full of stress, anxiety, and emotional turmoil, Swadharma offers a refuge—a way to find balance and clarity by aligning actions with divine principles.

Living in accordance with Swadharma helps us become more aware of our true nature. This awareness leads to emotional resilience and a deeper sense of fulfilment. Instead of reacting impulsively to life's challenges, those who practice Swadharma learn to respond with wisdom, patience, and love.

In this way, self-realization through Swadharma not only elevates the spiritual seeker but also fosters mental clarity, emotional balance, and a harmonious life. By transcending selfish desires and ego, we can live in a state of peaceful awareness, free from the stresses that plague the modern world.

The Role of the Guru in Swadharma

The practice of Swadharma is deeply connected to the relationship between the Guru (spiritual teacher) and the disciple. The Guru's role is to guide the disciple in understanding their true nature, helping them identify and fulfill their Swadharma. Through this sacred relationship, the disciple gains the wisdom to navigate life's challenges and align their actions with their divine purpose.

The Guru serves as a beacon of light, offering not just teachings but also practical wisdom drawn from their own experience. By imparting knowledge and providing spiritual guidance, the Guru helps the disciple overcome obstacles and stay steadfast on the path of self-realization.

In the words of the Bhagavad Gita, "*When the disciple is ready, the Guru appears,*" emphasizing the importance of the Guru in guiding the seeker towards their true path. The Guru-disciple bond is a sacred one, built on mutual respect, love, and a shared commitment to spiritual growth.

Reflective Questions

- How can you integrate the practice of selfless service into your daily life?

- What personal desires or attachments hinder your ability to practice Swadharma?

- In what ways can you be more compassionate and aware of the needs of others around you?

- How does your work or role in the community align with your spiritual duty (Swadharma)?

Call to Action

As we reflect on our individual paths, let us commit ourselves to living according to the principles of Swadharma. In a world often focused on personal gain, let us choose the path of selfless service, compassion, and righteousness. Every act of kindness, every selfless moment, brings us closer to the divine and to true spiritual fulfilment.

By aligning our actions with Swadharma, we contribute not only to our own spiritual growth but also to the well-being of the world. Each small act of love and service becomes a divine offering, a step towards inner peace and collective harmony.

Inferences

- Swadharma is the path of spiritual awakening through selfless service, compassion, and fulfilling one's duties with a sense of duty rather than attachment.

- The modern world's disconnect from purpose can be mitigated by embracing Swadharma, which helps individuals align their daily actions with higher spiritual values.

- Swadharma enhances mental health by fostering self-awareness and mindfulness, leading to emotional balance and resilience.

- The Guru plays a critical role in guiding the disciple towards their Swadharma, offering wisdom and insight to navigate life's challenges.

- Reflecting on our own Swadharma can lead to a deeper sense of purpose and fulfilment, helping us integrate spiritual practices into our modern lives.

Social Upliftment:

Swadharma offers a timeless path to spiritual fulfilment, transcending the boundaries of time and place. By understanding and embodying our own Swadharma, we not only elevate our spiritual lives but also contribute to the betterment of society. Through selfless service, compassion, and the guidance of a Guru, we can live in alignment with our true purpose, finding peace, joy, and divine connection in every moment.

Let us all strive to live in accordance with our Swadharma, embracing it as the guiding principle of our lives, and offering our service to the world with love and humility.

Prayer

O Divine Creator,
Guide us to walk the path of Swadharma with unwavering faith.
May we perform our duties with selflessness and devotion,
Bringing love, compassion, and light to all beings.

Bless us with wisdom to discern our true nature,
And grant us the strength to serve others without attachment.
May we, through our actions, experience the divine presence in every moment,
And fulfill our purpose as instruments of peace and harmony.

Om Shanti, Shanti, Shanti.

Chapter-31

The True Wealth – Purity of Heart

Nurturing Virtues:

"Man's real wealth is his goodness, his inner purity, and the virtues he cultivates throughout his life."

In the teachings of His Holiness Sri Vidyanarayana Theertha, the essence of life's wealth is not found in material possessions but in the virtues that reside within us. These virtues—goodness, purity, love, patience, endurance, forgiveness, charity, and sacrifice—are the pillars of true strength and character. Cultivating them leads to a life of peace, spiritual fulfilment, and alignment with the divine. This process of nurturing virtues, often referred to as *Samskara (spiritual discipline)*, is a lifelong endeavor.

The Bhagavad Gita (17.20) reminds us: *"A person is known by their actions, not by their external wealth."* This underscores that our deeds, shaped by virtues, define our essence and impact the world.

Sanctified Life:

"By keeping the heart pure, the entire life becomes sanctified. Therefore, it is essential to cultivate qualities such as goodness, purity, love, patience, and tolerance."

Purity of heart is the cornerstone of a meaningful life. It is a state of inner clarity and alignment where ego, desires, and attachments are transcended. This purity not only enriches the individual but radiates outward, inspiring others and fostering harmony.

In the teachings of His Holiness, virtues are not abstract ideals but practical tools for self-purification. They enable individuals to:

1. Develop emotional resilience and inner peace.

2. Strengthen relationships by fostering understanding and compassion.

3. Build a foundation for spiritual growth and divine connection.

Practical Steps to Cultivate Virtues

- **Daily Meditation:** A practice to quiet the mind and center the heart, creating space for inner purity.

- **Mindfulness in Actions:** Consciously align every thought and deed with higher principles.

- **Acts of Kindness:** Perform selfless acts without expectation, reinforcing compassion and love.

- **Reflection Journaling:** Regularly assess how well one's actions align with virtues like patience, tolerance, and forgiveness.

His Holiness advises: *"When we set our intentions on good deeds, we must act immediately, for delay may cause the thought to fade."* Regular practice makes virtues a natural part of one's being.

The Essence of Self-Transformation

> *"Self-transformation is the key to realizing the divinity within. Through constant effort, we can refine ourselves and realize our highest potential."*

True transformation is a gradual journey requiring dedication, discipline, and self-control. Spiritual growth is about refining one's thoughts and actions to align with divine will.

- **Patience** teaches endurance during challenges.
- **Tolerance** fosters acceptance in diversity.
- **Forgiveness** liberates the soul from anger and resentment.

Modern neuroscience supports this idea, showing that cultivating virtues like compassion and gratitude activates brain regions associated with happiness and connection, releasing hormones like oxytocin and serotonin. These findings affirm that virtues not only enrich spiritual life but also enhance emotional and mental well-being.

The Role of Prayer in Spiritual Growth

"Prayer is not merely a ritual but a means of expressing our deepest reverence and seeking divine guidance."

Prayer is a powerful tool for self-purification. It aligns the heart with the divine and cultivates gratitude and surrender. His Holiness describes prayer as a direct conversation with the divine:

"The light that permeates this universe, the consciousness that flows through all creation, is You alone. Everything, from the earth to the skies, is filled with Your divine presence. My heart responds to You with compassion, and every movement of my body reflects Your influence. Guide me with wisdom; meet my need."

This prayer exemplifies the devotee's surrender and reliance on divine grace, reminding us that prayer is not for rewards but for spiritual unity.

The Power of Faith and Devotion

"Through unwavering faith and devotion, the disciple strengthens their connection with the divine and experiences divine grace."

Faith and devotion are indispensable on the spiritual journey. Faith is not blind belief but an intuitive trust in the divine's wisdom.

Devotion involves surrendering to divine will and trusting the greater cosmic plan.

In moments of doubt, these qualities anchor us, enabling perseverance and deeper connection with the divine. As the Bhagavad Gita (9.22) states: *"Those who strive with devotion to purify their hearts are always under the protection of the Divine."*

Modern Relevance of Purity and Virtue

In today's world, where materialism and distractions often overshadow inner growth, virtues like patience, love, and forgiveness hold transformative potential. Cultivating purity of heart fosters:

1. **Emotional Resilience:** Virtues like tolerance and forgiveness reduce stress and enhance mental well-being.

2. **Ethical Leadership:** Leaders who embody purity inspire trust and foster harmony in their communities.

3. **Global Unity:** Purity transcends cultural and religious boundaries, offering a universal foundation for peace and collaboration.

The practice of virtues is not just for individual betterment but for creating a society rooted in empathy, equity, and mutual respect.

A Life of Selflessness and Grace

"May we all strive to live lives filled with goodness, love, and compassion. Let our hearts remain pure, and our actions aligned with divine will, so that we may experience the ultimate grace of the divine."

By cultivating virtues and living with purity of heart, we align ourselves with divine will. This alignment brings inner peace, joy, and fulfilment, enabling us to lead a life of selfless service and divine grace.

Inferences

1. **True Wealth is Inner Purity:** Life's ultimate wealth lies in cultivating virtues like love, patience, and tolerance.

2. **Samskara (Self-Improvement):** Regular practice of spiritual disciplines refines the heart and soul.

3. **Faith and Devotion:** These qualities are the foundation for divine connection and grace.

4. **Power of Prayer:** Prayer is a direct channel to the divine, offering guidance and gratitude.

5. **Modern Relevance of Virtue:** Purity of heart is essential for navigating today's challenges, fostering both personal and societal transformation.

6. **Selfless Service:** Serving others selflessly aligns us with divine will and purpose.

Prayer

Oh Divine Light, so pure and bright,
Guide my steps through day and night.
In Your love, my heart takes rest,
In Your grace, I feel most blessed.

Through every path, through every deed,
May Your wisdom plant the seed.
Of kindness, truth, and love so true,
Let all my actions mirror You.

With faith in You, I face each day,
Your gentle hand will lead my way.
Oh Lord of love, my heart's delight,
Fill my soul with Your endless light.

Chapter-32

The Universal Power of the Human Cell: A Reflection for All Humanity

Transcending Science:

In the intricate design of life, the human cell stands as a profound symbol of unity, resilience, and limitless potential. It is the foundation of all living beings, embodying lessons that transcend science, touching upon the spiritual, psychological, and societal realms. Inspired by the profound teachings of His Holiness Swamy Vidyanarayana Theertha, this exploration of the human cell offers a universal message for every individual, irrespective of their faith or station in life.

The Cell: A Masterpiece of Unity and Functionality

- **Anatomy and Physiology:** The human cell is a miracle of creation. It houses organelles like the nucleus (*the control center*), mitochondria (*energy generators*), and many more, each playing a specific role in harmony. This internal collaboration within a single cell ensures life's continuity and vitality.

  Universal Insight: The cell reflects the principle of coexistence. Just as its components work together for the greater good of the body, individuals in families, communities, and nations thrive through collaboration and unity. Each part, though distinct, contributes to the collective whole.

- **Swamy's Wisdom:** *"In one cell, how many parts: brain, nervous system, kidney, lungs, pancreas, blood, heart..."* This observation emphasizes the intricate interdependence of life's building blocks, urging us to appreciate the unity that sustains existence, both within the body and in the world around us.

Psychological and Spiritual Dimensions

- **Psychology:** Our thoughts and emotions have a direct impact on the health of our cells. Positive states like joy, love, and gratitude enhance cellular vitality, while stress, anger, and negativity can harm it.

  Message for All: Understanding the mind-body connection reminds us to cultivate positivity, mindfulness, and self-awareness—not just for mental well-being but for physical health too. Our thoughts shape our cells, and in turn, they shape our lives.

- **Spirituality:** Spiritually, the cell is a microcosm of the divine. Swamy Vidyanarayana Theertha explains: *"Amma sees; Amma is Amma. Amma accepted the cell."* This reflects the idea that life itself is an act of divine love, with every cell carrying a sacred purpose.

  Universal Truth: Regardless of religious belief, this insight highlights the sanctity of life and the interconnectedness of all beings. By honouring our own life, we honour the divine presence in all creation. Every cell is a manifestation of divine wisdom, contributing to the divine symphony that sustains life.

- **Divine Intelligence:** The cell's design and function are not the result of random processes but a manifestation of divine intelligence. The same intelligence governs the larger universe, reminding us that we are part of a grand, orchestrated plan. Just as each cell works in perfect harmony, so does the entire cosmos, driven by a force far greater than ourselves.

Sociology and Anthropology: The Cell as a Mirror of Society

- **Sociology:** Just as cells form tissues and organs, individuals form communities and societies. Healthy societies, like healthy bodies, depend on fairness, cooperation, and inclusivity. When each individual plays their part in harmony, the whole system thrives.

  Message for Humanity: Societies thrive when we recognize that every individual, like every cell, plays a vital role in the collective well-being. Disregard or harm to any part of society disrupts the whole. True societal health comes from the respect and care we show to each other.

- **Anthropology:** Across cultures and civilizations, the cell symbolizes life's shared origin. Swamy reminds us: *"Abdul Kalam, Swami Vivekananda, and Adi Shankara—all came from one cell."* This reinforces the idea that humanity is united by a common source and potential.

- **Universal Insight:** Greatness lies within every one of us. The same divine spark exists in every cell, urging us to nurture ourselves and others to unlock this inherent potential. The cell reminds us that the seeds of wisdom, greatness, and divinity are within all human beings.

A Call to Reflect and Act

1. **Embrace Diversity and Unity:**

   The cell teaches us that diversity within a system is its strength. Whether in our personal lives, workplaces, or communities, embracing different perspectives and talents fosters resilience and growth. Diversity in unity makes life vibrant and full of possibilities.

2. **Cultivate Holistic Well-being:**

Recognize that physical, mental, and spiritual health are interconnected. Practices like meditation, healthy living, and acts of kindness nourish not just the body but the soul. True well-being involves balancing the mind, body, and spirit, leading to wholeness.

3. **Honour Interdependence:**

The survival of the cell depends on its environment, just as our well-being depends on our relationships with others and nature. Live sustainably and harmoniously, respecting all forms of life. By taking care of nature and nurturing the earth, we safeguard our own health and the health of future generations.

4. **Pursue Wisdom and Self-Awareness:**

Swamy's words—*"You are given intelligence to analyze yourself; that is wisdom."*—urge us to look inward, understand ourselves, and act responsibly. Self-awareness allows us to make conscious choices that uplift ourselves and others, fostering a more compassionate and responsible world.

5. **Transcend Barriers:**

"God is not in temples, churches, mosques." This statement invites us to seek the divine in every aspect of life, from the smallest cell to the vast cosmos. By transcending labels and divisions, we connect with the essence of universal love and truth. The divine is within us all, and in recognizing this, we embrace the unity of all existence.

CELL-A Profound Teacher:

The human cell is a profound teacher, embodying principles that are universal in their relevance and application. It reminds us of our interconnectedness, shared origins, and immense potential. The cell, like every individual, is a testament to divine wisdom and harmony.

His Holiness Swamy Vidyanarayana Theertha's teachings inspire us to reflect on these truths and apply them in our daily lives. Whether we are leaders, followers, or simply seekers, the wisdom of the cell calls us to live in harmony, nurture our innate divinity, and contribute to the collective good.

In Swamy's words: *"Wait, watch, and win."* By practicing patience, observation, and decisive action, we elevate ourselves and contribute to a brighter future for all humanity.

A Prayer for Unity and Divine Wisdom

Divine light that fills the skies,
Your presence, in all things, lies.
In every breath, in every heart,
Your essence, never far apart.

The earth, the heavens, and the sea,
All move in Your divine decree.
In quiet prayer, I humbly bow,
Seeking Your grace in this very now.

Through every step, through every deed,
Guide me with wisdom, meet my need.

In Your vast love, I place my trust,
In Your will, I shall adjust.

Oh, Lord, Your light shines bright and true,
I surrender my heart to You.
Let all my actions, pure and wise,
Reflect Your grace that never dies.

Chapter-33

Understanding Time, Change, and the Nature of Existence:

Trials and Tribulations:

The Inescapable Nature of Time and Change

"Time is the force that governs the entire universe. Just as the seasons change, so too does everything in life change with the passage of time."

In this profound discourse, His Holiness Sri Vidyanarayana Theertha speaks to a devotee in deep sorrow, questioning the trials and tribulations of life. The devotee's anguish mirrors the common human struggle with life's inevitable transitions. His Holiness reminds us that time and change are fundamental laws of the universe. No one can avoid the effects of time—ageing, loss, and the fading of external honours are all part of its eternal rhythm. Resisting this flow is futile, as it contradicts the very nature of existence.

In the Bhagavad Gita, Lord Krishna says:

"Change is the law of the universe. You can either resist it, or you can grow with it." — (Bhagavad Gita 2.14)

The Impermanence of Material Attachments

"Everything, including our physical body, positions, and wealth, is transient. No matter how much we desire to keep things permanent, time takes them away from us."

His Holiness explains that all material attachments—wealth, relationships, social status—are fleeting. Time relentlessly brings change, and as we age, we lose things we once cherished. The desire to hold onto the impermanent is bound to bring disappointment and sorrow. Just as we cannot prevent the decay of our bodies, we must understand that clinging to anything temporary will only lead to pain. The pursuit of permanence in an ever-changing world is ultimately fruitless.

As the Bhagavad Gita states:

"Whatever is born will die, and whatever dies will be reborn. This is the eternal cycle of life and death." (Bhagavad Gita 2.14)

Acceptance of Change and Understanding the Natural Order

"Embrace the natural order of the universe, accept the flow of time, and live in harmony with it. Resistance leads only to pain."

In this teaching, His Holiness emphasizes the importance of accepting the cyclical nature of life. Everything follows the natural law of birth, growth, decay, and dissolution. While change can be painful, it is part of a divine plan, and understanding this brings peace. By embracing the flow of time, we reduce the suffering that comes from resistance. When we accept life as it is, we experience the harmony that comes with aligning ourselves to the natural order of the universe.

As Lord Krishna advises in the Bhagavad Gita:

"One who has mastered the art of acceptance, who understands the flow of time, is free from sorrow and worry." (Bhagavad Gita 2.14)

The Role of Suffering in Spiritual Growth

"Suffering, though painful, serves as a great teacher. It is in our deepest trials that we often find the greatest opportunities for spiritual growth and understanding."

His Holiness explains that suffering is an integral part of life, but it is also a catalyst for spiritual evolution. Rather than viewing suffering as something to avoid, we must learn to embrace it as an essential part of the divine design. It is through suffering that the soul purifies, and through this purification, one gains deeper insight into the nature of existence. By transcending the pain of suffering, we can achieve spiritual freedom and insight.

The Nature of Miracles and Spiritual Power

"Miracles are not the result of supernatural powers; they are the natural outcomes of deep spiritual practice and alignment with the divine will."

Miracles are often perceived as supernatural phenomena, but His Holiness clarifies that they are simply the natural consequences of deep spiritual practices. Those who dedicate themselves to meditation, selfless service, and devotion cultivate spiritual power that allows them to transcend the material realm. These *"miracles"* are the result of aligning one's will with the divine consciousness, not an external force. Through disciplined spiritual practice, the limitations of the physical world are transcended.

In the Bhagavad Gita, Lord Krishna states:

"With devotion and discipline, you can transcend the limitations of the material world." — (Bhagavad Gita 9.22)

Spirituality as a Guiding Force

"Spiritual practices and the understanding of the divine provide a lens through which we can navigate the world. Religion is not meant to divide, but to unify us with the divine."

His Holiness stresses that religion and spirituality should serve as tools for self-awareness and transformation, not sources of division. Spirituality's ultimate purpose is to realize the divinity within all beings. By viewing life through this lens, we stop seeing external differences and instead foster internal unity and peace. Religion is a means of recognizing the divine in all, guiding us toward harmony with ourselves and others.

As Lord Krishna reminds us in the Bhagavad Gita:

"The divine is within all beings; through this recognition, we transcend all divisions." — *(Bhagavad Gita 10.20)*

Detachment from the Material World

"The true goal is to perform our duties selflessly, without attachment to the results. This detachment leads to true freedom."

In this section, His Holiness advises that we perform our worldly duties—be it in work, relationships, or service—without attachment to the fruits of our actions. This attitude of selflessness is the essence of spiritual progress. When we relinquish our grip on outcomes and act with sincerity and devotion, we experience a deep sense of peace and contentment. True freedom comes from detachment, not from possession or attachment to results.

The Bhagavad Gita expresses this wisdom:

"Do your duty without attachment to the results. This is the key to inner peace and spiritual progress." — *(Bhagavad Gita 2.47)*

The Nature of the Divine and the Purpose of Life

"God is the ultimate source of all creation. Everything, from the smallest particle to the vast universe, is part of His divine will."

His Holiness teaches that the universe operates according to a divine plan, where every element of creation is part of this grand design. God, the Divine, is the source of all life, and everything exists through His will. Understanding this truth is the key to realizing our own divine essence. Aligning ourselves with this plan brings us closer to our true nature and ultimate fulfilment.

Lord Krishna states in the Bhagavad Gita:

"I am the creator of all things; everything is born from Me and exists through My will." — *(Bhagavad Gita 10.8)*

Faith in Overcoming Doubt

"Faith is the light that guides us through the darkness of doubt. In moments of uncertainty, trust in the divine plan."

His Holiness explains that faith is not just belief but a deep trust in the divine wisdom that underlies the universe. In moments of doubt and uncertainty, it is faith that sustains us. By trusting the divine plan, we can overcome fears and doubts, and move forward with confidence in the path ahead. Faith is the key to overcoming obstacles and finding clarity in the midst of confusion.

Unity with the Divine in All Aspects of Life

"The divine is not confined to temples or sacred places; it exists in every breath, every action, and every being."

His Holiness emphasizes that divinity is not something external to us, but an inherent part of everything in the universe. Each act, whether mundane or extraordinary, is an opportunity to express the divine. By seeing the divine in everything, we align ourselves with the highest truth and live with greater awareness and reverence for life.

Living in Harmony with the Divine Will

"By accepting the laws of nature, embracing change, and aligning ourselves with the divine will, we can live a life of peace, joy, and fulfilment."

In conclusion, His Holiness urges devotees to embrace the changes of life with acceptance and grace. The path to spiritual fulfilment lies in surrendering to the divine will, practising detachment, and understanding the impermanent nature of the material world. Through these practices, we can transcend sorrow and achieve lasting peace, joy, and contentment, regardless of external circumstances.

Reflection:

"Live in harmony with the divine plan, embrace change, and trust in the wisdom of the universe. This is the path to true peace and liberation."

Inferences:

1. **Time and Change are Inevitable:** The flow of time and the changes it brings are inescapable. Learning to accept them is key to spiritual peace.

2. **Attachment to the Material World:** Attachment to transient things leads to sorrow. Detachment brings freedom and inner peace.

3. **Suffering as Spiritual Growth:** Suffering, when embraced as a teacher, transforms us and leads to greater wisdom and spiritual growth.

4. **Miracles are Spiritual Achievements:** Miracles are the natural outcomes of deep spiritual practice and alignment with divine will.

5. **Spirituality as a Guiding Force:** Religion is a tool to connect with the divine, not a means to divide. It helps us live in harmony with the world and others.

6. **Selfless Action:** Performing duties selflessly without attachment to results leads to inner peace and spiritual progress.

7. **Faith and Overcoming Doubt:** Faith is the light that helps us navigate uncertainty and stay aligned with the divine plan.

8. **Divine Order:** All of creation is part of a divine plan. Understanding this truth brings us closer to our true nature.

9. **Unity with the Divine:** The divine is present in all aspects of life. Recognizing this brings us into alignment with universal consciousness.

Prayer of Divine Harmony

Time flows, change will come,
In its rhythm, we become one.
Release attachment, find the way,
In peace, our hearts will stay.

Suffering teaches, we arise,
With wisdom gained, we reach the skies.
Miracles born of truth and grace,
In divine will, we find our place.

Spiritual path, a guiding light,
Bringing harmony, day and night.
Selfless acts, in duty done,
Inner peace has just begun.

Faith will guide when doubts arise,
With trust, we reach for higher skies.
Divine order, a perfect plan,
Leads us back to who we are.

Chapter-34

The Divine Compass: Outer Contribution and Inner Realization

In its eternal quest, the human soul seeks not just to traverse the world but to unite with it—understanding that true peace and purpose arise not from isolation but from oneness with the whole of existence. This delicate and profound path calls us not to a life of conflict but to harmony and to honour the sacred within every being and every living thing.

The teachings of Sri Swamy Vidyanarayana Theertha remind us that we are not here to fight between faiths, but to live in accord with the divine truth that flows through all. Sanatana Dharma, ancient and boundless, is like the vast ocean that absorbs every stream and every river and yet remains pure. It teaches that devotion, when true, is not merely an outward expression but a silent, steadfast presence that is rare and needed more than ever.

Let us stand together—united in our reverence for the land that nourishes us, the heritage that shapes our identity, and the future that we build with wisdom and compassion. Let us rebuild India, not just with bricks and stones, but with the strength of our spirit and the beauty of our timeless traditions.

The Life of Sri Ramakrishna Paramahamsa: A Beacon of True Spirituality

Sri Ramakrishna Paramahamsa's life was a radiant testament to the divine unity that transcends all divisions. His spiritual journey, marked by an unquenchable thirst for truth, was not one of isolation but of inclusiveness. Ramakrishna embraced all faiths as rivers leading to the same ocean, demonstrating that the divine could be worshipped in countless forms. His simplicity was profound, for it spoke of a universal love that was not bound by rituals or dogmas.

In his teachings, we find the key to true spiritual freedom. Ramakrishna's message was one of love, humility, and surrender to the divine. Swami Vivekananda, his disciple, took this light and carried it across the seas to the West, unveiling the deep spiritual wisdom of the East to the world. Vivekananda showed humanity that true spirituality is not an abstract concept but a way of life—one that permeates every thought, every word, every action.

He brought forth a vision in which the essence of religion is realized not in external rituals but in internal transformation. He understood that the path to divinity is not separate from life itself; it is lived in every moment, every act of service, and every compassionate gesture.

The Inner Journey: Transforming the Mind and Heart

The outer world may be the stage upon which we play our roles, but it is the inner world—the heart and mind—that shapes our true identity. The brain, a marvel of divine creation, is not merely an organ of cognition; it is the vessel through which we connect with the infinite. When aligned with the divine, the brain and the heart become the tools through which we experience the sacred.

Shirdi Sai Baba, in his simple yet profound way, showed us that spiritual wisdom does not lie in renouncing the world, but in engaging with it from a place of detachment. He taught us that true wealth is not gold or property, but the peace of a heart untouched by greed. His teachings on detachment were not about renouncing material possessions but about realizing their fleeting nature—about seeing through the illusion and recognizing that the soul alone is eternal.

In his earthly manifestation, Sathya Sai Baba expanded this message through selfless service. He demonstrated that serving humanity is not an external duty but an expression of our divinity. Every act of kindness, every gesture of compassion, brings us closer to realizing our highest potential, our truest self. Sathya Sai's legacy reminds us that the divine is present in every act of love and every act of giving.

The Role of Money: A Tool for Spiritual Growth

Money, in itself, is neither good nor bad; what we do with it defines its true nature. Both Shirdi Sai Baba and Sathya Sai Baba taught us that material wealth is transient—like the river that flows and eventually merges with the sea. However, money can become a means of spiritual expression when used for the benefit of others. It becomes an offering—a gift that nourishes the soul of the giver as much as it uplifts the receiver.

The true value of money lies not in its accumulation but in its flow. It is like water: too much of it can drown, and too little will dry up the land. The key is to let it flow where it brings life—through charity, education, and service. In today's world, where the pursuit of wealth often overshadows the pursuit of wisdom, this understanding is more crucial than ever.

True Devotion: The Essence of Inner Realization

True devotion is not a mere ritual or external show; it is the silent surrender of the ego, the deep recognition of the divine presence in every moment. It is the understanding that every breath we take, every thought we think, and every action we perform is an offering to the divine.

The teachings of Sri Adi Shankaracharya remind us that the ultimate reality is not in the outer world, but within. In the universe's vastness and seemingly endless diversity of life, there is an underlying unity—an oneness that transcends all divisions. Through Advaita Vedanta, Shankaracharya taught us that to understand the nature of the world is to understand the self and to understand the self is to realize the divine.

In today's world, where the outer and inner worlds often seem at odds, these teachings call us to bring them into harmony. By living with compassion, practicing selfless service, and embracing the wisdom of our traditions, we can cultivate a spiritually rich and materially meaningful life.

A Call to Action

The divine is not distant; it is within us, in every thought, action, and gesture. The outer world and the inner world are not separate—they are interwoven, like the threads of a sacred tapestry. When we align our hearts with the divine and live with wisdom and compassion, we bring peace not only to ourselves but to the entire world.

Let us walk the path of spirituality not as an escape from life but as a way to engage more fully. Let us remember the teachings of those who have shown us that the divine is present not just in temples and sacred spaces but in every moment, every being, and the soil beneath our feet.

May we rebuild our world, not with the bricks of division, but with the stones of love and wisdom. Let each of us, in our own way, be a part of the divine symphony that plays across the universe, bringing peace, love, and understanding to all.

A Prayer for Universal Peace and Unity

O Divine Light,
Illuminate the path of every soul,
Guide us to see the unity in all,
To realize that we are one—
Not divided by borders, not separated by belief,
But bound by the eternal thread of love.

Grant us peace, O Lord,
Not just in our hearts, but in every land,
May our minds be free from hatred,
And our actions be rooted in compassion.

Let there be no wars, no suffering,
Let the earth sing in the harmony of our unity.
May every heart recognize the divine within,
And every soul find solace in your embrace.

O Divine, lead us to serve,
Not for fame, nor for gain,
But to uplift, to heal, to nurture
The divine spark in every being.

Guide us to live with love,
To give with grace,
And to walk the path of wisdom,
In every moment, in every breath,
For we are all one,
And the light of truth shines in us all.

Om Shanti, Shanti, Shanti.

Chapter-35

The Essence of Guru Parampara and the Path of Self-Transformation

Spiritual Enlightenment:

In the vast, sacred journey of self-realization, the significance of a true Guru cannot be overstated. The wisdom imparted by His Holiness Sri Vidyanarayana Theertha illuminates the path to spiritual enlightenment and self-transformation, emphasizing that a seeker must exercise discernment in choosing a Guru. In a world often clouded by pseudo-Gurus who mislead under the guise of spirituality, the clarity to identify a true guide is invaluable. Sri Vidyanarayana Theertha's guidance echoes the timeless wisdom: *"Paani Peena chaanke, Guru Banaana Jaanke"*— just as we drink water only after filtering, so too must we select a Guru after discerning his true nature.

The journey toward spiritual enlightenment is not one of haste or superficial engagement. It is a careful, deliberate process where a genuine Guru leads the seeker toward purity and self-realization. Once the Guru's guidance is accepted, it becomes the transformative force that binds the seeker's soul to the Divine, never to part.

The Essence of Guru Parampara

Guru Parampara—the unbroken chain of enlightened masters—is the foundation of spiritual growth in many traditions. Each Guru in this sacred lineage has walked the path of divine experience and, through their divine grace, passed down the light of wisdom to their disciples. This transmission of knowledge is not just academic but a sacred, transformative process through which the seeker is led to the highest truth.

The Guru is more than a teacher; he is the divine guide, imparting wisdom both through words and silence. As Lord Shiva is portrayed in the Dakshinamurthy Stotra as a silent teacher whose silence speaks volumes, so does the true Guru convey profound truths in the quiet moments of presence. The seeker is invited to experience the divine in its purest form through this silent transmission.

Sri Vidyanarayana Theertha's teachings remind us that one of the first steps on this spiritual journey is to cleanse society of ignorance, convert ourselves inwardly, and embrace the Guru's grace. Society may be stained with falsehood, but the heart of the seeker must undergo purification, aligning itself with divine truth.

Role of a Genuine Guru

A true Guru does not merely instruct but leads by example, guiding the disciple through the darkness into the light of spiritual awakening. The Guru's role is not just to teach but to shape the disciples, to mould them into a vessel that can carry divine wisdom. This sacred bond, forged in trust and surrender, is one of the deepest connections a seeker can experience.

Sri Sudheendra Theertha exemplified this principle when he chose Sri Raghavendra Swamy as his disciple. Before accepting him, he carefully observed Venkatanatha's character, spirituality, and inner potential. This act was not one of haste but of divine discernment—a reminder that a true Guru must carefully choose a disciple, just as a seeker must be prepared to receive the wisdom offered.

This relationship is reciprocal: while the Guru leads the disciple to higher planes of consciousness, the disciple must be ready to open their heart to receive the divine teachings with humility and devotion.

Spiritual Transformation: A Personal Responsibility

True transformation is not external; it begins within. A seeker must cleanse the mind and heart of negative emotions—jealousy, greed, and pride—so that divine grace can take root. The disciple's heart must become a sanctuary, a *Brundavanam,* where divine presence resides, free from the clutter of worldly vices.

Sri Vidyanarayana Theertha's teachings emphasize that the Guru's grace flows into a heart free from malice, ego, and ill will. Only then can the Guru's teachings take root, transforming the disciple into an embodiment of divine wisdom.

The path to self-realization is thus not a quest for mere knowledge but a profound inner transformation. The seeker must purify their heart, mind, and soul, becoming capable of embodying the wisdom imparted by the Guru.

Illuminating Path:

The journey to self-realization requires introspection, discipline, and the unwavering guidance of a true Guru. Through the Guru Parampara, passed down through generations, the seeker finds a light that illuminates the path to the Divine. As Sri Vidyanarayana Theertha teaches, only a pure heart can receive the Guru's grace, which leads to ultimate enlightenment, transforming the seeker into a divine being who resides in God's eternal presence.

Journey to the Divine

The path to truth is calm and clear,
A steady walk, no rush, no fear.
The Guru's touch, a gentle guide,
Lifts the soul to the Divine inside.
In silence deep, the wisdom speaks,
A sacred bond, the seeker seeks.
With every step, the heart aligns,
To wisdom's light, the soul inclines.

Purify the heart, the mind, the core,
In divine grace, we soar, we soar.
The Guru's love, a steady beam,
Guides us toward our highest dream.

Chapter-36

Watch, Wait, and Win: Insights from Sri Vidyanarayana Theertha

Self-Discovery:

In today's fast-paced world, where everything seems to demand instant results, the teachings of His Holiness Sri Vidyanarayana Theertha offer a different perspective: the path of *"Watch, Wait, and Win."* These three simple yet profound principles encapsulate the essence of spiritual growth, emphasizing patience, awareness, and divine realization. In an era dominated by the pursuit of instant gratification, these timeless teachings serve as a guiding light for spiritual seekers, offering a path that prioritizes self-discovery over worldly desires.

"The seed of wisdom is sown in patience, and it flourishes in the fertile soil of time."

— *Sri Vidyanarayana Theertha*

Watch: Observing with Awareness

The first step in spiritual growth is to observe—not only the external world but also one's own mind and actions. The art of watching is a call to introspection, to go beyond surface appearances, and uncover the deeper truths that reside within. By watching attentively, one begins to discern what is real and what is illusion. Sri Vidyanarayana Theertha teaches that self-reflection and awareness are essential for true growth. Through vigilant observation, we understand the subtle movements of our mind and can begin to correct course when necessary.

In a world that demands quick fixes, many students, leaders, and individuals chasing material success often resort to shortcuts, hoping to bypass the process of true growth. However, just as a seed does not sprout the moment it is planted, nor does a plant bear flowers and fruit immediately, spiritual growth also requires time. Instant results are an illusion, and the need for patience is essential. Whether seeking success in studies, leadership, or material achievements, one must recognize that everything has its season, and rushing through the process can lead to imbalance and frustration.

"Only those who observe patiently can distinguish the true from the false."
— Sri Vidyanarayana Theertha

Wait: Cultivating Patience

The second principle, *"Wait,"* speaks to the core of spiritual transformation. True spiritual progress cannot be rushed; it is a gradual unfolding of the divine within. Sri Vidyanarayana Theertha emphasizes that patience is key to spiritual success. Transformation takes time, and it is in the act of waiting—trusting in divine timing—that the heart is purified and made ready for the highest realization.

In today's world, impatience is a common trait. Many students and individuals, driven by the desire for material gains, are eager to take shortcuts to reach success. But this impatience only leads to disillusionment. Just as a plant needs time to grow, bloom, and bear fruit, spiritual growth demands a process of unfolding over time. Losing mental balance or patience, Sri Vidyanarayana Theertha reminds us, means losing God's grace. It is essential to trust the divine process, remain steady, and wait for the right moment, knowing that every step brings us closer to our true purpose.

"Patience is not the ability to wait, but the ability to keep a good attitude while waiting."
— *Sri Vidyanarayana Theertha*

Win: Attaining Spiritual Victory

The final principle, "*Win*," refers to the realization of one's true nature. This victory is not marked by worldly achievements or material success but by the recognition of the Divine within. By surrendering to the guidance of the Guru, enduring life's challenges, and practicing patience, the seeker achieves the ultimate victory: self-realization.

Sri Vidyanarayana Theertha teaches that true victory lies not in external accomplishments but in the inner triumph of realizing our oneness with the Divine. This realization is the highest form of success, as it brings lasting peace, contentment, and wisdom. Through this process, we experience the true meaning of spiritual victory—freedom from the ego and alignment with the infinite source of all creation.

"Victory over the self is the greatest victory of all."
— *Sri Vidyanarayana Theertha*

A Practical Reflection: Applying Watch, Wait, and Win Today

The principles of Watch, Wait, and Win are not merely abstract ideas but practical tools that can be applied in daily life. By observing our thoughts and actions with mindfulness, waiting patiently for the right moments and divine guidance, and striving for the inner victory of self-realization, we can navigate life's challenges with grace. When we align ourselves with the divine will and trust the process, success is assured, and the heart becomes a sacred space where God's presence resides.

"True success is not in reaching the destination, but in the journey towards it with patience and faith."
— *Sri Vidyanarayana Theertha*

Tips for Practicing Watch, Wait, and Win in Daily Life

1. Cultivate Awareness: Set aside time daily for self-reflection. Watch your thoughts, emotions, and actions without judgment. This awareness will help you understand where you need to grow.

2. Be Patient: Remind yourself that true spiritual growth cannot be rushed. Trust in divine timing and practice patience in your daily life, whether in your personal growth, relationships, or work.

3. Stay Balanced: Avoid the temptation to take shortcuts. Recognize when impatience or frustration arises, and refocus your mind on maintaining inner peace.

4. Trust the Process: Trust that every challenge, every moment of waiting, is part of your transformation. Be patient with yourself, and trust the journey.

5. Surrender to the Divine: Cultivate faith in the Guru and the divine process. Surrendering to the guidance of the Guru and divine will leads to true spiritual victory.

True Spiritual Success:

"Watch, Wait, and Win" is a philosophy that teaches us to observe with awareness, cultivate patience, and achieve victory by aligning ourselves with divine will. Through these principles, we can embark on a journey of spiritual growth and self-realization. The teachings of Sri Vidyanarayana Theertha remind us that true spiritual success lies not in external accomplishments but in the inner victory of realizing our divine nature. In this journey, the grace of the Guru

ensures that we emerge victorious, discovering the divine within and experiencing true peace and fulfilment.

In conclusion, the essence of *"Watch, Wait, and Win"* calls for a return to patience, a deep awareness of our inner world, and a faith that transcends the desire for immediate rewards. By relinquishing impatience and trusting in the divine timing of our spiritual growth, we can step into the victory of understanding our true, divine selves.

"In patience, we discover that divine grace is never late; it arrives exactly when we are ready to receive it."
— Sri Vidyanarayana Theertha

Prayer to God

O Divine Lord, in Your light we stand,
Grant us patience with Your guiding hand.
In every challenge, give us grace,
To find Your presence in every place.

Help us watch with open eyes,
And wait with faith, where wisdom lies.
Let our hearts in stillness win,
By trusting You, the path within.

With every step, in You we trust,
Guide us, O Lord, from dust to dust.
May Your grace forever shine,
As we seek Your will, divine.

Om Shanti, Shanti, Shanti.

Chapter-37

The Mystic Path: Love, Care, Trust, and Surrender as Pillars of Transformation

The Essence of Spirituality

Spirituality is not confined to religion; it is a universal way of life that seeks to uncover the divine truth within. In a world of diverse belief systems, clashing ideologies, and endless arguments, humanity often forgets the essence of its existence. The divine energy that manifests as Rama, Jesus, Shankara, Lalitha, Dattatreya, and countless other forms unites us all. These enlightened beings, each assigned their role by the Cosmic Mother, fulfilled their purpose with clarity and wisdom. They walked the earth as instruments of love, care, and divine truth.

In today's world, marked by rising intolerance, jealousy, hatred, and violence, society faces unprecedented unrest. These negativities disrupt harmony, erode relationships, and cloud the collective consciousness. Amidst this chaos, the timeless wisdom of His Holiness Sri Vidyanarayana Theertha offers a beacon of hope, emphasizing simplicity, authenticity, and devotion over rigid traditions and formalities.

Through the universal principles of love, care, trust, and surrender, Sri Vidyanarayana Swamy reminds us of the transformative power inherent in aligning with divine consciousness. By bypassing rituals and embracing inner devotion, we detoxify our minds and hearts, paving the way for peace, unity, and spiritual renewal.

This philosophy is not just a call to spiritual seekers but a message of healing and balance for a fractured world—a reminder that transformation begins from within, anchored in the mystic energy that guides us through life. In this age of division, the message of spiritual masters like Sri Vidyanarayana Theertha is clear: we must not squander our precious time in quarrels or conflicts. We are called to live fully, brightly, and with constant awareness, embracing love, care, trust, and surrender. These core principles transcend materiality and guide us toward spiritual enlightenment.

The Interconnection of Gurus and Their Cosmic Purpose

There is a divine system connecting all enlightened beings. Each Guru is assigned a unique role in the grand cosmic design. Their purpose is to serve as channels of divine energy, guiding others toward realization. As Sri Vidyanarayana Theertha teaches, we must acknowledge the interconnectedness of all yogis and Sadgurus. They work in harmony, each fulfilling their cosmic role with clarity.

For example, the bond between Ramakrishna Paramahamsa and his disciple, Vivekananda, exemplifies this divine connection. Ramakrishna, recognizing Vivekananda's potential, named him *"Vivekananda,"* symbolizing ripened wisdom (*Viveka*) and eternal bliss (*Ananda*). Together, they exemplified the unity of wisdom and love in the divine plan.

As Ramakrishna once said, *"The fragrance of a flower spreads naturally. Similarly, a Guru's wisdom and love radiate effortlessly, inspiring seekers to bloom in their own time."*

Love: The Universal Fragrance

Love is the essence of life and the foundation of all spiritual practice. It is a force that connects us to the divine and to one another. Divine love transcends all divisions, fostering unity and compassion. When we embrace love, it cleanses our hearts of hatred, jealousy, and fear, making space for peace and understanding.

Sri Vidyanarayana Theertha reminds us that the essence of love lies in its ability to transcend worldly differences. He emphasizes that quarrels over ideologies only waste the precious time we have on earth. *"Let your life be a message of love, for love alone heals the wounds of the world."*

Care: The Embodiment of Empathy

Care transforms the abstract feeling of love into tangible actions of kindness and empathy. Compassion is not bound by religion or creed; it is an expression of the divine purpose.

Vivekananda, during his travels, exemplified this kind of care. His deep compassion for the downtrodden and his ability to uplift others through his words and actions changed countless lives. As he said, *"The best way to find yourself is to lose yourself in the service of others."*

Care bridges the gap between individuals, reminding us of our shared humanity. By embodying care, we create a world where love and compassion become the guiding forces of life.

Trust: The Anchor of Spiritual Growth

Trust in the divine plan is the foundation for spiritual growth. Without trust, life becomes a series of restless doubts, and we lose alignment with the cosmic flow of energy. Trust purifies the mind, freeing it from fear and skepticism, and allowing one to open up to the divine wisdom.

"Trust the journey, for every step is guided by a wisdom greater than our own," says the ancient wisdom of the Vedas. Just as disciples

trust their Sadgurus, we, too, must trust the unfolding of life, knowing that the same divine source guides it.

Surrender: The Path to Eternal Bliss

Surrender is the pinnacle of spiritual practice. It is not a sign of weakness but the strength to release control and embrace the divine will. Through his total surrender to the Cosmic Mother, Ramakrishna Paramahamsa became an embodiment of divinity. His surrender led him to become a beacon of light, guiding seekers like Vivekananda toward their highest potential.

The teachings of the saints remind us that *"Surrender is not giving up; it is rising above."* True surrender is not the denial of self but the acknowledgement that we are instruments in a greater plan, and through this surrender, we attain eternal bliss.

Living Fully and Brightly

Time is fleeting, and life is not a guaranteed bond of 100 years. Sri Vidyanarayana Theertha calls upon us to live with constant awareness and to make every moment a step toward enlightenment. We are meant to live even after we die—not as physical beings but through the eternal fragrance of our actions, thoughts, and contributions.

He warns us not to waste our time arguing over theories, ideologies, and philosophies. These conflicts only lead to internal and external disturbances. Instead, we must focus on living brightly, fulfilling the divine purpose assigned to each of us. Life is about connecting to the divine source and embracing the lessons that each moment offers.

The Connection to ZERO to ZERO: The Mystic Circle

ZERO to ZERO: The Mystic Circle serves as a guide for this journey. The book captures the essence of the teachings of Sri

Vidyanarayana Theertha, showing us that all paths lead to the same divine truth. It emphasizes the importance of embracing love, care, trust, and surrender as we journey from the ego (*zero*) to the realization of the divine (*zero*).

The teachings in the book mirror the wisdom passed down by the ancient masters, reminding us to live fully and without attachment. As we transcend the material world, we become instruments of the divine will, part of the cosmic dance that connects all of us.

The Oneness of Mystic Energy

In the grand scheme of existence, all enlightened beings—whether they appear as Rama, Jesus, Shankara, or Dattatreya—are manifestations of the same mystic energy. They have come into this world to play their roles and fulfil their divine purpose. The same energy that guides them also guides us.

Life's essence lies not in debating differences but in living with love, care, trust, and surrender. These principles align us with the cosmic purpose, enabling us to rise above the noise of division and touch the eternal. When we realize that we are all connected through the same divine energy, we understand that the journey is not about individual success but collective awakening.

"In the grand symphony of life, let us play our roles with harmony and grace, for it is through our collective awakening that the divine truth shines brightest."

Through His grace, this book has manifested, and I hope it serves as a reflection of His divine light, guiding all who seek the truth. With deep gratitude, I dedicate this to Him and to all seekers who, through this work, may feel a connection to the higher purpose He reveals.

Prayer

Divine Mother, guide us on our journey,
From the chaos of doubt to the light of truth.
Grant us the wisdom to see beyond the illusion,
The strength to live with love, care, trust, and surrender.
May we become instruments of your grace,
Spreading your fragrance across the world,
And may we realize the oneness that binds all beings,
In the eternal dance of divine consciousness.
Aum Shanti Shanti Shanti.

Chapter-38

The Guru's Path

A Universal Journey of Self-Discovery and Inner Strength

"Search for a Guru, select wisely, and surrender fully. Cleanse society, convert yourself, and conceive the Guru's grace. Just as we filter water before drinking, examine the Guru before accepting. Once you accept, the Guru will guide you to purity and self-realization."

"The journey within is the longest and most meaningful one we will ever undertake. Across all cultures and traditions, spiritual mentors guide humanity toward self-realization, urging us to reconnect with simplicity, humility, and the divine within."

— His Holiness Sri Vidyanarayana Theertha Swamy

* * * * * *

Sri Vidyanarayana Theertha, an enlightened spiritual leader and physician, offers timeless teachings that transcend cultural boundaries. His reflections on the Guru's role, the body as a metaphor for society, and the practice of walking as a spiritual discipline resonate universally. By intertwining ancient wisdom with modern relevance, his teachings serve as a beacon for global seekers navigating the complexities of contemporary life.

The Universal Role of the Guru: Beyond Cultural Boundaries

In ancient Indian tradition, the Guru was revered as a guiding light—a bridge between ignorance and enlightenment. Sri Vidyanarayana Theertha reframes this role for the modern age, where societal dynamics have shifted.

- Then and Now: *"In ancient days, students and parents sought out the Guru. Today, the Guru must seek out students, teachers, and seekers,"* Swamiji observes. This shift highlights the increasing fragmentation of modern society, where spiritual guidance is often overshadowed by material pursuits.

This concept parallels the *Zen master's role in Buddhism,* the *spiritual director in Christianity,* and the *mentor-disciple relationships* in indigenous traditions worldwide. Regardless of culture, humanity's collective yearning for guidance remains unchanged.

The Body and Society: A Shared Metaphor

Swamiji likens the human body to society, where each part plays an integral role:

- *The "head" represents leadership and vision.*
- *The "heart" symbolizes compassion and emotional intelligence.*
- *The "limbs" signify action and progress.*

He warns, however, that society's *"coaches"*—those meant to lead—are often burdened with negative karma, failing to guide with clarity.

This echoes the Bhagavad Gita's teachings on duty and selfless action:

"One must act in accordance with one's dharma (purpose), free from ego and attachment."
— Bhagavad Gita 2.47

Globally, this metaphor aligns with the **Taoist principle of harmony**, which views the human body as a microcosm of the universe, urging balance in all aspects of life.

Walking as a Spiritual Discipline: Progress and Awareness

Swamiji emphasizes the power of walking, not just as a physical movement but as a spiritual act. *"Walking is the best engine,"* he says, *"the most natural way to strengthen the body and awaken the mystic cells within."*

Walking, in this sense, becomes a metaphor for mindful progress:

- **The Buddhist Path:** Thich Nhat Hanh's teaching, *"Walk as if you are kissing the Earth with your feet,"* mirrors Swamiji's vision of walking as an act of connection and awareness.

- **Global Practices:** From the sacred pilgrimage of the Camino de Santiago in Spain to the Indian Kumbh Mela, walking has long symbolized the human quest for purpose and enlightenment.

In a world dominated by sedentary lifestyles and digital distractions, walking reconnects us to our physical selves and the natural world.

The Inner Guru: A Universal Truth

Swamiji extends the concept of the Guru to the *"inner consciousness"* within each individual. _*"The true driver is the Guru, which is our own inner voice,"* he says, reminding us that spiritual mentorship begins with self-awareness.

This insight aligns with the teachings of global spiritualists:

- **Mahatma Gandhi:** *"The best way to find yourself is to lose yourself in the service of others."*

- **The Dalai Lama:** *"The ultimate source of happiness is within us."*

- **Sufi Mystics:** Who often describe the inner self as the ultimate guide to divine truth.

Lessons from Revered Gurus and Global Spiritualists

Swamiji's profound teachings draw inspiration from revered Gurus such as His Holiness Sri Sri Sri Chandrasekhar Bharathi and His Holiness Chandrasekaranadendra Saraswathi, who represent the synthesis of two complementary paths of spiritual realization:

- *The Path of Stillness* (Sitting like Brahma):

This path emphasizes deep contemplation and meditation, where the seeker remains in stillness to realize the eternal truth within. Just as *Brahma*, the creator, is depicted as seated in serene meditation in spiritual texts, the practice of sitting in silence

enables one to connect with the cosmic consciousness. It's in this space of quietude that the true self is discovered. This path teaches us the value of reflection, solitude, and the awakening of inner wisdom.

This is not merely a passive stillness, but an active receptivity to the divine presence that pervades all existence.

The *advaita* (non-dualism) philosophy of *Adi Shankaracharya* aligns with this approach, where silence and stillness reveal the oneness of the self with the Absolute.

- *The Path of Action and Movement (Walking):*

The second path of spiritual realization, exemplified by walking, stresses the importance of engaging with the world and carrying out one's duties with purpose and dedication. It's a dynamic path that emphasizes progress, awareness, and living one's spiritual principles through action. Through walking, we actively participate in the world, yet remain anchored in the awareness of the Divine.

The *Bhagavad Gita* advocates this path, calling on individuals to fulfill their duties without attachment to outcomes—

> *"Perform your prescribed duties without attachment"*
> — *(Bhagavad Gita 3.19)*

Walking, symbolizing progress, is a metaphor for moving through life while maintaining a deep connection to spiritual wisdom. The actions of *Mahatma Gandhi*, who advocated for nonviolent protest, or *Mother Teresa*, who served humanity with humility, are reflections of this path of dynamic action rooted in spiritual purpose.

Swamiji encapsulates the essence of both paths, recognizing that *stillness* and *movement* are not opposing forces but two aspects of the same journey toward spiritual realization. Just as the moon reflects light in stillness, it also travels across the sky. Similarly, we must balance our moments of inward contemplation with our outward actions, living our spiritual truth in both thought and deed.

This profound understanding connects *global spiritual traditions:*

- The *Zen teachings of Japan*, where the stillness of meditation complements the active mindfulness practiced in daily life.

- The *Taoist philosophy*, which speaks of the balance between *Yin and Yang*, emphasizing harmony between being and doing.

- *Christian mysticism*, where saints such as *St. Francis of Assisi* blended prayerful solitude with acts of love and service, teaching that divine realization comes through both communion with God and service to humanity.

This balance between contemplation and action finds echoes in the teachings of:

- *Swami Vivekananda, who said, "Arise, awake, and stop not till the goal is reached."*

  Vivekananda's call to action encourages us to embody spiritual ideals in the world. This aligns perfectly with the path of walking, where we are called to actively pursue our goals with purpose and determination while being grounded in spiritual awareness.

- **Christian contemplative traditions, which stress the unity of prayer and service.**

  In Christianity, contemplative practices such as prayer are deeply intertwined with the call to serve others. Godly persons like Mother Teresa exemplified this unity, combining prayer with selfless service to alleviate the suffering of others, a powerful reflection of the "walking" path of spiritual action.

The teachings of these revered Gurus and the wisdom embedded in global spiritual traditions illuminate the importance of integrating these dual paths into our daily lives, fostering a deeper understanding of our interconnectedness with the Divine and all of creation.

Spiritual and Realistic Inferences for the Benefaction of Society

Spiritual Inferences:

1. The Guru is Within:

   - The Guru's guidance is not external; it lies within each individual as the voice of inner consciousness. The external Guru merely helps awaken the divine wisdom already present.

   - *"The best way to find yourself is to lose yourself in the service of others."* — Mahatma Gandhi.

2. Balance Between Contemplation and Action:

   - Spiritual progress requires both stillness and movement. Meditation nurtures inner peace, while action allows us to apply that peace in the world.

   - Swamiji's teaching: *"One wins by sitting like Brahma, while another wins by walking"* reminds us that both paths of stillness and activity are essential in our spiritual evolution.

3. Body and Society as a Microcosm:

   - The human body is a reflection of society, and each individual has a unique role to play. Just as the head leads the body, society's leaders must guide others toward collective well-being, with humility and wisdom.

   - *"One must act in accordance with one's dharma (purpose), free from ego and attachment."* — Bhagavad Gita 2.47.

4. Walking as a Spiritual Discipline:

   - Walking is a metaphor for the progress we make in life. It is not just physical; it represents moving toward self-awareness, mindfulness, and spiritual awakening.

- Walking, as a daily spiritual practice, aligns us with the rhythms of the earth and strengthens our connection with our true self.

5. Reverence for the Guru's Path:

   - The Guru is a bridge between the seeker and divinity. Reverence for the Guru is a sign of respect for the divine wisdom that guides us.

   - *"The Guru is the eternal light that illuminates the darkness of ignorance."* — Guru Granth Sahib.

6. Living with Humility:

   - True wisdom lies in humility. It is not in the titles or material possessions, but in the ability to serve others with love and compassion.

   - *"Humility is not thinking less of yourself, but thinking of yourself less."* — C.S. Lewis.

Realistic Inferences:

1. The Role of Self-Reflection in Personal Growth:

   - Just as walking allows us to connect physically, introspection connects us mentally and spiritually. Regular self-reflection fosters awareness of our thoughts and actions, helping us live more consciously and with purpose.

2. Embracing Simplicity in a Complex World:

   - In a world filled with distractions, the practice of simplifying our lives—through mindfulness, conscious living, and spiritual practice—leads to deeper fulfilment.

- o Swamiji's insight about returning to simplicity—whether through walking, prayer, or contemplation—guides us toward a life free of stress and confusion.

3. Service as a Path to Spiritual Growth:

   - o Spirituality is not about withdrawing from the world but actively engaging with it in a way that uplifts society. Service is a natural expression of spiritual growth.

   - o True transformation happens when we contribute to the welfare of others, irrespective of their background, faith, or status.

4. Awareness in the Age of Technology:

   - o In today's fast-paced, technology-driven world, it is easy to lose touch with the deeper aspects of life. Practicing spiritual disciplines like walking or meditation can ground us in the present moment and reconnect us with our inner peace.

5. Inner Strength as the Key to Overcoming Challenges:

   - o When faced with challenges, we often look outside ourselves for answers. However, true strength lies within—our inner consciousness is the greatest resource we have for overcoming life's difficulties.

Inner Truth and Harmony:

Sri Vidyanarayana Theertha's teachings invite us to reflect on our connection to the world, to each other, and, most importantly, to ourselves. In a world that often emphasizes external achievements and distractions, his message calls us to seek and live in harmony with the inner truth. Whether through the Guru's teachings, the metaphor of the body as a society, or the simple practice of walking as a spiritual discipline, Swamiji emphasizes that the path to spiritual fulfilment is not difficult—it simply requires us to return to the basics of self-awareness, humility, and service.

Let us strive to embody these teachings in our daily lives, not just as a means to personal growth but also to benefit society and uplift humanity. In our quest for meaning, we can always return to the truth that resides within us, guided by the wisdom of the Guru and the light of divine consciousness.

Prayer:

"O Divine Guru,
Grant us the wisdom to walk the path of righteousness.
Guide us to seek not only knowledge but to live with compassion,
To serve with humility, and to see the divine in every soul.
May our actions reflect the eternal truth,
And our hearts be filled with love for all beings.
May we embody the grace of your teachings,
And lead the way for others to follow.

Om Shanti, Shanti, Shanti."

Chapter-39

Awakening the Divine Within

The Path of Wisdom, Devotion, and Unity

In the pursuit of self-awareness and divine understanding, we are often compelled to ask the most fundamental question: *Who am I?* This question transcends individual identities and unravels the deeper layers of our existence, propelling us on a journey that unites the soul with the cosmos.

The answer to this profound question is not one of simple labels or roles. Rather, it is a dynamic process of discovery, transformation, and realization. As we traverse this path, we encounter fellow seekers who walk alongside us, guiding us toward greater enlightenment. These companions are not just individuals but spiritual brothers and sisters, fellow travellers on the road to awakening.

In the spirit of this eternal quest, I, Dr Hari, the compiler, creator, and curator of this book, have had the privilege of walking this path with two extraordinary souls: Dr Swamy (Sri Vidyanarayna Thirtha), whose deep wisdom and spiritual insight guide me, and Dr Nagaraj, my yogic brother, known as *Naga Yogi Raj* by a hidden mystic saint of the Himalayas.

Each of us has embarked on a distinct yet interconnected journey that reflects the balance between stillness and action, contemplation and movement, meditation and service. Dr. Swamy, a revered guide, embodies the timeless wisdom of the Gurus and teaches us the value of profound silence and stillness in the pursuit of self-realization.

Dr. Nagaraj, the Naga Yogi Raj, represents the strength of inner wisdom and spiritual power, a living testament to the mystical teachings passed down through generations. And I, Dr. Hari, am the humble curator of these divine teachings, weaving together the threads of ancient wisdom and modern understanding to share with the world.

In this book, we explore the spiritual insights, lessons, and teachings that have shaped our journeys, as well as the universal truths that connect us all. Together, we reflect on the question of who we are—not as separate identities, but as part of the infinite, interconnected whole that is the divine expression of the universe.

This journey of self-realization is not a solitary endeavour but a collective awakening, a shared experience that transcends time, culture, and individuality. We are all one in the divine light, walking together toward the same goal: the realization of our true selves.

The Profound Triad: A Journey of Intellect, Devotion, and Spirituality

In a serene moment of reflection, His Holiness Sri Vidyanarayana Theertha revealed a profound spiritual insight about the interconnected roles of intellect, devotion, and guidance in the spiritual journey. Dr. Swamy spoke of three individuals—Dr. Nagaraj, Dr. Swamiji, and myself—as representations of universal energies working in harmony to achieve divine realization. What follows is an exploration of this revelation, its significance, and its implications for seekers everywhere.

The Symbolic Triad

Sri Vidyanarayana Theertha compared our roles to distinct yet interdependent aspects of a spiritual journey:

1. *Dr. Nagaraj – The Brain and the Driver*
   Dr. Nagaraj represents intellect, the faculty of reasoning and analysis. He is the "driver," steering the journey with precision and purpose. Intellect is essential in navigating life, discerning right from wrong, and understanding the complexities of existence. As the engine of thought and action, it powers the seeker's quest for knowledge and wisdom.

2. *Dr. Swamiji – The Guru and the Walker*
   Dr. Swamiji, embodying the role of the Guru, is the guiding force who walks with deliberation and clarity in the *"brain"* of the collective consciousness. The Guru is both external and internal—a spiritual teacher who awakens the inner conscience of the seeker. Swamiji's steady walk symbolizes a grounded approach to enlightenment, emphasizing mindfulness, simplicity, and deliberate effort over haste or shortcuts.

3. *Dr. Hari – The Devotee and the Atma Link* As the devotee, I serve as the bridge between intellect and divine guidance. Devotion (*Bhakti*) is the heart of this triad, the force that fuels the connection between the seeker and the Guru. The Atma link—a bond of the soul—unites the intellect and the Guru in a shared purpose, creating harmony and alignment in the spiritual journey.

The Vehicles of Progress

Sri Vidyanarayana Theertha likened our spiritual journey to various modes of transportation: aeroplanes, trains, ships, bullock carts, and even walking. Each represents a different approach to life's challenges and spiritual progress:

- **Airplane**: A swift, transcendent leap into higher consciousness, bypassing the ordinary.

- **Train**: Collective progress, emphasizing the importance of community and shared purpose.

- **Ship**: A steady navigation through life's emotional depths and uncertainties.

- **Bullock Cart**: A humble and patient journey, representing the simplicity of tradition and grounded living.

- **Walking**: Swamiji's chosen path, signifying conscious effort, mindfulness, and connection with the present.

The Guru's role as the *"walker in the brain"* highlights the importance of patience and deliberation in achieving spiritual growth. While modern vehicles symbolize speed and efficiency, walking reflects the timeless value of inner work and contemplation.

Unity in Diversity

The most profound aspect of Sri Vidyanarayana Theertha's insight lies in the statement: *"He is in me, I am in him."* This reflects the non-dualistic truth of Advaita—that the Guru and the seeker are ultimately one. The triad of intellect, guidance, and devotion merges into a singular essence, where the boundaries between teacher, disciple, and self-dissolve.

This unity is not merely philosophical but deeply practical. It teaches us that spiritual progress requires:

- The clarity of intellect to discern the path.

- The guidance of a Guru to illuminate the way.

- The devotion of the heart to sustain the journey.

When these elements work in harmony, the seeker transcends the limitations of individuality and experiences the oneness of existence.

A Personal Reflection

As I reflect on this revelation, I am reminded of the immense grace of Sri Vidyanarayana Theertha, whose wisdom transforms the ordinary into the extraordinary. His ability to see the divine in every interaction inspires me to strive for deeper self-awareness and greater spiritual alignment.

Through this triad, I have come to understand that the Guru is not merely an external guide but also the inner conscience that walks within us, directing our thoughts, actions, and aspirations. This realization is both humbling and empowering, a reminder that the divine is always present—within us and around us.

Truth Unites:

The journey of life is not about speed or efficiency but about alignment, mindfulness, and connection. Whether as the driver, the Guru, or the devotee, each of us has a role to play in the collective journey toward enlightenment.

Let us walk this path with gratitude, guided by the wisdom of our Gurus and the light of our inner consciousness. As Sri Vidyanarayana Theertha reminds us, *"He is in me, I am in him."* This truth unites us, transforming our individual journeys into a shared pilgrimage toward the divine.

Inferences for Reflection:

- **Intellect as the driver**: Rational understanding and clarity direct the seeker's journey.

- **Devotion as the heart**: Devotion is the fuel that keeps the spiritual journey alive.

- **Guru as the guide**: The Guru provides the wisdom and guidance necessary for spiritual awakening.

- **The interconnectedness of the Triad**: The mind, heart, and guidance must work together for the seeker to reach their highest potential.

Prayer for Divine Guidance:

O Divine Creator,
May we walk the path of wisdom,
With intellect sharpened by clarity,
With hearts fueled by devotion,
And with feet guided by the divine teachings of our Gurus.
Grant us the grace to realize the unity within us all,
To see Your divine light in every moment,
And to walk in the footsteps of truth, love, and compassion.
May we transcend all duality and realize the oneness of existence.
In Your divine presence, we find peace.
Hare Krishna.

Chapter-40

Doctors: Divine Healers on a Sacred Journey

A Pathway to Healing:

The field of medicine is often seen as a noble profession—a pathway to healing the body, alleviating suffering, and saving lives. However, its true potential goes far beyond physical treatment. As divine instruments of healing, doctors play a vital role in restoring harmony between the body, mind, and soul. In today's world, dominated by corporate healthcare, the spiritual and holistic aspects of medicine are often overlooked. This article aims to inspire doctors to reconnect with the deeper purpose of their work, integrate diverse healing practices, and advocate for a healthcare system that truly serves the well-being of every individual.

The Spiritual Calling of a Doctor

Medicine, at its core, is not merely the practice of diagnosing and treating physical ailments. It is a sacred journey that encompasses the soul, spirit, and body. His Holiness **Sri Vidyanarayana Theertha**, a revered spiritual guide, reminds us that doctors are not only healers of the body but also spiritual guides who assist in the **transformation of karma**. His teachings emphasize that the ultimate goal of healing is not just the alleviation of physical pain, but also the restoration of spiritual well-being.

Dr. Naga Yogi Raj, a revered figure who seamlessly integrates spirituality with medical practice, emphasizes a profound truth: healing is not just about curing physical ailments but also about guiding the soul. As an experienced doctor with a background in psychology and medicine and a former tutor at Government Medical College in Anantapur, he brings a unique perspective to healthcare. His life journey, documented in *Hidden Radiance,* reveals his deep understanding of the interconnectedness between the body, mind, and spirit.

The Role of a Doctor: Healers of the Body and Soul

Doctors are more than medical professionals; they are divine instruments, entrusted with the sacred responsibility of guiding souls toward healing. Every diagnosis and treatment offer an opportunity to heal not just the body but the deeper, hidden wounds of the soul. **Hospitals** should not be viewed merely as institutions of medicine but as **temples of healing**, where doctors serve as guides to help patients achieve both physical and spiritual restoration.

In this context, **pathology** becomes a profound inquiry into a patient's spiritual and karmic history. Tests, diagnoses, and treatments are not just about physical conditions—they are spiritual revelations that uncover the root causes of suffering. The role of doctors extends far beyond medical expertise; it is a divine calling that requires deep humility, compassion, and reverence.

The Challenges of Modern Healthcare: A Call for Holistic Integration

While the role of doctors is divinely significant, the modern healthcare system, particularly in **corporate hospitals**, often reduces medicine to a business. In many countries, healthcare has become commercialized, where profits outweigh the well-being of patients. Dr. Naga Yogi Raj expresses deep concern about the **unnecessary investigations** and **unwarranted treatments** that burden patients, especially the poor. These practices not only lead to physical harm but also generate a climate of **panic and anxiety** among patients, who often feel pressured into unnecessary procedures due to the fear of not receiving optimal care.

The cost of medical treatment in corporate hospitals further alienates the most vulnerable sections of society, creating a gap between those who can afford proper care and those who cannot. **Why should healthcare be treated as a business**, where the focus shifts away from the true essence of healing? Why do patients, especially in low-income groups, find themselves paying high prices for treatments that may not even be necessary?

Dr. Naga Yogi Raj strongly advocates for the **integration of multiple healing practices** under one roof. He asks why governments can't improve their healthcare systems to include homeopathy, Ayurveda, Unani, Siddha, and Naturopathy alongside conventional medicine. Many patients experience miraculous results with homoeopathy, while others find immense relief in Ayurveda. By embracing a variety of healing systems, doctors can cater to a broader spectrum of needs, enhancing their patients' overall well-being.

A Vision for the Future: Integrating Healing Systems for Comprehensive Care

Why not create government hospital complexes that accommodate all these different branches of medicine? **Imagine a hospital where homeopaths, Ayurvedic doctors, Unani practitioners, and allopathic physicians collaborate**. By fostering mutual respect among practitioners of diverse healing systems, we can create a system that serves every individual's unique needs. Every patient is different, and integrating these practices allows for a more personalized and holistic approach to healing.

Doctors, irrespective of their specializations, must recognize the value of all systems of medicine and work together, respecting each other's expertise. By doing so, they can provide **comprehensive, integrated care** that focuses on the whole person, addressing not just the disease but also the root causes and the emotional and spiritual health of the patient.

A Prayer to Lord Dhanavantri: Seeking Divine Guidance

Before embarking on their daily practice, doctors should take a moment to pray and seek divine guidance. Lord **Dhanavantri**, the Hindu God of healing, represents the ultimate source of health, wisdom, and restoration. Here is a prayer that doctors can offer to invoke his grace:

Inferences for Doctors: Key Takeaways

- **Doctors as Brain, Patients as Thoughts**: A doctor's wisdom shapes the thoughts of recovery, guiding the patient toward healing, not only of the body but also of the soul.

- **Doctors as Gurus**: The doctor's diagnosis is not merely medical; it is also spiritual guidance, helping the patient correct their karmic imbalances.

- **Hospitals as Temples**: Medical institutions are sacred spaces for healing, where both physical and spiritual restoration occur.

- **Pathology as Karmic Inquiry**: Diagnostic tests serve as spiritual inquiries, uncovering the karmic causes of physical ailments and offering insights into the spiritual journey.

- **The Role of Physicians and Surgeons**: Physicians provide wisdom, while surgeons remove blockages, contributing to holistic healing of the mind, body, and soul.

- **Embrace of Modern Specialties**: New medical fields are essential for addressing contemporary challenges, offering solutions to complex modern ailments.

- **Transforming Karma**: The ultimate goal of healing is not just physical well-being but the transformation of negative karma into positive actions.

Reflection Questions for Doctors

1. **Why do we, as doctors, solely focus on the physical body?** Are we overlooking the spiritual and karmic aspects of our patients' health?

2. **Can we, as healers, expand our understanding beyond the medical curriculum and embrace holistic healing practices?** How can we integrate alternative and complementary medicine into our practices to enhance the patient's healing journey?

3. **How do we, as physicians, engage with the divine aspect of our profession?** Do we see ourselves as instruments of divine will, and how does that influence our approach to patient care?

Quotes to Reflect On:

- "A doctor's wisdom shapes not just the body but also the soul, guiding patients to harmony beyond illness."

- "Healing is not confined to the body. It transcends the physical and reaches into the soul, balancing karmic forces and restoring divine harmony."

- "Doctors are the brain of society, patients are the thoughts, and together they must seek the wisdom of healing."

- "Medicine is the bridge between science and spirit—doctors, as healers, must walk both paths to restore balance."

- "A true healer does not merely cure. A true healer enlightens the soul, guides the spirit, and nurtures the body back to harmony."

A Call to Doctors Everywhere

The role of a doctor goes far beyond a profession; it is a divine calling, a sacred responsibility to heal not just the body but the soul. Doctors are entrusted with the profound duty of guiding individuals through both their physical ailments and their spiritual journeys. As Dr. Swamy and Dr. Naga Yogi Raj have so eloquently expressed, we must rise above the commercial pressures and the growing complexities of the healthcare industry. We must return to the true essence of healing—recognizing that true wellness is not just the absence of disease, but a harmonious balance between the body, mind, and spirit.

In this sacred role, doctors have the opportunity to touch lives in ways that transcend medicine. By embracing the holistic path of healing, doctors can guide their patients not only toward recovery but toward peace, purpose, and spiritual awakening.

Doctors, it is time to reflect on your sacred duty. By embracing **holistic, integrated care**, and honouring the ancient healing traditions alongside modern medical practices, you can **transform healthcare** and restore the divine balance that was always intended.

Let us move forward with the wisdom of **Sri Vidyanarayana Theertha**, the guidance of **Dr. Naga Yogi Raj**, and the strength of Lord **Dhanavantri** to elevate the practice of medicine, creating a healing system that truly serves humanity.

Prayer for Healing and Wisdom:

Om Namo Bhagavate Dhanavantraye Namaha

"O Divine Healer, Lord Dhanavantri,

We humbly bow before you with gratitude and reverence. You, the embodiment of divine health, guide our hands and minds as we walk the sacred path of healing. Grant us the wisdom to look beyond the physical ailments and to understand the deeper needs of the soul. Empower us to treat with compassion, restore balance, and help our patients find peace and vitality.

As instruments of your divine will, may we heal not only the body but also the mind and spirit. Inspire us to transform negative karma into blessings, leading our patients toward wholeness and renewal. May we always approach our work with humility and respect, honouring the sacred responsibility entrusted to us as healers?

May we, like you, serve the world with grace and devotion, guided by the eternal light of healing.

Om Namo Bhagavate Dhanavantraye Namaha."

Chapter-41

Embracing Life's Beatings: The Spiritual Path of Transformation

Life, with all its joy and sorrow, is a series of experiences designed to shape and refine us. For spiritual aspirants, these challenges, often called "beatings," are not obstacles but divine opportunities for growth. Through the wisdom of Swamy Sri Vidyanarayana Thirtha, we understand that life's trials are not only tests of endurance but also transformative experiences that can lead us to greater spiritual heights.

This article explores the deeper spiritual meaning behind life's *"beatings"* and how we can use them to advance on our path to divine realization.

The Spiritual Meaning Behind Life's "Beatings"

The term *"beating"* symbolizes the challenges and hardships that life inevitably presents. These difficulties are often viewed as obstacles, but in reality, they are essential for spiritual evolution.

1. Getting Beating: The Acceptance of Challenges

In the spiritual journey, the first step to growth is accepting life's difficulties. These challenges are not punishments but divine instruments that push us toward inner refinement. Swamy Sri Vidyanarayana Thirtha often shares that these difficulties are part of God's plan, meant to help us realize our higher purpose. The key is not to resist but to accept them as opportunities for learning and growth.

This acceptance leads to *spiritual progress*, for when we face challenges with openness, we allow our minds to become flexible, adaptive, and wise. When we surrender to divine will, we are freed from resistance, enabling spiritual energy to flow freely. This openness paves the way for us to become better instruments of the Divine, bringing us closer to our soul's purpose.

A prime example is Lord Rama's life in the Ramayana. His exile, along with the numerous hardships he faced, were not a result of divine punishment but part of a greater plan that led to the triumph of dharma (righteousness). Through these struggles, Lord Rama exemplified patience, humility, and unwavering faith in divine will. His journey shows how accepting hardship in service to the greater good can bring us closer to fulfilling our highest spiritual potential.

2. Baking in Beating: Refinement Through Suffering

Just as raw materials require heat to transform into something refined, spiritual aspirants undergo refinement through life's challenges. *Swamy Sri Vidyanarayana Thirtha teaches that when approached with the right attitude, suffering purifies the soul and brings clarity to the mind.* This process is essential for cultivating spiritual wisdom, allowing us to detach from worldly distractions and focus on the divine essence within.

In the context of real life, this process helps aspirants not only become spiritually mature but also resilient in facing real-world challenges. The ability to endure suffering with patience and faith strengthens character and deepens our connection to the divine purpose in our life.

Consider the life of *Saint Eknath*, a prominent Marathi saint, who endured numerous hardships in his lifetime, including the loss of loved ones and persecution for his devotion. Yet, he remained steadfast in his faith, using suffering as a means to deepen his connection with the Divine. Through his suffering, he became a beacon of wisdom and love for others, transforming his pain into profound spiritual lessons. This transformation through trials demonstrates how life's beatings refine not just the body but the soul.

3. Becoming Benevolent to Beating: Gratitude for Challenges

Instead of resenting hardships, Swamy Sri Vidyanarayana Thirtha encourages us to embrace them with love and gratitude. By viewing challenges as divine lessons, we can transform suffering into a source of strength. This approach allows us to see the greater wisdom behind our difficulties, helping us stay aligned with our higher purpose.

On a spiritual level, embracing hardship with gratitude helps us dissolve the ego. The ego thrives on complaints and resistance, but gratitude transcends it, allowing our hearts to open fully to divine wisdom. *This benevolent relationship with suffering also empowers us to be more compassionate and understanding toward others.*

A beautiful example from Indian spirituality is *Sri Ramakrishna Paramahamsa,* who faced severe physical suffering throughout his life. Despite his pain, he accepted each challenge with gratitude, believing that every hardship brought him closer to God. His ability to maintain a positive, grateful outlook in the face of adversity became an inspiration to his followers. This deep acceptance of suffering as divine grace is what enabled him to become a living embodiment of unconditional love and wisdom, guiding countless souls toward liberation.

The teachings of Swamy Sri Vidyanarayana Thirtha show that our response to life's challenges is crucial in determining our spiritual progress. Spiritual wisdom teaches us to view obstacles as divine lessons essential for our growth.

4. Balancing Beating: Equanimity Amidst Struggles

Balance is essential in life. Swamy often emphasizes that true spiritual strength lies in maintaining equanimity in the face of life's ups and downs. This equanimity allows us to remain unaffected by external circumstances, enabling us to find peace amidst chaos.

In real life, this inner balance helps us navigate not only personal trials but also the turbulence of modern life, such as work pressures, emotional challenges, and external conflicts. By remaining grounded in our spiritual practice, we are less swayed by the fleeting distractions of the material world.

Bhagwan Buddha's life provides a profound example of equanimity. Throughout his journey, he faced numerous challenges, from personal loss to the rejection of his teachings. Yet, he maintained perfect balance, teaching his followers to remain detached from worldly struggles and attain inner peace through mindfulness and meditation. *His ability to stay centered despite external circumstances is a powerful example for us to maintain peace and clarity even in the most challenging situations.*

5. Being Away from Beating: The Wisdom to Avoid Unnecessary Struggles

Not every challenge we face is necessary for our spiritual growth. Swamy Sri Vidyanarayana Thirtha encourages us to use discernment and wisdom to avoid unnecessary suffering. *Through meditation and self-awareness, we can align ourselves with divine will and avoid the pitfalls of unnecessary karmic entanglements.*

In real life, this wisdom helps us make better decisions, choosing paths that align with our true purpose, and avoiding distractions or situations that lead to unnecessary stress. This discernment aids in spiritual progress by allowing us to focus our energy on endeavours that bring us closer to the Divine.

The teachings of *Sri Krishna in the Bhagavad Gita* highlight this wisdom, advising Arjuna to not engage in battles that are not part of his dharma. By being aware of one's true purpose, unnecessary struggles can be avoided, leading to a more peaceful existence.

6. Being Near to Beating: Embracing Challenges as Divine Lessons

Rather than running away from difficulties, Swamy encourages us to face them directly and use them as stepping stones for spiritual growth. *Each challenge is an opportunity for transformation*, offering valuable lessons that can deepen our understanding of ourselves and the universe.

This approach is crucial both in spiritual life and daily existence. It helps us stay present in the moment, embrace our true self, and be at peace with life's inherent unpredictability. Embracing challenges with grace strengthens our resolve and builds spiritual maturity.

The life of Guru Nanak Dev Ji is a powerful example of this approach. Despite facing persecution, ridicule, and hardship, Guru Nanak remained steadfast in his mission to spread love and oneness. His ability to embrace challenges and use them for a higher purpose continues to inspire millions of people worldwide.

Transforming Suffering into Wisdom

The ultimate lesson in spirituality is to view suffering through the lens of love and gratitude. *Swamy Sri Vidyanarayana Thirtha teaches that when we surrender to the divine plan, every hardship becomes an opportunity for greater wisdom.* By embracing life's trials with open arms, we align ourselves with divine will, allowing us to rise above them.

In real life, this surrender allows us to let go of unnecessary attachments and the fear of failure. By trusting that every experience is part of the divine design, we can live with greater peace and acceptance.

An inspiring example of this is *Sri Aurobindo*, who faced many challenges in his life, including imprisonment and personal suffering. Yet, he transformed every trial into a means of spiritual growth, ultimately becoming one of India's greatest philosophers and spiritual leaders.

Inferences: Embracing the Path of Transformation

From Swamy Sri Vidyanarayana Thirtha's teachings, we can derive the following insights:

- *Challenges as Divine Lessons*: Every difficulty is an opportunity to grow spiritually, to learn more about oneself and the divine.

- *Equanimity is Essential*: Maintaining inner peace amid external circumstances is crucial for spiritual progress.

- *Gratitude Transforms Suffering*: We can turn our trials into stepping stones for growth and wisdom through gratitude.

- *Wisdom Prevents Unnecessary Suffering*: Discernment and mindfulness allow us to avoid unnecessary struggles, aligning us with divine will.

- *Embrace Challenges*: Life's difficulties are not to be feared but embraced as opportunities for transformation.

The Path of Spiritual Evolution

Swamy Sri Vidyanarayana Thirtha reminds us that the "beatings" of life are not to be feared, but rather embraced. Each trial holds the potential to refine us, transform us, and bring us closer to our divine nature. By accepting challenges with love, maintaining equanimity, and using them as opportunities for wisdom, we can progress not only in spiritual life but also in real-life endeavours. The path of transformation is not an easy one, but it is through these very challenges that we rise to our highest potential. *In the end, life's beatings are the tools that shape us into divinely radiant beings, prepared to fulfil our higher purpose.*

Prayer:

O Divine, in every test,
Guide me to grow, give me rest.
In every struggle, help me see,
The lessons you've laid out for me.

Through the pain, may I stay strong,
With patience, I'll move right along.
Let each challenge shape my soul,
And make my heart pure and whole.

Grant me peace in times of strife,
To walk with grace through this life.
Help me learn, help me grow,
In Your light, may I always glow.

Thank you, Divine, for every beat,
For every trial, every feat.
With love, I embrace Your way,
And trust in You, come what may.

Chapter-42

S-A-I

(Sacrifice-Attain-Intuition)

In today's fast-paced, material-driven world, spirituality is often relegated to the background, overshadowed by the demands of daily life and technological advancements. However, the teachings of Shirdi Sai Baba, as interpreted by Sri Sri Sri Vidyanarayana Theertha, offer a profound antidote to this disconnect, reminding us of the eternal truths that bind us all. Sai Baba's philosophy is simple yet profound, offering a path of love, service, faith, and compassion that transcends the boundaries of religion, culture, and time. His teachings hold immense relevance today, providing guidance not only for spiritual seekers but also for anyone seeking peace, harmony, and meaning in life.

Love: The Heart of Sai Baba's Teachings

At the core of Sai Baba's teachings lies an all-encompassing love. As Swamy Sri Vidyanarayana Theertha emphasizes, *"Sai is sugarcane, means love, love only, nothing greater than love. Love moves, love shares, love forgives, love soothes."* This simple yet profound statement encapsulates the essence of Sai Baba's teachings. Love, as he taught, is the driving force behind everything in life. It is the energy that heals wounds, bridges divides, and brings people together.

Sai Baba demonstrated through his actions that love is not just an emotion but a transformative force that can turn the hardest hearts into compassionate ones. In a world often torn by division and hatred, Sai Baba's message of love is more relevant than ever. As Swamy Vidyanarayana Theertha shares, *"In this world, where everything is temporary, love is the only eternal truth."*

The Role of Service in Spiritual Growth

Sai Baba's life was a testament to the power of service, or "Seva," as a path to spiritual enlightenment. He encouraged his followers to serve others selflessly, regardless of caste, creed, or religion. Service, for Sai Baba, was not just an outward act; it was an expression of love and devotion to the divine. Swamy Vidyanarayana Theertha elaborates on this by stating that service to the needy, in both the mundane and spiritual realms, is a means to purify one's heart and connect with the divine. *"Service is not just an obligation, it is the true path to spiritual growth and liberation."*

In our daily lives, we can embody this principle by offering our time, resources, and love to those in need. In doing so, we align ourselves with the divine will and contribute to the collective well-being of society. Service, in this sense, becomes a bridge between the individual and the universal, between the worldly and the spiritual.

Faith and Patience: Pillars of Sai Baba's Wisdom

Sai Baba's unwavering faith in God, combined with his infinite patience, serves as a powerful lesson for all of us. In an age of instant gratification and rapid results, Baba taught the importance of cultivating patience and surrendering to the divine will. *"Patience is the key to unlocking the door of divine wisdom,"* says Swamy Sri Vidyanarayana Theertha.

Faith and patience are not passive; they are active states of being that guide us through life's challenges. By trusting in the divine process and remaining patient, we learn to navigate the ups and downs of life with grace and resilience.

Sai Baba's Relevance in Modern Life

While Sai Baba's teachings are rooted in ancient wisdom, they remain deeply relevant in today's world. As modern challenges mount—whether they are social, political, or personal—the need for spiritual guidance becomes ever more urgent. Sai Baba's simple but profound teachings on love, service, and faith provide a timeless solution to the crisis of the human spirit in the modern age.

In contemporary society, where technology and materialism often overshadow human connection, Sai Baba's message encourages us to return to the basics: love, simplicity, and service. His philosophy offers a counterbalance to the stress, anxiety, and disconnection that many experience in the digital age. By incorporating Sai Baba's teachings into our lives, we can foster peace, harmony, and understanding in both our inner and outer worlds.

The Role of Sai Baba's Teachings in Mental Health and Well-being

Sai Baba's teachings also hold significant value in the realm of mental health and well-being. In today's world, where stress and anxiety are rampant, Sai Baba's emphasis on inner peace, patience, and surrender provides a spiritual framework for cultivating emotional resilience. By practicing mindfulness, faith, and love, individuals can reduce stress, enhance emotional stability, and foster a sense of well-being.

As Swamy Vidyanarayana Theertha states, *"When you are aligned with love and service, your heart becomes a vessel of peace."* In this way, the practice of Sai Baba's teachings contributes not only to spiritual growth but also to mental health and emotional healing.

Sai Baba and the Call for Social Justice

Sai Baba's life was a powerful challenge to the societal norms of his time. He stood against caste discrimination, inequality, and injustice, encouraging his followers to look beyond superficial divisions and see the divine presence in all beings. His message is as relevant today as it was during his lifetime. *"True devotion lies in the love you show to others, especially those in need,"* says Swamy Vidyanarayana Theertha.

In the current social climate, where inequality and division persist, Sai Baba's teachings encourage us to work towards a more just and inclusive society. By embracing his message of love, compassion, and service, we can contribute to a world that is more equitable, harmonious, and united.

The S.A.I. Framework: Sacrifice, Attain, and Intuition

Swamy Vidyanarayana Theertha has introduced the S.A.I. framework—Sacrifice, Attain, and Intuition—as a guide to spiritual and personal growth.

S: Sacrifice — The path to spiritual progress requires sacrifice, whether it be sacrificing ego, desires, or attachments to material possessions.

A: Attain — Through dedication, service, and love, we attain the ultimate realization of the divine presence within us and in all beings.

I: Intuition — Developing intuition allows us to connect with the deeper truth of existence, transcending the limits of the material world.

By embodying these principles, we walk the path of spiritual enlightenment and personal transformation.

Sai Baba's Message of Unity in Diversity

Sai Baba's teachings transcend all boundaries—whether cultural, religious, or philosophical. His message is universal, calling for unity and peace among all beings. He demonstrated that true spirituality recognizes no distinctions between individuals, casting aside the artificial divisions that separate us. *"I am with all who seek the truth, regardless of their path,"* said Sai Baba, reinforcing the idea that all spiritual paths lead to the same ultimate truth.

In a world increasingly divided by differences, Sai Baba's message offers a vision of unity, compassion, and understanding. By seeing the divine in all people, we can transcend conflict and build a world rooted in love and mutual respect.

Subtle Truths about Shirdi Sai Baba

There are many subtle aspects of Shirdi Sai Baba's life that remain little known to his devotees, though they offer deep insights into his divine nature. For instance, Sai Baba was known to perform miracles not to show his power, but to strengthen the faith of his devotees. One of the lesser-known facts is his practice of materializing objects out of thin air, such as sacred ash (vibhuti) and even food, to satisfy the needs of his followers in times of scarcity. Yet, he always emphasized that true miracles lie in the devotion of the heart, rather than external displays of divine power.

Moreover, Sai Baba's intimate connection with nature—whether it was the trees, the river, or the animals—reminds us of the interconnectedness of all life. His famous saying, *"I am with you wherever you are"* reflects his omnipresence, not just in the physical sense, but in the hearts of those who genuinely seek his guidance.

Enduring Lessons:

The timeless philosophy of Shirdi Sai Baba, as illuminated by Sri Sri Sri Vidyanarayana Theertha, offers profound and enduring lessons for both spiritual seekers and those navigating the challenges of the modern world. Through the transformative power of love, service, faith, and simplicity, we are invited to rise above the limitations of the material realm and connect with the divine essence that flows through all beings.

Sai Baba's teachings, which center around love and selfless service, are not mere spiritual ideals—they are invitations to live a life that reflects the highest virtues of humanity. His message, timeless and boundless, guides us toward personal transformation and societal harmony. In a world where the gap between spirituality and daily life grows wider, Sai Baba's teachings call us back to the heart of Sanathana Dharma—a heart that beats with love, compassion, and unity, transcending all divisions.

As Swamy Sri Vidyanarayana Theertha beautifully reminds us, *"In every heart, you can find Sai; in every act of love, you embody his spirit."* By embodying Sai Baba's teachings in our everyday lives, we do more than just transform ourselves—we become instruments of collective spiritual awakening, awakening the hearts of others to the light of compassion and understanding.

An Avadutha Bikshaku, whose boundless grace and wisdom have miraculously transformed barren lands into fertile soil, has shown us the path to enrich our lives in both the material and spiritual realms. Through his unwavering guidance and selfless service, he has uplifted humanity, especially in this Kaliyuga, where the world is crying out for compassion, peace, and healing.

We humbly offer our prayers, seeking God's presence to be with him always, granting us the eternal guidance that leads us to his holy feet. As the embodiment of Datta Guru, he continues to inspire, support, and guide all beings, helping us live in harmony, peace, and spiritual fulfillment.

Chapter-43

Awakening the Divine Within: The Infinite Power of Love

Embracing Divine Love in a Fragmented World

In today's fast-paced world, we are often caught in the relentless pursuit of material success, distracted by the constant demands of daily life. We chase after happiness, achievement, and fulfilment, yet many of us feel incomplete as if something essential is missing. In the noise of this constant striving, we overlook a simple, profound truth: Divine Love is the force that can guide us toward inner peace, fulfilment, and lasting joy.

Divine Love is not a distant, abstract ideal or a lofty philosophical notion. It is a profound, transformative energy—tangible and alive—that transcends all boundaries—religious, cultural, and societal. It speaks directly to the very core of our being, awakening the soul to its infinite potential. Though often hidden beneath the noise of daily life, this divine energy, when rediscovered, holds the power to shift our perspective completely. It has the capacity to illuminate the darkest corners of our minds, bringing clarity, inner peace, and an unparalleled sense of joy.

This chapter invites you to pause, reflect, and embark on an inward journey to reconnect with the divine energy that is always within you, patiently awaiting your recognition. We will explore how this infinite love can transform not only our individual lives but the world around us.

The Journey Within Reconnecting with the Divine Love Within

When we speak of Divine Love, we are not referring to human emotions or conditional affection. Divine Love is the purest, most profound energy emanating from the very source of existence. The unconditional force sustains all life, independent of our physical experiences.

To tap into this boundless love, the journey must begin within. In the rush of daily life, we often miss the quiet whispers of love that come from within. Through practices like meditation, mindfulness, and self-reflection, we uncover the layers of our being that connect us to this divine presence. In moments of stillness and introspection, we begin to recognize the love within, guiding us toward wisdom, peace, and greater harmony.

This journey is not about perfection but about embracing love in every aspect of our lives. It's about listening to our inner voice, trusting the divine guidance that flows through us, and allowing this love to transform our thoughts, actions, and relationships.

Sri Swamy Vidyanarayana Theertha's profound teaching—God is not in temples, churches, or mosques. Wait, watch, and win"— reminds us that the divine is not confined to external structures. It is within each of us, waiting to be acknowledged. Divine Love calls us to go beyond external worship and embrace the love that resides within, guiding us toward clarity and transformation.

The Five Elements of Transformation: Love in Action

Divine Love is not a passive feeling but an active, living energy that shapes our reality. The five elements—Earth, Water, Fire, Air, and Ether—serve as metaphors for the transformation that occurs when we align ourselves with this love. Each element represents a unique aspect of our spiritual journey, contributing to divine energy's holistic nature.

- **Earth**: Stability and grounding. Divine Love anchors us, helping us find balance in a chaotic world. Like the Earth that sustains life, love gives us a foundation to grow and thrive.

- **Water**: Fluidity and cleansing. Just as water purifies the body, Divine Love washes away fear, anger, and resentment, cleansing our hearts and minds.

- **Fire**: Transformation and passion. Fire symbolizes change. Divine Love ignites the passion within, inspiring us to act with purpose, to let go of what no longer serves us, and to rise with renewed energy.

- **Air**: Freedom and expansion. Air is the breath of life. Divine Love invites us to expand our horizons, live freely, and explore new possibilities.

- **Ether**: Spirit and connection. Ether bridges the physical and spiritual realms. Divine Love connects us to the infinite, allowing us to experience unity with all beings and the cosmos.

When aligned with Divine Love, these five elements create a harmonious flow of energy, guiding us toward greater wisdom, peace, and compassion.

The Zero of Divine Love: Unity with the Infinite

At the core of this transformative journey lies the concept of "Zero." While zero is often viewed as emptiness or nothingness, in the context of Divine Love, it represents the purest state of being—free from ego, attachment, and illusion. It is the state where all barriers dissolve, and only love remains.

In this state of "Zero," we are not lacking anything. We are everything. We become one with the divine, and through this union, we unlock our fullest potential. In this moment of clarity, we understand that

Divine Love is not something to be sought outside of ourselves but is something to be recognized and embraced within.

This realization transforms us, allowing us to live in a place of purity, connection, and oneness. As Sri Swamy Vidyanarayana Theertha teaches, *"In this state of awareness, the divine becomes evident, not as a distant entity but as the very essence of life itself."*

Embracing the Infinite Love Within

As you reflect on the teachings of this chapter, consider how you can begin to cultivate Divine Love in your own life. Start by creating moments of stillness, listening to your inner voice, and trusting in the divine guidance that resides within you. Know that each step you take toward this love is a step closer to your highest self and a deeper connection with the infinite energy that flows through all of existence.

Divine Love is not a destination but a continual unfolding—a journey of transformation that leads us back to our truest essence. In the state of Zero, we are aligned with all the elements of creation, and in this alignment, we experience the fullness of Divine Love. As you walk this path, remember that you are never alone—the love of the divine is always with you, guiding, nurturing, and transforming you into the highest version of yourself.

Inferences/Takeaways:

1. **Divine Love is Universal**: It transcends religious and cultural boundaries, residing within all beings.

2. **The Inner Journey is Key**: True transformation begins with looking inward, cultivating self-awareness, and reconnecting with the love already within us.

3. **Selfless Service Embodies Divine Love**: The life of Sai Baba exemplifies that Divine Love is active and transformative, demonstrated through selfless service and compassion.

4. **The Zero State**: Zero symbolizes the purest state of being, free from ego and illusion, allowing us to experience oneness with the divine.

5. **Practical Transformation**: By practicing love through service, kindness, and compassion, we can align ourselves with Divine Love and positively impact the world around us.

Message from Sri Swamy Vidyanarayana Theertha

"Do not look for love outside yourself. It has always been within you. It is the breath you take, the stillness that guides you, and the light that shows your way. Right now, understand that you are one with the divine. When you connect with this inner love, you will find peace and purpose. You will gain the strength to overcome any challenge. Love is not something distant to be sought. It is the essence of who you are, waiting to awaken. Trust this truth, and let it change your life from within."

Awakening the Divine Within

Divine Love is the highest power that exists within every one of us, and it is the key to transforming our lives. By embracing this love, we open ourselves to peace, wisdom, and a deep connection with all of existence. As we embark on the journey of recognizing the divine within, we align ourselves with the universe's infinite energy, unlocking our fullest potential. This transformation is not an end but a continuous unfolding—an invitation to become more loving, compassionate, and connected in our daily lives.

Let us walk this path with an open heart, trusting that each moment brings us closer to the divine truth that has always been within us. By living in alignment with Divine Love, we can heal ourselves, our relationships, and the world around us, creating a space for unity, peace, and eternal joy.

Chapter-44

Sai: The Mystic Energy That Ignites Your Soul

In a quiet yet profound conversation between His Holiness Sri Vidyanarayana Theertha and *Dr Hari, the nature of Sai and his divine* energy unfolded in a way that transcended the limitations of words. Their exchange, filled with deep insights, revealed Sai not only as a mystical figure but as a living, breathing energy that connects every soul to the divine. His energy pulsates through all creation, weaving a cosmic fabric that binds the individual self to the universal, eternal presence. The teachings shared by His Holiness Sri Vidyanarayana Theertha illuminated the path to understanding Sai's boundless, omnipresent power—a force that does not merely exist in the far reaches of the spiritual realm but vibrates in the very core of our being. As this discussion unfolded, it became clear that Sai's role is far beyond that of a distant figure; he is the force that flows within us, guiding us with his grace and wisdom toward our highest potential, aligning our souls with the divine rhythm of the universe. His presence is the unseen hand that gently nudges *us toward our true self, infusing every moment with light, purpose, and transcendence.*

In this context, Swamy shared a profound insight about Dr. C. Nagaraj, also known as Naga Yogi Raj, recognizing him as a pure energy, a hidden radiance, much like Sai. While Sai's energy is known to the world, Dr. Nagaraj's mystic energy remains largely unseen—reserved, unrecognized, and hidden in the depths of anonymity. Swamy described Dr. Nagaraj's life as an example of mystic energy, flowing with divine power yet remaining humbly veiled from the external world. "You call your brother Nagaraj; I call Sai, for He is a mystic energy, pure and unalloyed," said Swamy. In this, he drew a subtle parallel—both embody a sacred energy that transcends the physical and material world.

Yet, unlike Baba, who is widely known, Dr. Nagaraj has chosen to live a life of complete anonymity. His path is one of quiet contemplation and spiritual depth, untouched by the distractions of fame or recognition. This sacred energy flows through him, manifesting in silent acts of devotion and selfless service. In his very being, he embodies a force that is at once hidden and radiant, a testament to the divine truth that the most profound spiritual energies often remain unseen by the world, known only to those who seek with the heart, not with the eyes.

In this way, both Sai and Dr. Nagaraj represent the same unyielding mystic energy—one that exists beyond human understanding, bridging the soul to the divine essence that pervades all life. They are expressions of the infinite consciousness, each revealing a different facet of divine truth through their actions, presence, and energy. For those who are attuned to the subtle rhythms of the universe, both are mirrors reflecting the boundless, unmanifested force that sustains all life.

* * * * *

The Divine Force Within Us: Understanding Sai's Mystic Energy

Sai is not just a name; he is a divine force. He is an energy that exists everywhere—within every being and throughout the universe. Sai goes beyond time and form. To understand Sai is to connect with the powerful, mystic energy that flows through all of life. This energy is timeless, infinite, and always present. It moves through everything, connecting all souls to the divine.

Sai's essence is not something distant or hard to understand. It is a living, tangible force. Anyone who opens their heart to it can feel it. This energy connects us to the divine and awakens the hidden potential within our souls.

When we align with Sai's energy, we realize that it is not something separate from us. It is the very essence of who we are. This connection helps us discover our true nature and empowers us to go beyond the limits of our minds and bodies. It guides us toward spiritual awakening and divine understanding.

Sai's mystic energy is always with us. It flows through our lives, connecting us to the cosmic rhythm of the universe. When we align with this energy, we become one with the boundless force that sustains all creation.

Sai's Life: Living the Truth of Humility

Sai's life was a living testament to the purity of humility and selflessness. Though he lived in what many would consider poverty—begging for his sustenance—Sai was not bound by material needs. His life was not defined by what he received but by what he gave. With unconditional love and without measure, Sai gave everything he had to his devotees. Through this, he taught us that true wealth is found in the ability to give, not in the accumulation of riches.

Sai showed us that wealth is not in material possessions but in the heart's capacity to love, serve, and offer compassion to all. In the simplicity of his life, he demonstrated that when we seek nothing for ourselves, we possess everything that truly matters.

His actions revealed a profound truth: life becomes richer when shared. True fulfilment comes not from what we keep but from what we give away. The act of giving, without attachment, is the key to unlocking our highest potential. By living with this principle, we understand that the richness of life lies in our ability to share love and kindness—just as Sai did.

The Role of Suffering in Transformation

In today's world, suffering is often seen as something to avoid or eliminate. However, Sai's teachings reveal the profound role suffering plays in our spiritual journey. Through suffering, we undergo a process of purification—our minds and spirits are refined. Just as a seed must break open to sprout into a plant, we, too, must sometimes endure hardship to emerge as our true selves. Though this truth may be difficult to accept, its wisdom is transformative.

Suffering acts as a cleansing force. It reshapes our thoughts, refines our understanding, and illuminates the path toward a higher purpose. Without suffering, we would not fully appreciate the richness of life. The role of the Guru is not to eliminate suffering but to empower us with the strength to endure it. A true Guru shows us how to use suffering as an opportunity for growth.

Sai teaches us that challenges are part of the divine design. Instead of viewing them as obstacles, we learn to approach them with courage, faith, and peace. We recognize that they are stepping stones leading us to a deeper understanding of our true purpose.

Sai's Mystic Energy: A Force for Transformation

Sai's mystic energy is transformative. This divine force is not distant or abstract; it is a palpable presence that can be experienced by anyone who opens their heart to it. His energy awakens dormant potentials within us, guiding us toward wisdom, compassion, and divine realization. It is a living force that touches every soul with love, grace, and light.

When we embrace Sai's energy, we experience a profound shift in consciousness—a journey from confusion and chaos to clarity and peace. This shift brings balance and harmony into our lives, guiding us toward a deeper connection with the divine. By aligning with Sai's mystic energy, we tap into the universal flow of love that binds all beings together, experiencing a sense of unity and peace that transcends the limitations of the ego.

The Guru's Silence: Wisdom Beyond Words

One of the most profound aspects of Sai's teachings is the Guru's silence. In silence, the Guru speaks volumes. This silence is not emptiness; it is a space filled with divine wisdom, beyond the limitations of words. When in the presence of a true Guru, we do not just learn through spoken language but through energy, presence, and the divine vibrations that permeate the atmosphere.

The Guru's silence teaches us that the most profound truths are not always spoken aloud but often felt deep within. Wisdom does not come from accumulating knowledge, but from surrendering the ego and opening the heart to divine insight. In the sacred silence of the Guru, we realize that the answers we seek are not outside of us, but already lie within.

Trusting in the Divine Path

Devotion to the Guru is not just an act of faith; it is an act of surrender to the divine plan. The Guru is not here to solve our problems for us but to empower us to solve them ourselves. Through the Guru's guidance, we gain the strength to face life's challenges with courage and trust in the divine path that unfolds before us.

Sai's love for his devotees was unconditional. He never turned anyone away, regardless of their background, struggles, or faults. His love was all-encompassing, reminding us that every soul is precious and no one is ever truly alone. Through his energy, we are taught to recognize the divine within ourselves and in others, fostering compassion for all beings. When we embrace Sai's love, we move beyond our limited selves and into the realization of our infinite connection to the divine.

Sai's Begging: A Symbol of Giving

Sai's choice to live humbly, begging for his sustenance, was not born out of necessity but was a profound teaching. Despite having nothing, he gave everything to his devotees—unconditionally and without reservation. What need did he have for material wealth when he embodied the wealth of divine wisdom, love, and grace? His life was free from the burdens of worldly concerns, and his focus was entirely on serving humanity.

Through his simplicity, Sai taught us that true happiness does not come from external possessions but from inner contentment and the joy of selfless giving. His life exemplified the essence of his teachings: live simply, love deeply, and serve others without attachment to the outcome. In doing so, we discover that the wealth of the heart far surpasses any material possessions.

Conclusion: Embracing Sai's Energy

The journey to self-realisation is not always easy. We will face suffering, endure challenges, and navigate difficulties. Yet, with Sai's energy and the guidance of the Guru, these trials become opportunities for growth. Through them, we gain a deeper understanding of ourselves and the divine.

Trust in Sai's mystic energy, for it is through this energy that we unlock the divine power within. Sai's energy is not separate from us—it is who we are. When we align with it, we realize our highest purpose. In every trial, Sai's presence lifts us; through every challenge, his energy guides us toward peace and divine connection. The Guru does not promise a life without suffering but a life that finds strength through suffering, a life that sees the divine in every moment.

Embrace the journey. Through challenges, the grace of the Guru, and the power of Sai's mystic energy, we move toward ultimate realization—toward unity with the divine and inner peace. As you walk this path, remember that Sai's energy is always with you, lighting your way and guiding you to the fullness of your soul's potential.

Chapter-45

Living Grace

(Nurturing the Soul with Divine Love)

The Divine Grace Unfolded

In a world overshadowed by the complexities of modern life, where chaos often clouds the purity of our souls, the divine presence of a spiritual guide offers a profound sense of clarity and peace. His Holiness Sri Vidyanarayana Theertha, a beacon of divine wisdom, stands as a living testament to the eternal truths of the universe. Through his miracles, he not only reveals the boundless grace of the Divine but also imparts spiritual wisdom that transcends time and place. These miracles are not isolated events but reflections of the deeper spiritual law that governs all existence—the omnipresent, omnipotent force of love, compassion, and divine intervention.

"Miracles are not divine spectacles; they are the language of the Divine, spoken through faith, love, and surrender."
— *His Holiness Sri Vidyanarayana Theertha*

The Transformative Miracle in Chicago

In 2017, a devotee residing in Chicago faced an impending medical crisis—a severe heart ailment requiring an angioplasty. Overwhelmed by the fear of surgery and its consequences, the devotee, in a moment of prayer, sought solace in the grace of Swamiji. In response, Swamiji offered his blessings through a simple yet powerful WhatsApp message: "Blessings Blessings, Hare Krishna." Along with this message, the devotee received a photograph of Guru Govardhan and a sacred Shirdi Sai Bhajan, which opened the heart to divine connection and tranquillity.

The message, though brief, carried with it the weight of the divine and filled the devotee with a sense of peace and assurance that no medical intervention would be necessary. When the devotee underwent the final medical tests, they found that the heart condition had resolved miraculously, rendering the surgery unnecessary and nullifying the financial burden associated with it. This miraculous event was not merely the absence of disease but a tangible manifestation of Swamiji's grace, showing that divine will and love transcend the limits of human understanding.

"Faith is the bridge between human limitation and divine boundlessness. Healing begins when the soul aligns with the Divine."
— His Holiness Sri Vidyanarayana Theertha.

The Power of Yoga Siddhis

Swamiji's miracles are a living example of the power of Yoga Siddhis—the spiritual powers attained through deep meditation, austerity, and surrender to the Divine. These powers are not intended for spectacle or personal gain but are used as tools of compassion to uplift and guide humanity on the path of self-realization. Just as the sun's rays illuminate the world, Swamiji's divine energy illuminates the lives of those who seek his blessings with pure devotion.

The miraculous healing witnessed in Chicago is but one example of how Swamiji, with his boundless love and divine presence, operates beyond physical limitations. His powers are not confined to time or space; they reflect the very essence of the teachings of the Shrimad Bhagavad Gita, where Lord Krishna imparts the truth that all actions, when performed with surrender to the Divine, become part of the universal cosmic order.

"The true purpose of spiritual power is not self-glorification but selfless service to the suffering. Through compassion, divinity manifests itself."
— His Holiness Sri Vidyanarayana Theertha.

Lessons from Swamiji's Miracles

Every miracle performed by Swamiji carries profound spiritual lessons that guide us toward a deeper understanding of our divine nature. Miracles are not random occurrences but divine pointers that awaken our hearts and minds to the higher truths of existence.

Faith and Gratitude

Swamiji's miracles emphasize the power of unwavering faith and gratitude. The devotee in Chicago placed their trust in the divine, and through that faith, the impossible became possible. When we surrender ourselves to God and express gratitude for every moment, we open ourselves to receive divine blessings, no matter how small or grand.

"When the heart is open to Amma—the universal mother—miracles are but natural occurrences. Amma's grace flows unceasingly to those who hold her in their hearts."
— His Holiness Sri Vidyanarayana Theertha.

Forgiveness and Release

Swamiji's teachings, as exemplified in the Srimad Bhagavad Gita, emphasize the power of forgiveness. Holding onto grudges, resentment, or anger keeps us bound to the past, whereas forgiveness frees the soul and opens the heart to divine love. By forgiving, we release the chains of negativity and allow ourselves to experience the bliss of divine presence.

Living with Purpose

The miracles of Swamiji remind us to live a life of purpose and meaning. They teach us to perform our duties without attachment, to act selflessly, and always to seek the welfare of others. The path of Nishkama Karma, as Lord Krishna teaches in the Bhagavad Gita, is not about abandoning action but performing it with pure intention, free of ego and expectation. This is the way of spiritual liberation.

Yoga and Meditation

Spiritual practices like meditation, chanting, and selfless service are essential tools for transforming the mind and heart. Through these practices, we cultivate inner peace and connect with the divine essence. Swamiji's life serves as a living example of the transformative power of these practices, showing us that through discipline and devotion, we can experience the divine within and around us.

Nurturing Your Soul: Simple Practices for Daily Divine Connection

To cultivate spiritual growth and strengthen your bond with the Divine, try these simple, mindful practices:

- **Embrace Gratitude**: Start each day by acknowledging your blessings and offering heartfelt thanks to the Divine in whatever form resonates with you.

- **Meditate Daily**: Dedicate 10-15 minutes to quiet reflection, focusing on a word, mantra, or sacred phrase that brings you peace or inspiration.

- **Release the Past**: Liberate yourself from past wounds and grievances. Reflect on them, acknowledge their impact, and then consciously release them. Let go of the emotional weight, allowing healing to flow freely and create space for new beginnings.

- **Practice Selfless Kindness**: Perform one act of kindness without expectation. Whether it's a small gesture or a listening ear, give with an open heart.

- **Embrace Silence**: Create space for quiet moments each day. Let go of distractions and allow inner peace and clarity to emerge.

- **Live with Purpose**: Start your day with clear intention, embodying qualities like love, compassion, and humility.

- **Connect with Nature**: Spend time outdoors and reflect on the beauty and unity of all living beings, feeling a deep sense of interconnectedness.

These practices can help you align with the Divine and nurture your soul daily.

A Prayerful Invitation to the Divine

As we reflect on the miracles of His Holiness Sri Vidyanarayana Theertha, let us offer our hearts in sincere prayer, seeking his divine guidance and blessings:

"Swamiji, with a heart full of gratitude, we humbly bow before your sacred feet. We surrender our ego, desires, and attachments, asking for your divine wisdom to guide us on the path of righteousness. May your love light the way, dispelling the darkness of ignorance and leading us

towards spiritual fulfilment. Grant us the strength to forgive and release all past hurts so that we may live in peace and harmony with all. We seek your blessings, Swamiji, to transcend our limitations and experience the boundless grace of the Divine. With faith and trust, we surrender ourselves to your will, knowing that you will guide us toward the highest Living in Divine Light.

The miracles of His Holiness Sri Vidyanarayana Theertha transcend the extraordinary, revealing the presence of the Divine in every moment of our lives. Swamiji's life is a living testament that miracles are not rare events but are woven into the fabric of our daily existence, waiting to be recognized when we live with faith, devotion, and love. These divine revelations guide, protect, and bless us, urging us to awaken to the ultimate truth that the Divine is ever-present.

As Bhagwan SRI RAM 'SIR" wisely shares, the Bhagavad Gita is not merely a collection of verses but a transformative guide that transcends sectarian boundaries. SIR emphasizes that the mere accumulation of knowledge, without its practice, is of no value. True wisdom lies in embodying the teachings, not just speaking them. The Gita is an invitation to deepen our understanding and, more importantly, to transform our very essence, aligning with the Divine purpose that governs all life. Through devotion and surrender, we open ourselves to divine grace, guiding us toward the realization of our highest potential and the truth that resides within each of us.

His Holiness Sri Vidyanarayana Swamy beautifully reflects on the timeless wisdom of Lord Krishna, urging us to live free from ego, selfishness, desires, and anger. Lord Krishna's teachings, especially Nishkama Karma (selfless action), offer practical guidance applicable to all life aspects—whether in business, social service, or education. These teachings remind us that by embracing love, trust, and acceptance of the Divine, we can lead a lighter, more fulfilling life. The Gita's wisdom invites us to see the world as one family—Vasudhaiva Kutumbakam—and celebrates the universal message of peace, forgiveness, and trust in the divine guidance that leads us to harmony and success.

Geeta Jayanti is not only a time to celebrate this universal wisdom but also a day to honour those who guide us on the right path, much like Lord Krishna did for Arjuna. His teachings urge us to forgive the past, live fully in the present, and trust that the Divine will lead us toward peace and fulfilment.

With the blessings of His Holiness, may we walk this sacred path, embodying purity of heart, clarity of mind, and strength of spirit as we discover the divine within and share that light with all beings.

Igniting Divine Light Within

As the sun sets on our earthly doubts and fears, Swamiji's miracles awaken our souls' inner light, transforming darkness into a canvas of divine brilliance. Each miracle, a message from the Divine, calls us to rise above our struggles and remember that we are never alone—our journey is always guided by unseen hands. With Swamiji's grace, let us walk fearlessly on this sacred path, becoming beacons of the divine light that not only leads us to our highest truth but also radiates healing and hope to the world around us. May His Holiness' blessings ignite within us a relentless pursuit of spiritual awakening, unfolding peace, love, and boundless transformation for all.

"A Humble Offering of Divine Wisdom"

To

His Holiness Sri Vidyanarayna Thirtha

With utmost humility and reverence, I offer my humble respects to His Holiness Sri Vidyanarayana Theertha, whose divine guidance, wisdom, and holy spirit have been the true source of inspiration behind the creation of ZERO to ZERO: The Mystic Circle. *In truth, I have only been a humble instrument entrusted with the task of compiling, crafting, and curating the sacred teachings that flow from His infinite grace. To* "**compile**" *is to gather fragments of divine truth from the vast sea of wisdom, to* "**craft**" *is to shape them with love and devotion, and to* "**curate**" *is to present them with reverence, ensuring that the essence remains untouched by the ego. It is through His blessings that these words have taken form, and this work is not my own creation but a humble offering of His eternal wisdom.*

Through His grace, this book has manifested, and I hope it serves as a reflection of His divine light, guiding all who seek the truth.

With deep gratitude, I dedicate this to Him and to all seekers who, through this work, may feel a connection to the higher purpose He reveals.

*— **Dr Hari, Chinthakunta***